GEORGIA POW CAMPS
IN WORLD WAR II

DR. KATHRYN ROE COKER & JASON WETZEL

The History PRESS

Published by The History Press
Charleston, SC
www.historypress.com

Copyright © 2019 by Dr. Kathryn Roe Coker and Jason Wetzel
All rights reserved

Front cover: German POWs sing as they march to work. *Courtesy NARA collection.*
Back cover: POW German officer on a ship going to American captivity. *Courtesy NARA collection.*

First published 2019

ISBN 9781540239822

Library of Congress Control Number: 2019937044

Notice: The information in this book is true and complete to the best of our knowledge. It is offered without guarantee on the part of the authors or The History Press. The authors and The History Press disclaim all liability in connection with the use of this book.

All rights reserved. No part of this book may be reproduced or transmitted in any form whatsoever without prior written permission from the publisher except in the case of brief quotations embodied in critical articles and reviews.

CONTENTS

Acknowledgements	5
Introduction	7
1. America's World War II Prisoner of War Program	11
2. Reeducation Program	37
3. Camp Gordon	49
4. Camp Stewart	79
5. Fort Benning	89
6. Camp Wheeler	115
7. Fort Oglethorpe	139
8. The Prisoner of War Story in Georgia Newspapers	147
9. Daily Life for Prisoners of War	167
Conclusion	239
Appendix A: Death Rates of World War II Prisoners of War	241
Appendix B: Key to Map of World War II Prisoner of War Camps in Georgia	243
Notes	245
Bibliography	267
Index	275
About the Authors	287

ACKNOWLEDGEMENTS

Many people assisted in the completion of this little-known aspect of Georgia history. The reference archivists at the National Archives and Records Administration (NARA) were instrumental in locating textual and photographic records. Reference Archivist Nathan Jordon at NARA's Atlanta Branch located the Chief of Ordnance records pertaining to the Atlanta Ordnance Depot and Augusta Arsenal.

Command Historian Steven Rauch at the U.S. Army Signal Corps and Fort Gordon aided in locating records in the installation's archives. Historic Preservation Specialist Edward Howard of Fort Benning was delightful to work with, as he provided period maps of the installation and the prisoner of war (POW) camps along with outstanding photographs. He even went to the local library to find relevant articles.

Reference Assistant Librarian Alicia Owens at Macon's Middle Georgia Regional Library was so gracious and effective in locating Camp Wheeler photographs in the local history collection. Reference Archivist Jennifer Brown at Georgia State University assisted in obtaining Camp Wheeler photographs from the Tracy O'Neal Collection. Collections Manager Lauren Virgo at Aiken County Historical Museum and Executive Director Brenda Baratto provided material on the Aiken, South Carolina, POW branch camp. Communications Director Jana Wiggins at the University of Georgia's Carl Vinson Institute of Government supplied maps and assistance with copyright permission. A special thank-you goes to Christine McKeever, executive director, Sixth Cavalry Museum, Fort

Acknowledgements

Oglethorpe, Georgia, for her research assistance with Fort Oglethorpe's POW history.

So many people, like Pat McAlexander, editor of the *Athens Stroller*, published requests for information on the project. Individuals such as Kelly Gailey responded to those requests. She provided a photograph of her father, Gary Reeves, who contracted with the federal government to hire German POWs to work at Sumter County's Southerfield. Gregory C. White also responded with beneficial details. Savannah freelance writer Kim Wade and her associate, Andria Segedy, were intrigued with the subject, providing encouragement. Sieglinde (Linda) Bauer Gillespie, whose father was a German POW in Russia, and Anja Gillespie provided excellent German-to-English translations of letters and text.

Both Faye Beazly and her brother, Dr. Ed Heard, contributed valuable oral history interviews of their experience with German prisoners of war in Bainbridge, Georgia. Father Radbert Kohlhaas, a former POW at Camp Gordon, sat for a revealing interview on his return visit in 1989. Joe Buck, Albert D. Cromer and Edna Tatter contributed indispensable interviews.

Our friend, Jan Jewett of JkJ Design, expertly drew a graphic layout of Jason's map providing the locations of Georgia's POW camps. Sincere appreciation is extended to these and all others who offered assistance.

Special appreciation is extended to Pamela Ottesen, Jason's sister, for her ideas about the book's title, her excellent proofreading and her ongoing encouragement. Kathy extends her gratitude to her family and friends for their reassurance throughout the book's development.

INTRODUCTION

Have you ever been on a treasure hunt or antiquing when you suddenly, quite casually spy what appears to be a plain item? But it catches your attention—you *must* have it! Well, this happened to one unassuming Georgia woman strolling through an auction. The detective work began when she spotted a blank document enclosed in a plastic bag. Immediately, it grabbed her attention. As the curious woman peered intently at the form, she read the title, "Prisoner of War." Her inquisitiveness ever mounting, she read:

*Date of capture*_____

Place (or sector) of capture _____

*Unit making capture*_____

At the form's bottom was "(over)." Further captivated, the woman turned to its reverse side and read "Instructions for Use." The text below revealed the importance of this little rectangular piece of paper. The user was told: (1) "This tag will be accomplished at the division collection point" or at other specified places "at which point, each prisoner of war will be tagged (loop card around neck)"; (2) "Prisoners of war will be warned not to mutilate, destroy, or lose their tags."[1] Instructions were in English, German, Italian and Japanese. Then she noted that this was a U.S. government form printed in 1942. This was a tag prisoners of war completed and wore around their necks!

Introduction

The woman's mounting fascination led her to Googling. She learned for the first time that during World War II there were prisoners of war (POWs) detained in camps across the American homefront, including Georgia. She knew that the government had interned Japanese American citizens. She also was familiar with the Confederate army's POW camps in Sumter and Andersonville, Georgia, during the Civil War. But World War II POWs and POW camps in Georgia! How could that be? Why were they here? How did they get here? What did they do? How long were they here? Her mind raced with these and more questions.

As the self-made history detective discovered, in World War II the U.S. government confined approximately 425,000 German, Italian and Japanese POWs in the Zone of the Interior (homefront).[2] They were part of the three million prisoners the Allies held during the war. Between 1942 and 1945, the government set up at least 511 POW camps on America's homefront. Almost every state, especially in the South and Southwest (with its warmer climate and more rural areas), had one or more camps. Most were German soldiers, but not all were Nazis. She even learned that Camp Wheeler in Macon, Georgia, housed POWs. That was particularly interesting since her grandfather was stationed there in World War I.[3]

What about that tag? The woman wrote, "As for the POW form, I can only assume that someone kept it as a relic from the war. So much history embedded in such a slim piece of paper."[4] What an understatement! The history of prisoners of war living on the American homefront during World War II is unfamiliar to many Georgians and to most Americans. POW administration and programs were important to Georgia's "wartime economy and captor/captive relations" in the twentieth century.[5] As in other wars, diverse issues and controversies surrounded prisoners of war. But this time POWs were in the backyards of Georgians.

"Grateful for it for the rest of my life," is how former German POW Radbert Kohlhaas recalled his incarceration at Camp Gordon, Georgia, during his visit in April 1989. While a POW, he decided to become a Benedictine monk. If Kohlhaas had not eluded the Nazis, his dream would have died with him.[6] This nostalgia may seem odd for an experience that might invoke gloomier memories. At least since the American Revolutionary War, controversy has surrounded the status and treatment of POWs. Unlike the Korean War, Vietnam War and the Persian Gulf wars, this calamity of war came closer to home for Americans, as Axis prisoners of World War II were sent to camps across the United States. Kohlhaas's recollections and those of many other former POWs provide perspectives into America's

Introduction

Ms. Faye Beazly as a young teenager.
Courtesy Faye Beazly.

administration of POW camps and what life was like for the prisoners of war living virtually in the backyards of most Americans.

Memories of Georgians, like Faye Beazly and her brother, Ed Heard, help to tell and to preserve this intriguing story. As young children, they clearly remember watching German prisoners at work on their father's farm in Bainbridge. Guards such as Shiroku "Whitey" Yamamoto, a member of the 442nd Antitank Company, have stories to tell too. He recounted his job in Georgia:

> [W]*e were assigned to take…*[the Germans] *over to Georgia and Alabama to harvest the peanuts….And that was quite an adventure….And after we take them to the individual farmlands, we become the…standby guards, to be sure that none of them will escape. And…they don't have time to escape because they have a good deal as…the war is over for them….* [T]*hey find out that we were Japanese Americans and* [chuckles]

9

Introduction

there was a kind of humorous event...that takes place. We said, "Gee, how come that you're German, and we're Japanese descendants, and we supposed to be allies [chuckles], *but here we are, you're Germans, and we're Americans, even though we're Japanese Americans." But that's a light moment of humor that we enjoyed talking to them.*[7]

These reminiscences and those of other U.S. Army personnel, government officials and camp inspectors, as well as sundry documents like the one found in an auction, testify to this largely unknown and ignored part of Georgia's and America's history. This notable history is fading and in jeopardy of vanishing, as members of the Greatest Generation dwindle. Why do we need to remember this piece of Georgia's history? Prisoners of war in American history are receiving increasing attention and interest given incidents like those at Abu Ghraib and ongoing issues surrounding the Guantanamo Bay detention camp. Researchers scrutinize our country's previous administration, policies, treatment of POWs and public reactions. They expect their studies to provide insights on contemporary matters and concerns. From there we can learn lessons from the past to improve our present and future perspectives, understandings and experiences. Historian of the World War II European Theater of Operations Colonel William Ganoe warned, "History is the last thing we care about during operations and the first thing we want afterwards. Then it is too little, too late and too untrue." His words are haunting. Almost seventy-five years later, we still did not have a single historical account of the POW story in Georgia. This book hopes to fill that void and foster further research.

Chapter 1

AMERICA'S WORLD WAR II PRISONER OF WAR PROGRAM

Geneva Convention

The story of prisoners of war (POWs) in World War II is exceptional to the history of wartime detainees. The 1929 Geneva Convention Relative to the Treatment of Prisoners of War was the first effective treaty dictating the basic entitlements of both civilian and military wartime prisoners. Major world powers had learned lessons from the largely inoperable Hague and Geneva Conventions of World War I. Forty nations meeting in Geneva signed the treaty on July 27. With the exception of Japan and Russia, all the key belligerents in World War II were signatories to the accords.[8]

The Geneva Convention established the universal principle that POWs were to receive humane treatment. In particular, they were protected from acts of violence, retaliations, affronts and public curiosity. Signatories agreed to provide detainees with food and clothing, medical care, safety and other guarantees, such as religious freedom, mental and physical recreation, labor opportunities, mail and repatriation. Prisoners were not to be placed in hazardous situations nor were they allowed to work in war-related industries. Article 79 authorized the International Red Cross Committee to send its representatives to visit and inspect POW camps. The YMCA and the Swiss Legation were among other humanitarian organizations visiting compounds.[9]

Developing America's POW Policy

Acting Provost Marshal General Brigadier General Samuel Rockenbach had orders to outline plans for a military police corps ready for assembly upon the president's command. Rockenbach's 1937 proposed manual included guidelines for handling POWs. It placed the provost marshal general in charge of POWs and explained numerous heretofore undefined features of prisoner life, like using them as laborers. The manual was shelved.

With war on the horizon, in late 1941 President Franklin D. Roosevelt declared that the military would guard, if necessary, American shipping. That prompted Provost Marshal General (PMG) Major General Allen W. Gullion to ask permission to construct an internment camp. The first POW was captured on a mini-submarine on December 7, 1941—at Pearl Harbor.[10] Prisoners were now a fact of war.

President Roosevelt. *Courtesy NARA collection.*

Efforts to establish an all-inclusive prisoner of war policy were filled with missteps as various government agencies with overlying authorities (e.g., War Department, State Department, Provost Marshal General Office) asserted the right to administer a POW program. This intergovernmental mess went unresolved until the Provost Marshal General Office (PMGO) ultimately obtained control over all POWs remaining in America; that came as the war ended.[11]

Notwithstanding the intergovernmental agency conflicts, according to the adopted POW plan an interdepartmental board comprising the Departments of State, War, Navy and Justice made policy decisions. Actions then flowed downward from the War Department to the PMGO and, finally, to the U.S. Army. The army became the actual manager of the prison camps. The commanding generals of the army's nine service commands controlled the establishment and daily operations of POW (or PW) camps. An Internees Section within the State Department's Special War Problems Division worked closely with the various government offices involved and with humane organizations, including the American and International Red Cross, the Swiss Legation and the War Prisoners Aid of the International YMCA.[12]

North African Campaign and Its Impact

The North African Campaign (June 1940–May 1943) affected America's POW policies. In August 1942, England asked America to house prisoners captured in Northwest Africa. There simply was no way Great Britain could care for the 250,000 POWs in its custody. The initial request was for 50,000 POWs, mostly Germans, to be taken on one month's notice. After debate, the Joint Chiefs of Staff agreed. They later decided to accept another 25,000 prisoners the British had captured in Kenya.

At the time, there were only thirty-six military police escort guard (MPEG) companies and a few equipped camps. Gullion's refusal to accept African American soldiers into the MPEG companies exacerbated the lack of guards. He believed that using black soldiers would result in enemy retaliations. The PMG blocked a plan in 1942 to form two MPEG companies of black soldiers. This broke the government's promise to allow African American soldiers to serve in all branches of the U.S. Army. Assistant Chief of Staff Brigadier General Harry L. Twaddle and Operations Division Chief Major General Dwight David Eisenhower objected to Gullion's policy. Both emphasized using "Negro troops" as MPEGs. Eisenhower "stressed the need to decide in principle 'the source from which personnel for future…[MPEG] companies will be obtained'" and the "desirability of designating certain of such companies as colored units." Eisenhower first raised the issue in April 1942. Nevertheless, Gullion's policy remained in effect until MPEG companies were disbanded in April 1944. Thereafter, the nine army service commands

Recently captured German troops in North Africa. *Courtesy NARA collection.*

selected personnel to guard POWs in the United States—including some African American soldiers. In contrast, by 1944 African American soldiers commonly guarded POWs in North Africa and Europe.[13]

If the British had not stalled implementing the agreements, the PMGO would have faced a virtual flood of prisoners. With the extra time, the PMGO, even with its all-white soldier MPEG strategy, was prepared with enough guards and beds to accommodate the POW influx. As 1942 ended, the U.S. Army had transported 431 POWs to the American homeland. Mobilization of an extensive POW camp program was not required—yet.[14] But the situation was changing fast. Rommel's successor, General Hans-Jürgen von Arnim, surrendered on May 13, 1943. The agreements with the British, the Allied victory in North Africa and the invasion of Normandy thirteen months later inflated the number of prisoners, creating unparalleled problems.[15]

Capture

German noncommissioned officer Radbert Kohlhaas was an Afrika Korps soldier who once served in the Korps' Intelligence Division. He became a POW at Camp Gordon, Georgia. Kohlhaas described his apprehension:

> I was captured after the German surrender on Cape Bon in Tunisia on May 11, 1943. Our captors, the British 18th Infantry, from India, treated us honorably and manly and would even share their own provisions with their prisoners....Although families were told one thing, the German news service reported that Tunis was now a Stalingrad. Every house is a fortress. We are fighting to the last man.[16]

Soldiers searched the captives and then took them to the centers. To some it seemed as if "Axis captives drove themselves to…prison camps." One reporter noted, "Evidently, the master race prefers allied captivity to Axis freedom."[17]

Who were these prisoners America was accepting? A British correspondent watched a German battalion raise the white flag and tramp into the British lines—unusual for these elite, young, professional Afrika Korps soldiers. They were distinct from the older, volunteer soldiers fighting in Normandy and from those coming later who were less susceptible to Nazism. As POWs,

German prisoners captured at Cape Bon, on a British ship. *Courtesy NARA collection.*

Afrika Korps troops kept their military principles, manners and their Nazi philosophy—characteristics coloring the atmosphere of camps where they were predominant, which caused problems for the U.S. Army. The camps where the Normandy soldiers predominated were quite different.[18]

Overseas Processing

As officials in America scurried to meet the demands of the POW influx, the U.S. Army in North Africa established processing centers to hold the POWs. The centers resembled small towns. Since there were few African American combat units, POWs first met black soldiers who drove the trucks to the processing centers. Other black soldiers guarded the POWs on the way to the centers and protected them from antagonistic residents of recently freed countries. A former German POW remembered how the soldiers sheltered them from French citizens as they traveled to the coast in 1944: "Had they not acted so vigorously, we would have fared quite badly. On this occasion, we experienced for the first time how much compassion the colored Americans had for us. We were only able to solve this mystery after having our experiences with them in America."[19]

Once at the processing centers, the POWs underwent a "labyrinthine registration procedure." They completed a form resembling the U.S. Army's Basic Personnel Record; a medical examination; finger printing; photographing; and an interrogation. Army officials sent to the International Red Cross and the Swiss Legation copies of the registration forms, a personal and medical history, serial number, list of personal belongings and details of capture. These two organizations then contacted the prisoners' families. The registration process did not always go smoothly, especially when the area surrounding the processing centers was under attack. Problems included the lack of interpreters, the failure to assign serial numbers and the sometimes poor attitudes of the American guards. Such issues were not unique to the overseas centers. They were transported along with the POWs to camps in America. One glaring difficulty was the frequent inability to separate Nazis from non-Nazis. This obstacle later plagued Georgia's Camp Gordon and its Aiken branch camp along with other POW camps across the homefront. After lessons were learned, the U.S. Army sent the staunchest Nazis to Oklahoma's Camp Alva.[20]

Journey to the United States

The Geneva Convention required prompt removal of POWs from the front. Because of limited resources in North Africa, immediate transportation to the United States was essential. Embarkation locations were at Casablanca, Morocco, and Oran, Algeria. The prisoners spent time reading, writing letters home or anxiously walking about until transportation to America was available. Liberty ships became the most cost-effective means of transportation. Other modes of transportation included cargo ships and even passenger ships.[21]

Once aboard the ships, traveling in convoys, American MPs guarded the POWs and kept order with help from German officers and noncommissioned officers. Army nurse Second Lieutenant Yvonne E. Humphrey was assigned to care for the prisoners on one convoy. Humphrey described what she considered the Germans' severe concept of discipline: "If a soldier failed to salute a superior with sufficient snap he would be severely reprimanded or perhaps confined to quarters. One young German, who violated the wartime regulation by throwing something overboard—in this case, nothing more instructive to the enemy than apple peelings—was instantly thrown into solitary confinement on bread and water for three days....Their officers came close to arrogance.'"[22]

During the typical six-week-long voyage from North Africa or the two-week journey from Europe, the prisoners, like American military personnel, coped with cramped facilities and other adverse conditions. They landed at Camp Shanks, New York, or Norfolk, Virginia.[23] Kohlhaas described his voyage to America:

Georgia POW Camps in World War II

We were shipped by rail from Tunis to Constantine, Algeria, and finally turned over to the First Army at Algiers, where we embarked on the USS Samuel Griffith [Griffin], *a liberty ship, on Sept. 25* [1943]. *We sailed in a convoy of about 100 units. It took us three weeks to cross the Atlantic. The sea was calm, so we could stay on deck from sunrise to sunset every day. There were 400 of us in the mail hold of the boat. Those three weeks in the sunshine may have saved my life, because I was utterly exhausted at the time.*[24]

Camp Locations

Deciding where to locate the POW camps was complex. Predictably, to the PMGO security was the chief consideration. Many Americans feared prisoner escapes and prisoner sabotage. Camps could not be in blackout areas some 170 miles inland from either coast or along a specified 150-mile zone of the Canadian and Mexican borders. Initially, camps were in rural, sparsely populated and isolated areas with landscapes not offering hiding places for escapees. Nor could camps be near war-related industries. The PMGO also considered the area's proximity to transportation, labor needs and the availability of military installations. Among other specifications, the Geneva Convention mandated that prisoners were to be held in environments comparable to the climates where they were captured. Adherence to these requirements meant that two-thirds of the camps were located in the South and Southwest under the Fourth, Seventh and Eighth Service Commands.[25] The Fourth Service Command included Georgia, South Carolina, North Carolina, Alabama, Florida, Tennessee and Mississippi. As we will see, Georgia's base camps had branch camps in several of these states.[26]

In January 1942, the PMGO requested the formation of the first two compounds. The proposed sites were Roswell, New Mexico, and Huntsville, Texas. Local politicians had pressed hard to have a camp located in their respective city, pointing to the availability of bargain-basement-priced land, the region's remoteness and labor demands. And the areas met the Geneva Convention's climate requirements.[27] As America's manpower shortage became acute and security concerns diminished, more camps were located in the North and near less remote areas.

The PMGO had established internment camps following Pearl Harbor to contain Japanese Americans and a few German Americans. Since one-fifth of these stood idle, the PMGO rapidly converted them into POW camps. One was located at Fort Oglethorpe, Georgia. The military assumed control of Depression-era Civilian Conservation Corps (CCC) camps. The War Department decided to use existing military installations with extra space to house additional prisoners.[28] Eventually, every state had at least one camp, save Alaska, Hawaii, Nevada, Montana, Vermont and North Dakota. Alaska and Hawaii were too far away from the mainland, increasing transportation expenses and creating unnecessary escape risks. Nevada, North Dakota, Montana and Vermont were less populated and did not have significant military bases.[29]

To house even more POWs, an extensive construction program began. As of September 15, 1942, nine permanent internment camps were completed, another nine were under construction, six more were authorized and ten were designated as temporary camps. The largest camps held between 5,300 and 19,000 prisoners. Intermediate size camps confined about 500 POWs. Larger compounds were known as "base camps." Smaller "branch camps" spun off them, corresponding to accessible work for the prisoners. By the end of the war, there were more than 500 camps across America. In February 1945, America detained 12,619 German officers; 67,154 NCOs; and 226,413 enlisted soldiers.[30]

BASE CAMP SPECIFICATIONS

Following the Geneva Convention, stockades were built according to American military camp standards. The typical new base camp could accommodate between two thousand and four thousand prisoners. It was divided into one or more compounds separated by a fence. The facility was built (or its adaptation) separate from the camp's headquarters. (This would be a bit of a problem for the POW camp on Camp Gordon.) Four companies of prisoners, or about one thousand men, were housed in each compound. The standard layout included five barracks, a latrine with showers and laundry tubs and an administration building for each company. Each compound typically had a dining hall, a canteen, a recreation building, an infirmary, a workshop and an administration building. The camp itself had a chapel, a station hospital and an outdoor recreation area. If a station hospital were not available, the prisoners used designated wards in the post hospital.[31] The U.S. Army often adapted

View from guard tower at an unnamed POW camp. *Courtesy NARA collection.*

existing buildings and facilities to house POWs. As we will see, this was true of Camp Gordon's POW compound. American soldiers guarding the POWs received orders to remain outside the stockade and to have minimal contact with the prisoners.[32] Georgia had five base camps:

- Camp Gordon (Augusta)
- Fort Benning (Columbus)
- Camp Stewart (Savannah)
- Fort Oglethorpe (Oglethorpe)
- Camp Wheeler (Macon)

BRANCH CAMPS

As events unfolded, housing needs outgrew the base camps. The answer was smaller, subsidiary branch camps. Branch camps accommodated between 250 and 750 prisoners. The diverse housing included tents, auditoriums, mobile units, fairgrounds, armories, schools and sometimes privately owned facilities. Hospitals and prisons also lodged POWs. Branch camps were located near farms, factories and other areas where prisoners were employed. Georgia's five base camps had numerous branch camps across the state in areas most in need of farm and industrial laborers. One of Camp Stewart's branch camps was in Statesboro, Georgia. In 1944, the *Bulloch Times* reported that the camp was an answer to local labor needs.[33]

Georgia POW Camps in World War II

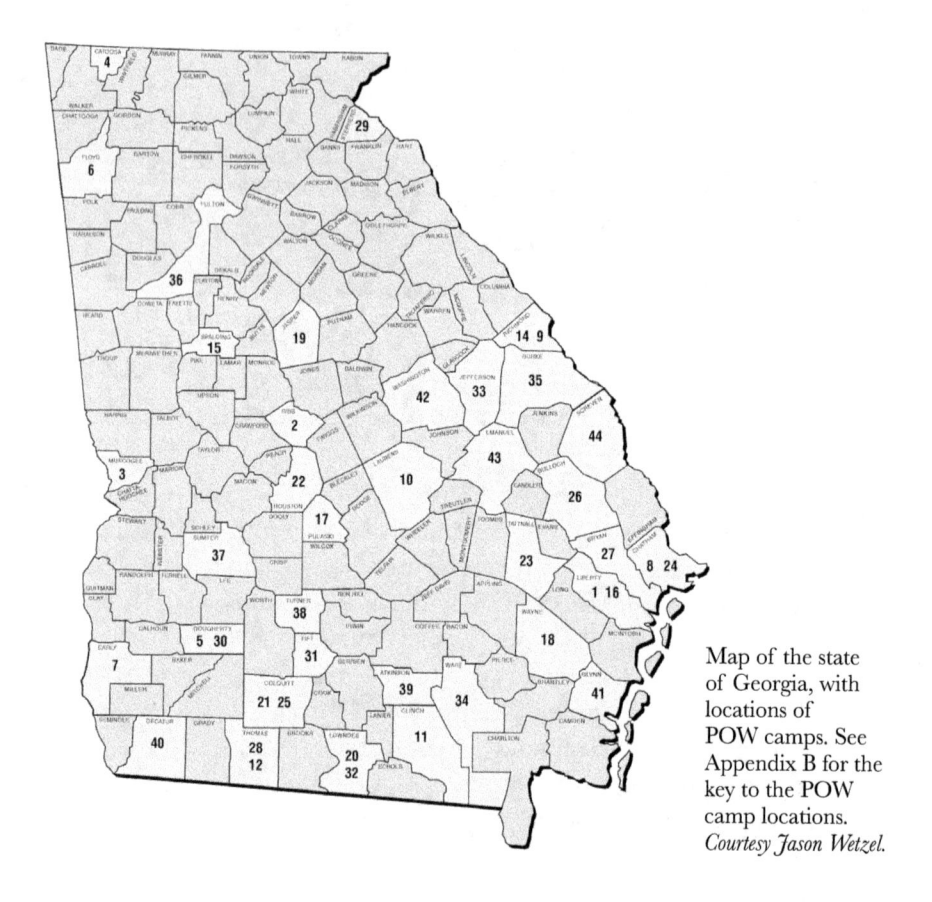

Map of the state of Georgia, with locations of POW camps. See Appendix B for the key to the POW camp locations.
Courtesy Jason Wetzel.

As of August 1, 1943, there were three base and branch camps in Georgia. By June 1, 1944, Georgia was home to fourteen camps.[34] Georgia's Camp Gordon POW base compound, for instance, administered or sent details to several side camps including:

- Waynesboro and Reidsville, Georgia
- Aiken, Charleston and Fort Jackson, South Carolina
- Wilmington, North Carolina
- Dade City, Florida[35]

Eventually, Fort Jackson became a base camp and administered the Charleston camp along with others.[36] By the end of the war, Georgia was home to five base camps, thirty-seven branch camps, seven hospitals, two internment locations and two cemeteries.

Arrival in America

The Port of Embarkation's commanding officer determined how the ships were to be unloaded. Kohlhaas recalled the day after the USS *Samuel Griffin* docked on October 15, 1943, at Staten Island:

> *We were searched getting off the boat in groups of ten.... There was one National Guardsman who did the searching with his submachine gun at the ready and there was a huge trash can that was for the things they would take away from us. I was the third one from the end. I didn't have much, just a few hankies and a little underwear, but some books too. Among the books were a dictionary, a Greek edition of Sophocles, and [a commentary] on Sophocles' tragedies.*
>
> *The first thing the man grabbed from my few belongings was that book. He opened it. "Wow, what's that?" I told him, that is Greek. "Don't you pull my leg. That's Greek to me," he said. It is Greek.* [Kohlhaas chuckled in a 1989 interview.] *"How come you speak Greek?" We learned that at school. "Let us check him out in speaking English. How come you speak English?" You asked me, didn't you? The guard didn't know what to do at that point. That was the end of the search,* Kohlhaas mused.[37]

POWs preparing for arrival in America. *Courtesy NARA collection.*

Train ride to the POW camp. *Courtesy NARA collection.*

Then the POWs encountered another maze of processing. "We...were by the Staten Island Ferry taken to lower Manhattan, for processing," Kohlhaas added.[38] All POWs were disinfected. Black soldiers usually did the job of covering the stripped-down prisoners with a white powder. The Military Police Corps interpreted orders and guarded the prisoners. The Quartermaster's Office collected, stored and returned the prisoners' personal belongings and their disinfected clothing. The Transportation Corps and railroad representatives coordinated arrivals, departures and destinations. After that, Military Police Corps soldiers placed the prisoners on trains for the journey to the prison camps. Before the war ended, more than 425,000 prisoners had gone through this process.[39]

Train Ride to Camps

Much to their surprise, the POWs traveled to the camps in Pullman passenger cars, where black waiters "in spotless white uniforms" served them. On the trains "headed south or west...they [POWs] soon discovered that America was virtually another world. Used to destruction and death, these veterans of battles such as El Alamein, Sicily, and Normandy were astonished at a nation which seemed almost unreal—no bombed-out cities, cars everywhere, and roads and spaces that seemed to have no end." Georg Gartner, a former Afrika Korps soldier/POW, commented, "America was startlingly large, and I...shrugged off any serious thoughts of getting back [escaping] to Germany on my own." (He did escape from a camp, assumed a new identity as Dennis F. Whiles and was never recaptured. After forty years, he revealed his true identity.)[40] They also noted the numbers of black railroad workers. A former POW recalled, "[A] crew of colored workers cleaned the windows of the trains with a hose and a broom. From a black worker I received my first American cigarette. He laid his hand gently on my shoulder. From that moment, I knew I would meet good people in captivity, too."[41]

Historian Fritz Hamer wrote, "[F]or most POWs the chance to escape the war was more important than going home. Furthermore, there were other material benefits such as the quality and quantity of food and shelter which the German army had not provided since early in the war. Until spring 1945 three meals a day, food variety, and generous commissary privileges were common in POW camps."[42]

It is captivating to compare the story of a typical train ride from the perspective of a young American soldier, Private First Class Norm Saunders, who was an artist, and from Radbert Kohlhaas. Saunders's story, along with his drawings, appeared in the November 1943 issue of the National Picture Monthly. They are duplicated here.[43]

Remembering his twenty-four-hour train trip to Camp Gordon, Kohlhaas wrote:

> *We...were by the Staten Island Ferry taken to lower Manhattan for processing, and later to Jersey City Penn Station. We were marched to our train by National Guard's men, one to each group of ten prisoners, and got onto the platform during the early evening rush-hour. As we were still wearing the rags of our Afrika Korps Khakis, the rush-hour crowd mistook us for US soldiers returning from the European theater of war and gave us a hearty welcome.* [The guards told them not to answer the crowd.] *The train, consisting of coaches, left at 5 P.M. We were seated in groups of three to each four-seat bay, with one guard at both ends of the aisle. The day-time trip through Virginia and the Carolinas seemed endless to me. We finally arrived at the Camp Gordon rail terminal in the late afternoon of Sunday, October 17, 1943. After the long trip from northern Africa, it did feel like Sunday to me.*[44]

Camp Arrival

Kohlhaas recalled that a few soldiers in dress uniform met him and his fellow prisoners at the train depot and then marched them the short distance to the Camp Gordon POW compound.[45]

Georgia POW Camps in World War II

I Guard Nazi Prisoners

by Pfc. Norm Saunders

This account of life aboard a U. S. train carrying Nazi prisoners to internment camps is an authentic bit of after-the-battle reporting by an Army MP who was a civilian artist. That his eye missed no telling detail is evident from both his first-person story below and his on-the-spot pencil sketches on these pages.—EDITOR

ONCE IN THE U. S. AXIS PRISONERS ARE HERDED INTO TRAINS BOUND FOR CAMPS IN INTERIOR. UNIFORMS ARE A MOTLEY OF THEIR OWN AND ALLIED ARMIES

Until I was assigned as an Interior Guard on a Prisoner of War train, the only German soldiers I had seen were in newsreels and training films.

The thousands I have seen since then look and act much as the first 50 did. They are shorter than American soldiers by half a head or more, and they are younger—their ages vary from 15 to 40, but the majority appear to be 18 or 19.

After being herded into a coach and placed three in a double seat, the first thing they look for is the water cooler. After Africa, they have little faith in any water supply.

And hungry! They're the hungriest lot I ever saw. At meal time, we bring bread, then potatoes, then meat, and next salad or other vegetables, with coffee last. Sauerkraut and frankfurters are a real treat to them, and ice cream just tops everything. They simply can't believe ice cream.

Picnic plates and utensils amaze them, and they say "America must be *kaput*"—nothing left but paper plates. When we throw the dishes away, they are flabbergasted by our extravagance! After washing and shaving, they'll dry themselves with a dirty old towel day after day, rolling it up and restoring it to their packs. They never use the paper towels furnished them until we show them how.

Their craving for candy and chewing gum is as great as for cigarettes. They are allowed to smoke for 30 minutes after each meal. The miserliness with which they save butts speaks for the quality and quantity they are used to.

NAZI CAPTIVES EN ROUTE EAT AS IF STARVED. THEY'RE CRAZY ABOUT ICE CREAM

EACH COACH CARRIES 30 PRISONERS. ONLY ONE MAY MOVE ABOUT AT A TIME

The Nazis are extremely curious about America—they gaze out the windows constantly. Each trainload usually includes one or more Germans who were in the U. S. before the war—and some lived in Brooklyn. Twice I have been asked, "How're the Dodgers doing?"

These more-traveled Germans point out various towns to their fellow-captives. Those who have never been here before are most curious and eager to see Indians, cowboys, the Mississippi river, and Chicago. War plants along our routes are the real eye-openers to the Nazis—those factories blazing away as we travel across America day after day. At first the prisoners look with mere interest and curiosity, then they stare unbelievingly, and before we reach the camps they just sit dumbfounded at the train windows. They have lost their arrogance and are a lot quieter and not so sure that Germany will win the war.

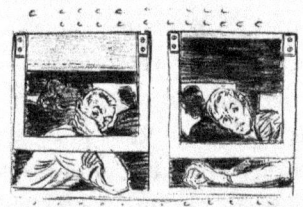

CONSTANTLY STARING out the windows, the Nazis lose confidence in Hitler's might as they pass countless war factories. Note the wooden stops permitting windows to provide ventilation but not means of escape.

WOUNDS SUFFERED BEFORE CAPTURE ARE DRESSED BY U. S. MEDICAL OFFICERS

ARTIST SAUNDERS TITLES THIS "A GOERING AIR-BORNE TROOPER IS GROUNDED"

JOURNEY'S END IS AN ISOLATED U. S. PRISON CAMP, WARY OF THE TOMMY-GUNS. PRISONERS LEAVE THE TRAIN QUIETLY—STILL CURIOUS BUT NO LONGER ARROGANT

CLICK
THE NATIONAL PICTURE MONTHLY
NOVEMBER, 1943•p. 16

ARTIST Norm Saunders juggles sketch-pad, tommy-gun.

Georgia POW Camps in World War II

The response of Americans to POWs arriving in their backyards ranged from anger to curiosity. Historian Arnold Krammer described the arrival of prisoners in Mexia, Texas: "[T]ownspeople lined up along Railroad Street to stare, awestruck, at the seemingly endless stream of German prisoners who disembarked from the train: 3,250 men in short pants, desert-khaki uniforms, and the large-billed cloth caps and goggles which came to symbolize Rommel's elite."[46] A resident recalled, "The line of prisoners stretched the full three miles out to the camp!...Remember that we were a town of only 6,000 people and we had just seen our population increased by 50%—and they were foreigners on top of it!"[47]

Not surprisingly, some onlookers were furious with Nazis in their city, "especially while their...[relatives] were overseas fighting Nazism." Former lieutenant William Arthur Ward recalled one of his experiences: "I only met one such person...but it was enough to make me take the matter seriously....I once had to escort a group of about 300 POWs....While waiting for our military bus...I bought cokes for all the guards and POWs. To my shock, the woman behind the counter at the general store went wild: she yelled and cursed, accused me of sympathy for the enemy, and damn near physically hit me. It was an unnerving experience."[48]

Hamer found that some Americans, particularly farmers, were more accepting of the new arrivals who spoke strangely:

> *When the first POWs were brought into the state* [South Carolina] *in the fall of 1943 the expected apprehension about enemy soldiers seemed outweighed by genuine curiosity. In September 1943, when 250 German POWs were brought to a temporary camp in Bamberg County* [South Carolina], *the county agricultural extension agent wrote: "there was almost a steady flow of traffic by the camp. People from miles around came to see what was taking place. (Even after they were banned from the camp area)...they never lost interest in the camp and its prisoners of war." Within a few weeks the Bamberg county agent reported that POWs were even "entertained" in local residents' homes! Despite the fact that these were prisoners who had recently fought to kill American troops, if not the sons of the Bamberg families that employed them, the bond between Germans and Americans grew during their weeks of association.*[49]

Opposite: "I Guard NAZI Prisoners." *Courtesy artist Norm Saunders, juggling a sketch pad and tommy gun*, National Picture Monthly, *November 1943, 16, reprinted on Oldmagazinearticles.com.*

POW with farmer's child.
Otto and Linda, 1945.
Courtesy NARA collection.

Many American farmers and their POW laborers did develop a rapport. With the persistent labor scarcity and competition from the higher-paying war industrial jobs, farmers and others like those in the pulpwood industry welcomed the POWs as a labor pool they could use.[50]

CAMP LIFE

U.S. Army personnel tried to segregate the POWs by nationality, branch of military and rank. Nationality was determined according to the soldier's uniform and identification card. Using this criterion, the army documented all POWs as either German or Italian. So, the Wehrmacht-subscripted Russian, Polish and Yugoslavian soldiers were recorded by the army as Germans. Initially, U.S. Army officials made no attempt to separate Nazis from anti-Nazis since all Germans were seen as Nazis. Unfortunately, these early decisions and misconceptions later had unforeseen, troublesome consequences.[51]

Usually, the army did separate German officers from enlisted men, placing them in separate camps. Officers had no less than 120 square feet of living space, while each enlisted man had 40 square feet. In camps with both officers and enlisted men, the army followed the Geneva Convention's requirement calling for the separation of the two groups into distinct commands. The PMGO wanted to safeguard the enlisted prisoners' need to follow their chain of command. The War Department directed that every three thousand prisoners were to have access to approximately thirty-two of their officers.[52]

The *Lagersprecher*

The U.S. Army urged prisoners to manage themselves in nearly all daily affairs. The POWs chose one of their comrades, known as the *lagersprecher* (spokesman), to communicate on their behalf to the camp's American officials. Supposedly, popularity decided the choice. But fear, bullying and despotism frequently determined the selectee. If Nazis were in the majority, the *lagersprecher* typically was a Nazi. Consequently, the *lagersprecher* bolstered the Nazis' grip on the camp. He represented their needs and viewpoints. Non-Nazi POWs saw the *lagersprecher* as a Gestapo member. The *lagersprecher* was nonetheless crucial to the camp's efficient operation and fulfilled other significant roles, such as serving as the delegate to the Red Cross, the Swiss Legation and the YMCA. He also had authorization to probe possible violations of the Geneva Convention. If issues arose, he could demand contact with the military district leaders and insist on action against the camp's administration.[53]

Prisoners deal with American army guards through their own liaison officers. Camp Gordon, Augusta, Georgia. *Courtesy NARA collection.*

Georgia POW Camps in World War II

Daily Schedule

The federal government enforced an exacting daily schedule, guaranteeing compliance with the Geneva Convention. The day began promptly with reveille at 5:30 a.m. The prisoners donned their navy blue fatigues with the white "PW" stenciled on them. (See front cover.) Their thirty-minute breakfast started punctually at 6:00 a.m. The prisoners showered and cleaned their living areas. Camp authorities inspected the barracks daily. Prisoners with projects inside the camp began their workday at 7:30 a.m.; those detailed to jobs outside the camp were driven to the worksite. The one-hour lunch began at noon. POWs performing agricultural tasks outside the camp received their lunch in the fields. At 1:00 p.m., work restarted and continued until 4:30 p.m. After showering, the POWs, often clad in their German or Italian uniforms, ate dinner from 6:00 p.m. to 7:00 p.m. The day ended with lights out at 9:30 p.m. After 11:00 p.m., the prisoners were restricted to their barracks.[54]

POW preparing a meal. *Courtesy NARA collection.*

Georgia POW Camps in World War II

Laborers

The Geneva Convention's labor-related articles required enlisted prisoners to work and specified the working conditions. The War Department's *Policy with Respect to Labor of POWs*, issued on January 10, 1943, put the matter in "a nutshell": "Any work outside the combat zones not having a direct relation with war operations and not involving the manufacture or transportation of arms or munitions and not unhealthful, dangerous, degrading or beyond the prisoner's physical capacity, is allowable and desirable." The government closely followed the Geneva Convention, establishing the Prisoner of War Employment Review Board, managed by the War Department.[55]

Wages

The Geneva Convention stipulated that enlisted POWs receive a fair wage. Originally, the pay rate matched an American army private's wages, sixty cents an hour, plus ten cents per day for necessities. As the war progressed, the rate was changed to eighty cents an hour. Officers were not required to work but did receive salaries ranging from twenty to forty dollars per month.[56] Using POW labor had drawbacks, like the language barrier, the possibility of escapes and unfamiliarity with the job (e.g., harvesting peanuts, cropping tobacco). Yet prisoners were readily available and proved to be hard workers. The government applied part of the wages in scrip to pay for the POW system. The prisoners were free to use the remaining scrip in the camp's canteen. The Geneva Convention required confiscation of all cash, along with other individual possessions (to be returned at war's end) during in-processing. This avoided using money in any attempted escapes.[57]

POWs at Fort Benning used these chits to purchase items in the canteens. *Courtesy World and Military Notes.*

With canteen proceeds, POWs bought an array of items, including musical instruments and library books, funded construction ventures and purchased writing materials. The latter was very important to prisoners, who wanted to write home, as was their right under the Geneva Convention. Until the summer of 1943, the government permitted them to "write two letters and one postcard per week." By that time, censoring their mail became difficult since the Office of Censorship had become so inundated. Consequently, noncommissioned officers and enlisted men could write home once per week. Yet this reduction did not affect the officers' privilege of sending five letters and postcards. In time, the censorship office read "every twentieth letter."[58]

Types of Labor

POWs were employed in three primary areas: agriculture, forest preservation and building infrastructure like roads and airstrips on military installations. Labor was divided into three classes. Class I was work needed to sustain the POW camp (other than enhancement and beautification). There was no pay for jobs in the mess hall and the laundry, repairing buildings and equipment and performing clerical duties in the administrative office.

Class II was contract employment for private companies or individuals. At first, contract labor was negotiated directly between an employer and the PMGO. In December 1942, the PMGO allowed camp leaders to execute contracts directly with employers. Finally, recognizing that the War Department was not in a position to effectively manage POW employment, beginning in October 1943 the PMGO coordinated efforts with the War Manpower Commission.[59] To avoid competition with American labor, private contractors first had to determine that no local labor was available. Contractors paid the federal government to use the prisoners. Many prisoners worked on farms, while others operated sawmills, constructed roads and did various jobs as needed.[60]

Farmers and other employers faced a "tremendous amount of red tape." First, they had to contact the county agricultural agent. Then the agent forwarded the request to the local War Manpower Commission or the cooperative extension office. From there, the request went to the state's regional office, which forwarded it to the provost marshal. Even after an employer managed to hire POWs, there was more red tape before the prisoners began working. The U.S. Army "charged employers $3.50 per day for each POW used. Eighty cents went to the prisoner and the remainder went to the government for the upkeep and maintenance of POW compounds and services." Employers signed a contract with the army, agreeing to abide by its specifications. A farmer had to live within thirty miles of a camp. Some

POWs working on south Georgia farm with American guard. *Courtesy Faye Beazly.*

farmers worked out a deal with the U.S. Army to provide transportation. Generally, farmers used their own transportation.[61]

Class III labor was beneficial but not critical on or associated with military bases. POWs maintained the physical plant; cleared land; constructed roads, sewage lines and other infrastructure; worked in mess halls, laundries and motor pools; and performed other needed tasks. The approximated value in 1944 of this labor was $70 million. By June 1945, POWs were executing 61 percent of all jobs on military bases. For a three-year period, the labor was computed to be as great as $131 million. Agriculture, the second-largest employer, amounted to just 18 percent of the entire workforce.[62]

Recreation

Because of the strict adherence to the Geneva Convention, American officials shaped camp life to prevent the prisoners from becoming bored when they were not working. Recreational activities included watching newsreels and films. Larger compounds had extensive film libraries. At Georgia's branch camp Blakely, the prisoners asked for and received films. The commanding captain procured two American films for them, along with a German film featuring trapeze artists. According to Heinz Gaertner, his fellow captives welcomed the distraction and enjoyed the films, especially the German ones.

POW soccer team. *Courtesy NARA collection.*

POWs often organized orchestras or bands and attended concerts and choral recitals. They read books from the usually "well-stocked camp library." Certain camps created theater ensembles and offered extravagant performances. For example, the theater group at Texas's Camp Hearne presented *The Merry Widow*, *The Flying Dutchman* and *The Student Prince*. American servicemen and civilian employees frequently attended these quite accomplished productions. Occasionally, POWs performed before local residents.[63]

The Geneva Convention required that prisoners have access to "sporting pursuits." Sports ran the gamut from chess to cricket, ping-pong, handball, *faustball* (a form of volleyball) and track and field events. Soccer was the prisoners' favorite sport. Most were not interested in American sports. Some camps allowed prisoners to have pets or animal pens.[64]

EDUCATION

Article 17 of the Geneva Convention called for POW access to intellectual discussion. In that spirit, camp authorities offered an assortment of educational opportunities. POWs took classes like English, German literature, shorthand, chemistry and mathematics. At a Kentucky camp, POWs enrolled in a course covering allegory in American comics. At Kansas's Camp Wabaunsee, courses in Hebrew were very popular.[65] The Fort Benning, Georgia camp offered a curriculum with courses on different educational levels. Those included a baccalaureate preparation program; first-semester university-level courses (e.g., medicine and law); teacher's

POWs in class. *Courtesy NARA collection.*

training; and correspondence courses through several universities. Among the educational opportunities at Georgia's Camp Gordon were classes in Spanish, history, electricity and architecture, leading to a bachelor's degree. A camp inspector considered Camp Gordon's educational program to be "one of the most ambitious educational programs along modern lines, both in lower and higher grades," that he had seen in any POW camp. The instructors were POWs proficient in particular subjects. In May 1944, the Reich's Ministry of Education announced that it would extend high school diplomas and college credit for courses. To the POWs, these courses meant better chances at success in their postwar lives.[66]

ESCAPES

Despite frequently slack garrisons, escapes were rare. In fact, there were no more than 2,200 recorded escapes across America (less than 1 percent). Some were on the run for over two or three days. Gerd Gutzat, who tried to escape twice from the Aiken, South Carolina branch camp, was an exception. As the war continued, with the chances of German victory fading, escapes almost vanished.[67]

Repatriation

By November 20, 1945, only 73,178 German prisoners had been repatriated, even though the Geneva Convention obligated America to guarantee the repatriation of all critically ill and wounded prisoners. There had been some agreements between the United States and Germany on POW exchanges, but not all had been enforced. On May 18, 1945, the U.S. Army Service Forces announced that approximately fifty thousand German POWs held in America were to be repatriated since they were "of no use." Among this group were commissioned and noncommissioned officers who "could not be forced to work," "rabid Nazis…and the sick or insane."[68]

The continued agricultural labor demands of the summer and fall of 1945 adversely affected repatriation. The War Department stepped in to accelerate repatriation, announcing in late 1945 that all POWs were to be "entirely out of private contract from military work by the end of March, 1946." The War Department also revealed a transparent, systematic plan to ship prisoners back home rather than depend on the heretofore "haphazard train schedules and available shipping space."[69]

The agricultural community was in an uproar. South Carolina congressman L. Mendel Rivers demanded Provost Marshal General Lieutenant General Blackshear Bryan explain the War Department's strategy. Finally, on January 25, 1946, President Harry S Truman responded to the keen political forces at play and from his own uneasiness over the tense situation. He placed a sixty-day hold on repatriating those POWs occupied in essential sectors of the economy. Truman later refused to consider any further delay.[70]

The United States agreed to an Allied plan transferring 1.3 million of the more than 2 million POWs it "owned" in Europe to the French. These prisoners were "to be used in labor battalions to help rebuild that country." Other nations (e.g., Britain, Scandinavian countries, Yugoslavia and Greece) received "supply prisoner labor." In the end, the United States transferred 700,000 prisoners to France alone. It is unknown how many POWs in America were sent to Europe. Some German POWs

Georgia POW Camps in World War II

Private First Class Clarence K. Ayers of Evansville, Indiana, reads the news of V-E Day as newly arrived POWs stand on a New York City pier, May 8, 1945. *Courtesy NARA collection.*

remained as "supply prisoner labor" for as long as three years before reaching their homeland.

To make the events of 1945 even worse for POWs, news of the liberated concentration camps prompted the federal government to dramatically reduce rations and food types in the compounds. Before repatriation, prisoners had to watch films about the concentration camps. Antagonism from camp guards was problematic. One former POW remembered:

> *For me...it was less the change of diet which upset me, than the hostile treatment we received from the guards. We had always eaten in the same mess hall with the American personnel—their only privilege being able to go directly to the head of the line. After May [1945] that all changed, and we now ate different diets....Moreover, we could no longer buy cigarettes at the PX and there were several surprise inspections to confiscate our earlier tobacco purchases. Fortunately we outsmarted these inspections by hiding our...cigarettes...but we knew that our relationship to our guards had certainly changed.*[71]

As we shall see from Radbert Kohlhaas, however, the majority of former German POWs have fond memories of their internment in America's homefront and considered the experience beneficial. Many left the country with money they had earned, which helped them in the postwar German economy.[72] Most had not felt hatred from Americans. A November 1943 poll showed that 74 percent of Americans blamed the German government, not the German people, for the war. As a boy, Mel Luetchens had an opportunity to rub shoulders with POWs while they worked on his father's farm. "They played games with us and brought us candy and gum," he recalled. "They were the enemy, of course....When you know people as human beings up close and understand about their lives, it really alters your view of people and the view of your own world. They were people like us."[73]

The history of World War II's Axis prisoners of war, former enemy combatants, confined in camps dotting America's and Georgia's homefront, is told in the following chapters so that this era of our history will not be forgotten.

A people without the knowledge of their past history, origin and culture is like a tree without roots.

—Marcus Garvey

Chapter 2

REEDUCATION PROGRAM

For now more than ever, we must keep in the forefront of our minds the fact that whenever we take away the liberties of those we hate, we are opening the way to loss of liberty for those we love.
—Wendel L. Willkie, One World

AMERICANS' VIEWS OF GERMAN POWS

The POW Reeducation (Ideological Diversion) Program was one of the government's most popular and controversial programs. The American public and POW camp commanders generally thought that all German soldiers were rabid Nazis. That was not true. The "average German soldier, and, thus, the average German prisoner of war...was not a fanatical... [Nazi]." He was a nationalist and fascinated "by the mystique and omnipotence of Hitler's leadership." But they were not all members of the elite Afrika Korps, "indoctrinated by the Nazi regime."[74] These were the first prisoners to arrive in America—straight from North Africa. These were the German soldiers most familiar to Americans. They were the soldiers who controlled countless stockades located virtually in Americans' backyards.

Nazi Control

There were numerous reasons why the Nazis took control at the camps, including problematic communications. Most qualified interpreters were in the Military Intelligence branch. Consequently, the PMGO used German prisoners who spoke English as camp spokesmen. Regrettably, most were Afrika Korps soldiers. Making them the camps' spokesmen only strengthened the Nazis' grip on the camps. Also, the camps' army staff typically were unfamiliar with German politics and culture. That naïvete empowered the Nazis. Segregating them from anti-Nazis was not a priority. Camp commanders had more on their minds, like managing the stockade with minimal and underqualified staff. So, "Nazis took over and terrorize[d] anyone who disagreed with them...under the noses of the Americans." They made it hell for anti-Nazis, moderates and apolitical prisoners. To make matters worse, hidden among the first group of POWs to arrive in America were members of the Gestapo and SS. It became precarious "to be seen as anything but a follower of Hitler. Outside the barbed wire was America, inside was Nazi Germany."[75]

Nazi-manipulated camps ran smoother, producing less glitches for already beleaguered American administrators. "It was a long time before American officials realized the Nazis were the minority in the camps and retained control of the majority through brute force. Until then, concessions [by camp officials] were made to keep the camp quiet."[76] These concessions "helped solidify" Nazi power in the camps.[77]

Nazi domination went beyond "brute force." "If a prisoner did not go along with the program or was suspected of disloyalty to the *Fuhrer*, then he risked being killed." There were at least five murders. Nazis held kangaroo courts and organized "suicides" to purge the camp of "troublemakers."[78] Nazi "vigilantes [mostly of the Afrika Korps] prowled the camps at night inflicting 'Holy Ghosts' [a German military term for severe beatings] on anyone who opposed them."[79]

Anti-Nazis and apolitical prisoners feared going to American officers because they were unsure of obtaining their protection. Indeed, complaints usually were ignored. In one case, a prisoner, fearful for the life of his non-Nazi friend, told the camp commander about his concern. Not understanding the gravity of the POW's alarm, the commander took no action. He compared the situation to opposing Democrats and Republicans, thinking, "'We don't go around killing each other.' The friend was found murdered the next morning."[80]

The fact that most American guards and other personnel spoke no German made it almost impossible to air complaints. After all, as noted, the camp spokesman was normally a Nazi. "Anyone who bucked the system was labeled a troublemaker." One former German POW, Heino Erichsen, described the atmosphere:

> *Top military brass in Washington, D.C., were pleased to find that they were not faced with the chaos of hundreds of thousands of uncontrolled individuals, but rather a tight obedient military unit in which each rank was responsible to its direct superior for its actions. This disciplinary tactic seemed sound to the captors, but it led to a disastrous strengthening of German militarism and Nazism in the camps.*[81]

Nazis used less dramatic methods of manipulation too. Nazis working in the library hid Third Reich books banned by the PMGO. While performing administrative tasks, they withheld forms or changed the form's information. Nazis tried to discourage church attendance. "Every Sunday morning…a self-appointed camp monitor at Fort Dupont, Delaware, tried a more direct approach to dissuade church attendance: The Nazi, posted himself, pencil and paper in hand, outside the compound church…and warned would be churchgoers that if they entered he'd note their names and they would discover the consequences when they got back to Germany."[82] These were a few of the tactics Nazis used to tighten their stranglehold on the camps.

Nazis also controlled the camps' educational program. Historian Judith Gansberg found that they "monopolized camp media, censored reading and film material, quashed any signs of anti-Hitlerism, and threatened violence to anyone who protested." In other instances, "German medics refused to [treat]…prisoners who declined to return a Hitler salute." German chaplains denied services to "Anti-Nazis who died under strange circumstances [alleged accidents or suicides]…and no German mourners were at their graves. One POW was not allowed to be buried among his 'purer Hitlerian ex-comrades' for fear he would contaminate them."[83]

Public Awareness

Eventually, the American public learned about these crimes and deaths. Infuriated "that Nazis were being allowed to commit and get away with such acts inside the borders of the United States," they lobbied their representatives.[84] Captain Joseph Lane of Iowa's Camp Cascade was an exception. He professed to a *New York Times* reporter, "My private suggestion is that you just kill them all and save the world a lot of headaches for the next couple of generations. Most of them are just hopeless."[85]

As Germany's defeat seemed more certain, public opinion changed even more. There was mounting concern over the nature of postwar Germany's government. Americans read articles promoting the importance of winning Germans away from Nazism and converting them to democracy.[86] To most Americans, National Socialism was a "malignant political philosophy which expressed itself in militarism, persecution, oppression, conquest, and sadistic cruelty."[87] Americans called for a German POW reeducation program in the camps. Many thought, "If the Germans were not offered an alternative political ideology, then it might be possible for another dictatorship to take control as it had after World War I."[88]

Popular syndicated columnist Dorothy Thompson wrote, "Men who put up provocative signs on the walls, bragging that they will win the war, and go around giving the Nazi salute are Nazis....They will go home in excellent health, having been well fed and cared for. And meanwhile, on American soil, we shall have kept alive all the symbols of their party."[89] Citizens formed committees like the Seger Committee, arguing that the world would be better off by replacing Nazism with democratic standards. The Harvard Branch of the American Defense Organization lobbied Secretary of War Henry Stimson, advocating the reeducation program. But Stimson opposed the idea.[90]

Eleanor Roosevelt Takes Action

In early 1944, Thompson, who led a group of female columnists, told her friend First Lady Eleanor Roosevelt about the Nazi activities in the camps. She learned about the "suicide" of two German POWs at Kansas's Camp Concordia. The two died at the hands of Nazi POWs "because of their curiosity about American culture and willingness to cooperate with camp officials."[91]

The enraged Mrs. Roosevelt, in her customary style, investigated the situation for herself. She invited for dinner at the White House Major Maxwell McKnight, the recently promoted chief of the POW Camp

Operations' Administrative Section. She wanted McKnight to corroborate what she had learned about Nazi activities. But Mrs. Roosevelt understood that McKnight did not have the consent of his superior officer, Assistant Provost Marshal Bryan. After the first meeting, Bryan told McKnight to "hold nothing back." Mrs. Roosevelt discussed the Nazi matter with President Roosevelt, who initially opposed reeducation. The president's own inquiry resulted in revitalizing the reeducation program that Brigadier General S.L.A. Marshall, Major Edward Davison and Colonel Dave Paige had developed in March 1943. As 1944 came to an end, a German POW reeducation program was becoming a reality.[92]

SPECIAL PROJECTS DIVISION AND THE "FACTORY"

The PMGO's Prisoner of War Special Projects Division (SPD), led by Major Davison, took measures to regain control of the camps and execute a reeducation program set up under Article 17 of the Geneva Convention. Government officials decided to keep the program secret, hoping to avoid reprisals against American POWs.[93]

In October 1944, the Special Projects Division moved to Fort Kearny, Rhode Island, its last location. One of the division's branches was called the "Idea Factory," or the "Factory." The Factory's staff included eighty-five highly specialized, educated anti-Nazi POWs. They took an eight-week training course, graduating in July 1945. These prisoners, along with the American staff, chose the reeducation program's subjects, instructional material and course outlines to be implemented in the camps. The Factory shaped a syllabus examining the histories of Germany and America and the development of America's democracy.[94] Describing the Factory's environment, Gansberg wrote in *Stalag: USA*, "It was a relaxed atmosphere conducive to the creation of a newspaper with antifascist views."[95]

Davison and a select group of leaders and teachers envisioned a plan to raise the level of interest among POWs about American culture and institutions. "Literature, films, newspapers, music, art, and education courses would be used to introduce the POWs to the power and resources of the Allies, in particular America and its democracy."[96] The curriculum was akin to an American citizenship course, with concentrations in history, civics, geography and English. Krammer found that "thousands returned to Germany fluent in English and 'having a new love and respect for the United States.'"[97] Arthur Smith wrote in *The War for the German Mind: Reeducating Hitler's Soldiers* (1996), "Davison brought together an extraordinary collection of German prisoners to help in the preparations and course work. Writers, newspaper editors, professors, and journalists by profession, they would have a profound impact upon postwar Germany."[98]

DER RUF

The Factory divided its reeducation program into three phases, called "Projects." Project I included designing courses and creating the newspaper, *Der Ruf (The Call)*. The Factory's commanding officer, Captain Robert L. Kunzig, said that the chief job of the POWs working for the Factory was "writing Der Ruf."[99] They first published *Der Ruf*, "written by POWs for POWs," on March 1, 1945. *Der Ruf* urged German POWs to give up National Socialism and concentrate on rebuilding their country. By *Der Ruf*'s seventeenth edition, November 15, 1945, it was carrying articles contending that the "true patriotism of the German involved making plans to rebuild Germany after the war."[100]

Der Ruf was the Factory's prototype for camp newspapers. The Factory recommended the papers be "used as a medium for self-education and a source for factual information. The editors of the papers should be impartial and objective."[101] Fort Benning's *Wille und Weg (Will and Way)* was one of eighty camp newspapers the Factory scrutinized.[102] Camp Hearne's (Texas) nine-page *Der Spiegel* carried updates from Germany, camp sports, film reviews, crossword puzzles, music theory and prisoners' letters to the editor.[103]

Reactions to the diverse camp newspapers were mixed. Some prisoners boycotted them and staged walkouts in the mess hall. These actions only helped to identify pro-Nazis. In time, German POWs who supported democratic principles outnumbered Nazis. Promotion of Nazism ended, as did the "reign of terror."[104] New arrivals to the camps told their fellow prisoners about Germany's impending defeat, further weakening any rationale in supporting Hitler's regime. Most of the camp newspapers, with *Der Ruf* in the forefront, endorsed this reality and encouraged the prisoners to begin preparations to rebuild their homeland.[105]

The achievement of Fort Kearny's pilot school led the War Department to create the United States Army School Center. The center had two training facilities: the administrative school (Special Project II) at Rhode Island's Fort

Getty, authorized on May 19, 1945, and a police training school (Special Project III), hosted at Fort Wetherill, Rhode Island, approved on June 2, 1945. Civilian and military teachers chosen by the Special Projects Division staffed these Factory-run experimental schools. They trained meticulously screened German POWs for administrative professions and for careers as military policemen in postwar Germany.[106]

FORT BENNING'S "UNIVERSITY OF DEMOCRACY" MODEL

Fort Benning's "University of Democracy" actually was the model for America's reeducation program. Fort Getty selected some of Fort Benning's POWs for enrollment in its program and invited Colonel George M. Chescheir's assistant executive officer, Captain Myrvin C. Clark, for a visit. Clark told Chescheir, "They are polishing off the selected prisoners of war in a credible manner for their return to Germany." The Fort Getty staff, Clark wrote, "display and co-opt" some of the Fort Benning materials. Continuing, Clark stated, "I am very much surprised and pleased to learn that the War Department is taking a great interest along the same lines that you and I think of importance."[107]

Clark also notified Chescheir that one former Fort Benning anti-Nazi prisoner was Camp Getty's spokesman. Fort Getty's program, Clark thought, "is practically along the same lines that we have established...however, I haven't seen any visual aids here that will compare with ours." A Fort Getty officer believed that Benning's camp newspaper, *Wille und Weg* (*Will and Way*) was "four times better...as a piece of journalism than *Der Ruf*."[108]

Later, Clark was transferred to Camp Wheeler. There he became the Intellectual Diversion Program's assistant executive officer at the base camp and at its three branches. He wrote Chescheir of his disappointment: "[T]he attitude of [these] Prisoners of War is incomparable with your Prisoners of War...and...the American leadership at...[Glynco, Reidsville, and Chatham Field] Camps has not been the same type of leadership that you had in your Branch Camp Offices."[109]

The SPD knew that it had to control the reeducation program. So, the division required one officer to serve as the administrative executive officer (AEO) in each of the nine service commands. The SPD wanted the AEOs

Eager to learn about the American form of government, these POWs are studying the history of democracy. Out of their earnings from work at the camp, they bought textbooks, and prisoners who know English prepare classes for other POWs. A great majority of the prisoners agree that a democratic form of government is needed for a new Germany. *Left to right, front row*: Armin Beudler, Alfred Kretschmer and Jakob Hofstetter. *Left to right, back row*: KarlHeinz Schollbach and Helmut Widman, October 14, 1945. *Courtesy NARA collection.*

to be journalism and film specialists who respected American and German culture. The U.S. Army's job description for AEOs stated that they "were supposed to speak German fluently, have a college education preferably in liberal arts, and should possess imagination and good judgment." The challenge in locating men with these credentials led to dropping the requirement to speak fluent German. The SPD instructed each service command to send a designated number of men for AEO training. The next obstacle confronting the SPD and the army was the attitude of numerous AEOS. Many officers were given their AEO training assignment unwillingly. Some preferred to "kill" POWs rather than attempt to "reorient them." Nonetheless, AEO training began in late 1945 at Fort Slocum, New York. AEOs attended a weeklong conference of "lectures, discussions, seminars, and a tour of a POW camp."[110]

The SPD sent 262 officers and 111 enlisted men to the service commands. The enlisted soldiers were the AEOs' aids. Basically, the AEOs' success depended on the camp commander's view of the reeducation program. Certain commanders claimed that since the POWs could not be helped, their only job should be helping to fill the labor shortage. They thought that reeducating the POWs was squandered time and manpower. Often a commander refused to allow the AEO to do his job, assigning him to unrelated duties.

The AEOs faced other obstacles in the camps. They learned about the Nazis' tight control; experienced "Holy Ghosts" incidents; observed *Mein Kompf* as a textbook in POW-instructed classrooms; witnessed the prohibition of frank political discussions in classes; and ran into resistance from the German Red Cross (which sent packages stuffed with propaganda) when censoring books and other materials. The AEO's chore of gaining the anti-Nazi prisoners' confidence was challenging given the Nazis' threat to anyone thought to be cooperating with the Americans. The AEOs had help from new prisoners arriving in the camps after D-Day. "The devastating news from Europe combined with the efforts of the reeducation program were instrumental in breaking the Nazi hold." Thereafter, the AEOs were more assertive and more effective.[111]

The SPD kept the AEO's task a secret. McKnight explained why: "We put them there since the AEO spoke German and the CO didn't. The Germans accepted this in terms of translating for the CO. It seemed to be natural. No one suspected they were there to carry out a so-called reeducation program to open the camp to free information."[112]

The SPD spurned books containing "contempt for America as a country without its own culture, without a soul, a country which is only interested in making money." Any book "which misinterprets...the significance of the contributions of all races to the formation of American culture and civilization must be rejected." Using these guidelines, "AEOs swept through the camps removing any material deemed offensive." That included Nazi propaganda, which "emphasized and distorted such subjects as Anglo-American imperialism, capitalistic decadence, race supremacy, and the glory of military conquest. To establish a balance...they [POWs] must be shielded from any emphasis of these subjects which in any way parallels Nazi propaganda."[113] The AEOs were instructed to use books representing "the contribution to civilization of countries," with no Nazi influence, and those stressing the contributions of nineteenth-century German culture. The government disseminated to the camps timeless literary works that the Nazis prohibited. The SPD also censored magazines and newspapers. By May 1945, the censorship program was becoming successful.[114]

The SPD offered about three hundred courses, spanning from elementary English to engineering. At Kansas's Camp Concordia, POWs took classes in theology, history, geography, government and physics. After V-E Day, courses concentrated only on Factory-supplied material. Certain classes were canceled and replaced with those focusing only on democratic ideals. POW-instructed courses (taught by former professionals like university professors, public school teachers and engineers) ended.

"Why We Fight." *Courtesy NARA collection.*

Before the reeducation program began, the camp spokesman frequently selected films unfavorable to America. That changed in May 1945, when the SPD established a broad film program, showing the "American scene without distortion" and venerating America's "democratic institutions."[115] Documentaries like the popular seven-part *Why We Fight* series were shown first to American soldiers and later to POWs. Newsreels tracked the war's progress, including the allied bombing of Germany. Obviously, those were difficult for the POWs to watch. Some prisoners claimed that the newsreels were merely propaganda.

As the war began to wind down, the War Department mandated that POWs watch films of Nazi atrocities in the concentration camps. The results were diverse. Countless POWs were traumatized to the point of disbelief. Others refused to accept any guilt or responsibility, claiming ignorance or contending that the crimes occurred after their capture. Numerous Nazis gave up supporting their party. Some believed or wanted to believe that it was American propaganda. Yet the evidence was simply too overpowering to deny, evoking shame and distress among most of the holdouts. The films made replacing Nazism with democracy much easier. By the fall of 1945, Nazi emblems and articles had vanished from the camp newspapers. Anti-Nazis ultimately dominated the camps. In June 1945, the PMGO declassified the POW reeducation program. Finally, the American public learned about what many had been advocating.[116]

Success or Failure?

As to the overall success of the program, one of the Special Projects Division's directors jokingly wrote:

> *Many people will ask, of course, whether the prisoners have actually changed.... [I]t is our firm conviction that they have also* [in addition to gaining weight] *become aware of the spiritual powers of this great country. Go into any camp and you will find them jitterbugging to the latest recording of America's great jazz, or perhaps with an ear cocked attentively to the radio from which the humanitarian and courageous career of Ma Perkins is being expounded. And certainly most of them know that there is only one superman and that he is an American reporter on the* Daily Planet.[117]

Gansberg thought "there was a lot of truth in that sarcastic statement—a touch of the best and worst of the program."[118] Some contemporary sociologists and psychologists had projected its failure. To the contrary, one of the top illustrations of the reeducation program's success was a SPD Conference for the AEOs, held at Fort Benning in October 1945. Two POWs from the base camp and prisoners from the thirteen branch camps gave a three-day forum of "classes, plays, and lectures by democratized prisoners." They eagerly displayed the program's achievements. In a unique edition of *Wille und Weg* titled "Nevertheless, We Will Carry On," the POWs printed the oath each had signed on October 25, 1945:

> *We accept the reeducation program "American Government and Democracy" to develop a new basis for the spiritual reformation of the Germans and the reconstruction of the German Nation. Since the inner collapse of our people was at last due to a systematic seclusion from the word and ideas of Western Democracy, we saw our first task...to create for ourselves...a glance into the construction and life of a state, which from the beginning of its history had one desire, the freedom of its citizens, the welfare of their life, and the peace of all those who lived within its borders.*[119]

Perhaps to most German POWs, the program's greatest advantage was more practical than ideological: democracy meant a more affluent lifestyle in their postwar homeland.[120]

Chapter 3

CAMP GORDON

ESTABLISHING A POW CAMP

On October 4, 1942, the War Department instructed the U.S. Army Chief of Engineers to provide POW housing and facilities at Camp Gordon, Georgia. One month later, the Army Corps of Engineers authorized $50,000 to begin the project. The Corps converted the existing American soldiers' barracks into a POW camp on the post by adding barbed wire fences and making adaptations to meet the standard plan for POW camps. Six twelve-foot guard towers surrounded the stockade, and another four smaller towers were placed strategically around the recreation area. "An excellent line of fire was available to the guards in the towers," found one camp inspector. But the camp commander was "afraid" to use the machine guns in the towers because the American barracks were "within forty feet of the fence line and the main road was within a few feet of the camp's eastern boundaries."[121]

The U.S. Army activated the Camp Gordon internment facility on January 8, 1943. One month later, the stockade commanding officer, Colonel Walter Anderson, notified the Fourth Service Command of deficiencies and of his proposed changes in the camp's construction. Anderson wrote about the problematic locations of the guard towers until as late as January 1944. An officer with the Provost Marshal General Office's Aliens Division recommended the camp's abandonment due to, among other reasons, structural defects. The recommendations went unheeded. On July 14, 1943, the compound was re-designated as Camp Gordon's POW Camp.[122] It could house 3,000 prisoners. There were 31 American officers and 445 enlisted men assigned to the garrison. The average POW population was over 2,000. By October 1943, there were "about 1200 prisoners, 4 companies of about 100 each to each of the three compounds."[123]

Former Afrika Korps soldier and POW Radbert Kohlhaas later remembered that the compound was located:

> *near the freight-yard....The PW-Camp site seems to have been the site of the present post stockade, consisting of three interconnecting rectangular compounds opening with their shorter sides towards a connecting road parallel to the main fence running along a large field we could use for soccer games once in a while. Outside the fence, there was a PW-Camp HQ, a chapel and a movie theater.*[124]

POWs Arrive

When Kohlhaas and his fellow POWs arrived at Camp Gordon in October 1943, Father Gerald P. O'Hara, then the bishop of Savannah/Atlanta, was expecting them. Father O'Hara was searching for priests to establish a German chaplaincy. Kohlhaas recalled in a 1989 interview that "[t]here was a priest, indeed, Msgr. Joseph Manefeld of Mainz, W. Germany, who was appointed to the Catholic community on the spot." Kohlhaas became his assistant.[125] "We were introduced," Kohlhaas said, "to a life that was incomparably better than we had known as German soldiers."[126] The POWs found housing comparable to American soldiers' barracks. On the bed, they discovered personal items, such as new underwear and soap. "Whatever you had been longing for weeks and months was there." The men then were marched to dinner at the mess hall. Smiling, vividly recalling, almost reliving the event, Kohlhaas sprightly said:

Radbert Kohlhaas, German POW. *Courtesy Kathryn Coker's collection.*

We couldn't believe it. That was at a level which we hadn't known for years in Germany. Not only in the Army, I mean in general. There were things on the table which you know from your cookbook, but not from experience. Many of the prisoners thought, "Well, they are trying to catch us somehow and let's take some of the food along for tomorrow, perhaps, for even next week."[127] *The mess sergeant told them not to remove any of the food, fearing it would spoil. "The next morning at breakfast," Kohlhaas exclaimed, "it was like Christmas again!"*[128]

On "feast-days," the POWs used the chapel in the headquarters area. On other days, the POW library, located on the second floor of the "first barracks as you entered the compounds," served as the chapel. There were recreational areas. "According to the Geneva Convention," Kohlhaas explained, "our camp was a regular U.S. Army Camp with all facilities including PX. To us it was like heaven after living in hell."[129]

CAMP LIFE

Kohlhaas stated that "[d]aily life...was comparable to regular Army life [starting] with roll call....Then we would go out to work [until four or five o'clock] and for me, that meant going to the gate and reporting to Chaplain [Captain Alden C.] Baughman's office." In addition to serving as Monseigneur Manefeld's assistant, from November 1943 to February 1944, Kohlhaas worked as Chaplain Baughman's secretary. Chaplain Baughman supervised both the German POW Catholic chaplain and the Protestant chaplain.[130]

After working, the men had dinner and then were free until around ten o'clock. "That," said Kohlhaas, "is when we went to the PX, had a beer, some ice cream or whatever else." Kohlhaas spent much of his spare time reading. In November 1943, the inspector found "one library for the whole camp...an advantage over the other camps where there usually is one library per sector." Books came from, among other sources, the Red Cross and donations. Prisoners bought books in the camp exchange. The library grew to at least four thousand volumes. Prisoners also subscribed to newspapers and magazines. The POWs had their own weekly (later monthly) news bulletin.[131]

An International Red Cross Committee member visited the compound on November 28, 1943. These reports offer eyewitness accounts, some

Georgia POW Camps in World War II

German POWs attend Lutheran service in one of the camp's chapels. Of the prisoners in this camp—one of many in the United States—approximately 45 percent are Catholics, 53 percent are Lutherans and the remaining 2 percent are of various denominations, April 1944. *Courtesy NARA collection.*

eloquently written, of life at the POW camps. The committeeman wrote that the three recently constructed two-story, steam-heated, "very clean" barracks had indoor showers, basins and toilets. "The food is excellent and sufficient," commented an inspector; the prisoners "have all the clothing they need." Another inspector thought the POWs' daily meal costs had "reach[ed] the rather high figure of $0.65 [which] certainly indicates that they are being well and generously fed." Clothing ranged from the blue denim work clothes to their German uniforms.[132]

International YMCA agent Edouard J. Patte was one of the most expressive representatives. In his December 1944 report, he wrote:

> *The buildings of Camp Gordon are simply stately. Not every camp can claim twenty-two dormitories, all with two floors, showers, toilet, hot water and forced heating, ten mess halls, some of them artistically decorated,*

three recreation centers, one school building, with bookbinding shop and an exquisite library, one theatre and one church just outside the wires, but so placed that they are available for the POWs. The beautifully clear skies of this region of Georgia add to the camp a certain softness that one does not find further south or north.[133]

Medical Treatment

American and German doctors located in two wings of Camp Gordon's hospital treated the POWs with modern medical equipment. Illnesses ranged from pneumonia to malaria and typhoid fever. German and Italian prisoners requiring prolonged treatment were referred to Augusta's Oliver General Hospital. Four barracks were reserved for POWs and other army prisoners. Initially, the two groups were not separated. In June 1944, that situation was being changed. Those with the most serious cases like shrapnel wounds and mental illness were scheduled for repatriation. Several deaths did occur from natural causes such as cancer, heat stroke, tuberculosis and accidents. Deaths from accidents included a gunshot wound and drowning. Prisoners also died from accidents related to wood cutting, stacking lumber and pulpwood details. Suicide and murder were among the other causes of other deaths.[134]

Recreational and Social Activities

Recreation included football, soccer, handball, tennis and boxing. The POWs enjoyed tournaments between the base camp and the side camps. Patte believed that the "[s]ports activities are well taken care of, but it is to be noted that the sports grounds are available only on limited times." He discovered a "very active theatrical group undertook to play a comedy written in camp." However, the transfer of some prisoners stopped any further progress. "The orchestra gave regular afternoon concerts during the summer…a concert was broadcasted from an outdoor platform…to the whole camp." But the scant supply of German music sheets hindered the conductor's ability to plan concerts. The prisoners used their own funds to buy musical instruments, including a grand piano. They could

Georgia POW Camps in World War II

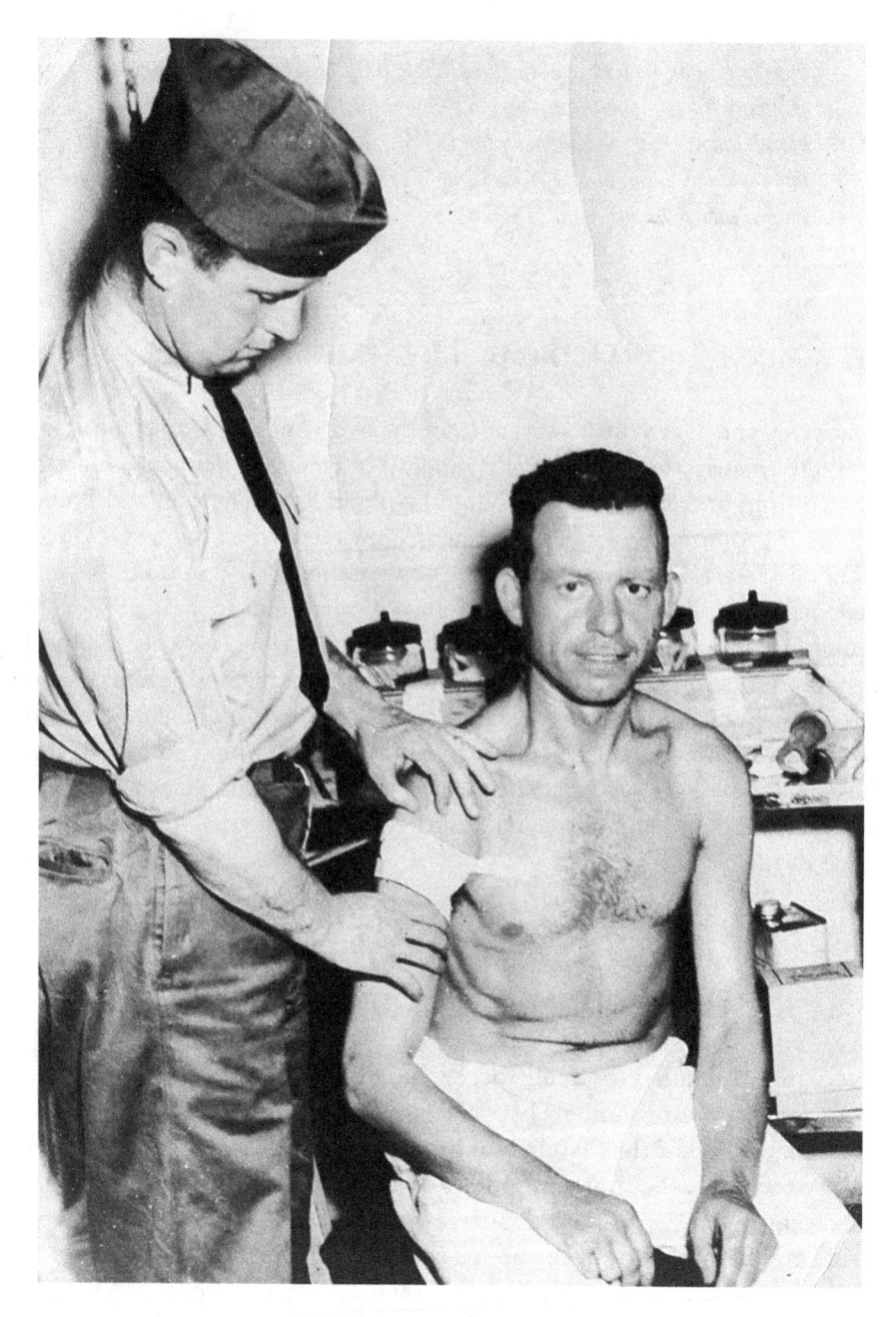

An American doctor is shown treating an injured POW. *Courtesy NARA collection.*

watch movies once a week. Patte thought that the movies would become "more popular, when German films…[were] available." The camp had an active church choir. The camp choir, however, became inactive with the transfer of the conductor and other key members. The string quartette, specializing in classical music, "was also disbanded, unfortunately, for the same reason; it was replaced by a trio which gave a concert of Mozart's chamber music." The lack of paper forced the camp's newspaper to go from a weekly to a monthly publication. Twenty "gifted artists" had "painted, decorated, sculptured or carved numerous works of decided interest, one being a crucifix of exquisite workmanship," for the chapel. Patte stated that religious services were "fairly well attended." Although he did not have time enough for a long chat with the POW chaplains, "they wished…to express their gratitude for all the facilities given to

In the evening, many German prisoners in the United States attend classes, taught by fellow prisoners. This group has chosen to learn English. Classes are not compulsory. *Courtesy NARA collection.*

them, and for the spirit of Christian fellowship shown by the camp U.S. chaplain."[135]

An educational director and twelve "professional teachers" provided courses. Patte wrote, "Courses have been well planned; for instance, young POWs under 20...who have not selected their life-work, receive general formation where German, history, geography and...[mathematics] have the main part." Sixty students in the camps had passed "their B.A. or B.S. in Germany and would like to continue their studies through correspondence courses, with American universities. The educational leader," Patte added, "would like to gather at the base camp, all the students now in the side-camps, and start with the whole group some sort of community school project; this studying together, coupled with the advantages offered by a good library." Patte thought this "would be a decided incentive for all undergraduates and graduates."[136]

After his inspection, Patte met again with Colonel Anderson. Anderson "in a very cordial way, invited...[his] remarks and suggestions." He believed Anderson "was an exceptionally kind host, [who] was good enough to have one of his officers take...[him] to a sub-camp 50 miles away in an army car, to help...[him] with a rapidly decreasing number of [his allotted] gasoline coupons." Patte ended his report thanking Anderson and his officers for a "most enjoyable" time. He hoped that his visit "will have proven helpful also to the POWs."[137]

NAZI RULE

But there were problems in the camp. Kohlhaas revealed that he was "forced by the Nazi NCOs in control of the compound to give up...[the] job that would remove...[him] from their watching eyes and ears." The Nazis knew that he wanted to become a Benedictine monk. Consequently, he was "a suspect and a potential traitor in their minds." At one point, the Nazis tried to court-martial him. The visiting International Red Cross team wanted Kohlhaas, who was exhausted from working on the Catholic Christmas program, to report to the hospital for repatriation. But Kohlhaas wanted to continue developing the program. So, he asked to stay. "Some of our Gestapo friends," Kohlhaas disclosed, "overheard me so, they drew up a document that I had refused to be repatriated.... [O]ne of them stopped me on the road, [warning], 'Well, don't forget you are a German soldier.'" Kohlhaas replied, "I think that is over. Oh, boy!" he exclaimed. Continuing, Kohlhaas described what happened next:

> It took about a week and then they set up a real court-martial in our Catholic Chaplain's office. One afternoon, they were all there, six or seven of them. They closed the door from the inside and then they started threatening me with taking steps against my family in Germany. They would...find means...to do it by way of some soldier who was going to be repatriated. They would give him the documents necessary for the police to interfere in Germany. That is the way they would do it.[138]

Once Kohlhaas managed to free himself from their grip, he told Chaplain Baughman about his harrowing ordeal. Baughman advised him to keep a low profile for a week or two "and then to forget about it." Coerced to do other jobs, Kohlhaas worked as a janitor at the installation's motor pool, in warehousing, on a night shift at the post laundry, at the "Post Engineers' flying saw-mill" and in peanut farming.[139]

Community Reactions

Kohlhaas noted, "It took about two weeks for all the trucks [in the motor pool to be] manned by German drivers. They [the Americans] were afraid of us in the beginning. The Prussians, dangerous men," he laughed.[140] Were Augustans afraid of the POWs in their backyards? According to area newspapers, documents, county farm officials J.W. Chambers and Fred Sims, area famers and businessmen, most in the community welcomed them. Secretary of the Augusta Chamber of Commerce Lester Moody lobbied the War Department and the Fourth Service Command to locate a POW camp in Augusta. In late August 1943, the "hopes of the farmers [were] buoyed" on learning that POWs "would be in the fields about Richmond county." Farmers needed all the help they could get—even from POWs—to harvest the peanut crop before severe weather threatened their livelihood. Farmers did not know for certain when POWs would be "permitted to go into the cotton fields." Responding to the labor crunch, the Fourth Service Command sent an undesignated number of Italian POWs from Camp Wheeler to Camp Gordon.[141]

Early in September 1943, the *Augusta Chronicle* included the article "German Prisoners Harvest Peanut Crop in Aiken Area: War Captives Go About Tasks in Fields with Will; None Shows Displeasure at Work." Reporter Maurice Getchell wrote:

> *With Aiken counties 13,978 acres of peanuts in the ground ready for harvest and the growers faced with a critical shortage, the United States army came to the rescue with 250 German POWs to help the farmers prepare their crops for market.... [T]here has been no evidence of laziness or attempts to shirk their tasks. They go about their work with a will, sing and whistle and joke with one another in their native tongue.... There are no weaklings in the group of war prisoners...here. Each is a fine specimen of physical manhood.*[142]

A "fine specimen" possibly succinctly characterized the attitude of many farmers toward the POWs. After all, farmers desperately needed the prisoners: laborers and interesting novelties of observation. At least, this is the impression given by some of the early newspaper accounts.

One month later, the same reporter coauthored an article about a funeral given for the accidental death of a POW. Getchell questioned, "His name? Well that matters little." Then the reporters described the ceremony near Camp Gordon's gate no. 2. "He was a captured soldier. Captured honorably and as such was given a military funeral, a tribute that one soldier accords another, whether friend or foe." That seemed to echo the attitude of many American soldiers.[143]

CLOSE ENCOUNTERS

Nonetheless, not all welcomed POWs in their backyards. Some of that feeling stemmed from several escape attempts. On May 11, 1944, the *Augusta Chronicle* revealed that a POW thought to have escaped was hiding in the attic of a POW stockade. Several citizens reported seeing him "in many, many places in Georgia and South Carolina."[144] In December 1944, Augustans read "Nazis Recaptured in Bibb County." They learned that three German prisoners who had fled from Camp Gordon had been caught near Macon, Georgia. The Germans had been on the run for four days. The *Augusta Chronicle* reported the details:

GEORGIA POW CAMPS IN WORLD WAR II

> *As* [Frank] *Sims* [a civilian guard at Warner Robbins Air Force Base] *and* [Private First Class Jack] *Bingham were driving toward the field* [Warner Robbins] *they noticed three men who leaped into a roadside ditch when they observed the approaching automobile. Stopping to investigate, the guard and the soldier found the three prisoners still in coveralls with PW identification....It is believed that the three escapees had hoped to make their way to Mexico; evidently believing they could return to Germany from that country.*[145]

In early April 1945, the newspaper ran the article "German War Prisoner Chased from Yard by Irate Woman." The reporter noted that "the nomadic habits of the German POWs, stationed in the Forest Hills vicinity, are causing quite a stir of alarm among the residents." While working in her backyard, one woman suddenly spied "a man standing there with his back to her. The big PW across his shirt gave her a momentary feeling of alarm, but she quickly recovered and slipped quietly into the house." Once inside, she found her husband's pistol and ran back into the yard. When the POW "found himself looking into the dangerous end of a gun he turned and ran, half stumbling in his haste, down an embankment." The woman chased him and came upon a group of about thirty POWs with no guard in sight. After she yelled for the guard several times, he appeared. She was unsatisfied with the guard's reply to her questions as to how the POW escaped. She scolded him: "[T]he prisoners should be kept in barbed wire enclosures and not allowed to bother anyone. This is not the first time we have been annoyed by prisoners wandering around our grounds." The fuming woman informed the guard of another episode of a POW in her yard, adding that her children and her neighbors' children were scared to play in their favorite area for fear of the POWs. Military personnel gave the woman permission "to fire a warning shot at prisoners found roaming around her grounds, if the laxity of assigned guards permits them to annoy her a Georgian."[146]

Motorists passing an excavated area across from Augusta's Daniel Field grumbled that the POWs "[w]hoop and yell at all passers-by." Various people cited an editorial referring to "a ruckus" in Arizona and in Washington, D.C., caused by Arizona's Senator McFarland. The senator had read "half a dozen irate letters" ranting about German POWs "roaming at large, pilfering from homes, stealing and displaying the Nazi swastika." One Arizona judge thought the prisoners did not escape from the guards but "just walked off from the job." Alluding to the editorial, the *Augusta Chronicle* harangued, "Vigilance in guarding the PWs should be maintained. And civilians should be extremely wary of prisoners." A federal judge in Michigan mentioned that women were jailed for having "illicit dates with prisoners." He warned that "aiding war prisoners could be punished with the death penalty." All civilians were reminded that "PWs are potentially dangerous criminals with whom they should have no dealings."[147]

The *Augusta Chronicle* cautioned Augusta Arsenal employees to abide by the "published regulations regarding prisoners of war." One employee was discharged for failing to follow the rules. Augusta Arsenal POW Camp commander Colonel J. Thompson issued a stern statement: "Any employee found guilty of violating the rules laid down concerning POWs will be subject to prosecution in federal courts for giving aid to the enemy."

The government forbade fraternization. POWs were not to come close to female employees. In fact, "Dividing partitions...[were] required between women work areas and POW work areas." Even talking to prisoners was banned. Colonel Thompson added, "It has been found that most trouble which occurs in dealing with POWs is caused by the civilian element rather than a failure of prisoners to observe rules and regulations....The inborn discipline of the German prisoner especially causes his observance of regulations."[148] So, the attitudes of Augustans varied. Kohlhaas believed that relations were good between the POWs and the civilian population. Many agreed with him.[149]

POW Labor

The prisoners worked in several locations and in sundry capacities. Kohlhaas remembered, "[I]n the beginning, we would work on the base only, but later on, we would go out with one...escort per detail, to work for civilian contractors." POWs toiled in the installation officer's kitchen and mess hall, in the bakery and in the laundry. They worked in the motor vehicle shop and motor pool and with the installation's quartermaster. POWs served as cooks and orderlies in the military hospital. And they labored on the installation's farm.[150]

Georgia POW Camps in World War II

POWs working in a lettuce field. *Courtesy NARA collection.*

Farmers and businessmen were among the groups welcoming the POWs. On December 10, 1944, the *Augusta Chronicle* ran the story "War Prisoners Used for Labor: Captives Work on Farms and in Industry Here." The article noted:

> On farms, in factories and plants and at the various army installations in the vicinity they help ease the labor shortage. [Rome Compress company employed twenty-one Germans who were] *busy these days loading and unloading cotton for shipment. While at Castleberry's Food Company, about 15 prisoners are employed in the packing department. Here they operate the nailing and packing machines, as the boxes of canned meats come down the line, and then stack them for shipment.*[151]

Evidently, Castelberry and the War Manpower Commission reached an agreement on wages. The company had asked the War Manpower Commission to certify using forty POWs. The commission insisted that the prisoners be paid not less than forty cents an hour. Castelberry had feared a strike from its workforce of two hundred American civilians, who earned thirty-five cents an hour.[152]

Ten POWs worked at the Georgia-Carolina Tile and Brick Company. They loaded "wheelbarrows of brick in the kilns after the new brick is cooled, which they wheel to the freight cars where the brick is unloaded and stacked for shipment." Before the Fourth Infantry (Ivy) Division left for overseas, Staff Sergeant Percy Tatter led a POW detail to Wadley, Georgia, to harvest peanuts. Some helped farmers dismantle houses. Thirty-five worked as woodcutters on Pierce Anderson's farm near Grovetown. "Working in groups of three," the *Augusta Chronicle* told its readers, "they saw down trees and cut the timber into 63-inch lengths for pulpwood. The wood is piled in standard cords. One prisoner is kept busy filing the saws for the other woodcutters." Others worked in area forestry and logging.[153] Continuing, the article read:

> At Camp Gordon, Daniel Field, and Oliver General hospital, government money is saved by the employment of this class of labor. In addition to the money saved, the prisoners' labor aids the labor shortage also. At Daniel Field and Camp Gordon prisoners are kept busy at the salvage yards sorting the items that can be used again on the post and preparing the other salvaged material for shipment. They also are engaged at many other tasks.[154]

AUGUSTA ARSENAL, GEORGIA

The base camp sent work details to the Augusta Arsenal and Oliver General Hospital. Kohlhaas thought that Augusta Arsenal employed the largest number of POWs. About two to three hundred men worked there daily. Augusta Arsenal "took on a new life" as it expanded to meet wartime demands. "German POWs were housed there by the hundreds." Local policemen Bill Chavous and Rufus Lanier were guards. One civilian contractor, Albert J. Cromer, used prisoners in construction projects. "They knew the Geneva Convention," Cromer recalled, "and knew what they could and could not do." Their morale was high, save when rations and privileges were curtailed following the news of German atrocities at the concentration camps. "The Nazis tried to create trouble and had to be sent back to the compound. But," added Cromer, "that was a small percentage."[155]

AUGUSTA NATIONAL GOLF CLUB

Another work detail was sent to the Augusta National Golf Club. In 1942, the Augusta National, home of the Masters Golf Tournament, became a casualty of war when it closed. Instead of golfers, two hundred head of cattle rambled the fairways. The idea was to "provide munching privileges to the steers so as to eliminate mowing." The plan called for selling the fattened cattle from which "the club [Augusta National Golf Club (ANGC)] would turn a 'small profit,' all the while adding more meat to the table of a country that was in short supply of almost everything....Meanwhile, the steers... not realizing where they were, continued to devour azalea and camellia bushes at an alarming rate." When the ANGC lost money on the cattle project, Superintendent Simk Hammack proposed turning the course into a "turkey farm." Luckily, the more than one thousand turkeys "had a diet that wasn't as indiscriminate nor destructive as the steers and, surprisingly, returned a fiscal gain that offset the earlier loss inflicted by the roaming herd of cattle."[156]

With Allied victory in sight, on November 19, 1944, the ANGC publicized its intention to reopen the club to members next month. But the widespread cattle- and turkey-ravaged fairways made resuming tournaments seem surreal.[157] The ANGC turned to Camp Gordon for help. The POW compound sent forty-two German prisoners who worked for six months to "return the course to its former glory." The ANGC provided transportation to pick up the prisoners every morning and return them at the end of the workday. These POWs had served with Rommel's "engineering crew...in North Africa, part of the Panzer division responsible for building bridges that enabled German tanks to cross rivers."[158] The prisoners built a wooden truss bridge over Rae's Creek close to the thirteenth tee. A wooden sign with a soldier-carved inscription marked the bridge's location. That bridge lasted until the club removed it in 1958.[159]

The Germans worked tirelessly to restore the Augusta National to its pre–"beef venture" condition.[160] "The voracious cows had devoured much of the Augusta National's character—its stunning flowers—while littering the premises with cow chips."[161] A club member who brought fruit to the POWs remembered that they told him "the army had sent them out 'mostly just to give them something to do.'"[162]

"I was only 10 years old at the time," said William S. Morris III, who became a member of Augusta National and publisher of the *Augusta Chronicle*. "I never got out here to see what was going on, but I'm told the German prisoners took care of a lot of the heavy work that preceded the reopening of the course once the war was over....Augusta National is where men come in peaceful combat to compete, not with rifles and grenades, but with the weapons of golf—drivers, irons, wedges and putters."[163]

Georgia POW Camps in World War II

Other Work Details

In April 1944, Camp Gordon ordered 278 prisoners to Wilmington Island, Georgia. They worked in dairying and in a fertilizer plant. Later, the POWs cut down trees, gathered vegetables and cared for livestock. In July 1944, the Charleston, South Carolina branch camp employed its 500 prisoners in mosquito abatement and woodcutting and in sawmills.[164] On April 1, 1944, Camp Gordon sent 250 POWs to Dade City, Florida, to work in the citrus industry. On April 14, residents read the *Florida Times-Union*'s account of their new "neighbors":

This historical marker in Dade City, Florida, is evidence of the POW camp initially under Camp Gordon's supervision. *Courtesy Georgia Historical Society, via waymarking.com.*

> A unit of 250 German prisoners arrived on a special train this week from a camp in Augusta, Ga. And have been moved into the camp on the eastern edge of Dade City. Buildings to house the prisoners and the force of sixty military police have been built under the direction of Army engineers. The military personnel of the camp are permitted to live off the reservation when not on duty and many of them have been joined here by their families and have taken apartments in Dade City. The prisoners were brought here to work at the plant of the Pasco Packing association and the mill at Lacoochee, operated by Cummer Sons Cypress Co. Most of the prisoners are young and groups of them in the camp last evening were singing. An officer remarked that they would no doubt soon be singing "God Bless America," as they seem rather content to be here.[165]

The compound was about a mile from downtown Dade City, "very close to the geographic divide of the 'white' and 'colored' areas."[166] Florida's POW Camp Blanding later managed the Dade City camp.[167] A historical marker on Martin Luther King Boulevard reminds citizens of this branch camp.[168]

U.S. Military Personnel

Some POW camp inspection reports included the strength and capability of the American military personnel at the camps, often soldiers "who by lack of qualifications…[were] not needed elsewhere." The International Red Cross Committee concluded in a November 28, 1943 inspection report that Camp Gordon Commander Colonel Anderson was receptive and "very interested in the prisoners.…[A]n efficient cooperation ha[d] already been established between the Authorities and the prisoners."[169] In January 1944, inspectors found the twelve officers and seventy enlisted men assigned to the camp to be "satisfactorily instructed" in the Geneva Convention's provisions. Colonel Anderson voiced his concern over the guards' too affable feelings toward the prisoners, "brought about by the guards working with the prisoners daily and getting to know the prisoners as individuals."[170]

Nonetheless, one month later, First Lieutenant John J. Buckley of the Advisory-Liaison Branch, Military Police Division, Fort Custer, Michigan, toured the compound and had a distinctly different opinion of Anderson. He wrote, "The Commanding Officer does not appear to be capable of handling the POW camp. He appeared to me to be indecisive in his decisions, uninformed of the local camp regulations and apprehensive of what newspaper columnists, especially Walter Mitchell, would say of the manner in which he operated the camp."[171]

Buckley thought the staff was "made up of retread officers who were both unimpressive and unorganized." He found that the enlisted men had no confidence in their officers. Morale was "sub-zero." The Military Personnel were overworked and unable to guard the number of prisoners detailed to them. Colonel Anderson told Buckley that he was aware of the problems but could not correct them without more men. Buckley recounted several incidents including fraternization between Anderson's staff and the POWs. One prisoner had escaped when a guard mistook a piece of paper for an official pass. "No discipline exists among the German POW." Other incidents reported to him had been "hushed up."[172]

Other Disciplinary Problems

Among the less serious disciplinary troubles were car thefts, stolen laundry, hiding to avoid transfer to another camp and speeding. Disciplinary measures included court-martials, hard labor and partial forfeiture of monthly allowances. Eberhardt attributed some problems, notably escapes and camp administration, to the American guards' negligence and the staff's questionable abilities. Of a December 1944 visit, Eberhardt reported, "It seems obvious that the Camp Commander has been greatly handicapped by…too many subordinates lacking qualifications for successfully carrying their share of the burden of administration. Several instances indicating that the hearts of subordinates were not in their work came to the writer's notice."[173]

Inspector Major Edward C. Shannahan was disparaging of the camp's administration and also found low staff morale. He questioned the camp commander's apparent habit of berating his officers in front of others, including the prisoners. Shannahan thought the staff needed more instruction about their duties.[174] What did Kohlhaas think? "He [Colonel Anderson] was an elderly gentleman, respected by both the HQ-detachment and the prisoners for his pleasant ways."[175]

Relocating POWs

Kohlhaas recalled that when Camp Gordon's POW population dropped in early 1945, the prisoners were relocated to Augusta's Daniel Field. The U.S. Army transferred the German Catholic priest to Camp Blanding. The Catholic POW community then became part of Augusta's St. Mary on the Hill. Daniel Field became a branch of Camp Wheeler in Macon, Georgia.

By August 1945, there were about 298 POWs at Daniel Field who worked in area industries and agriculture. The side camp sent work details to Merry Brick, the local brickyard. Joe Buck was a civilian contractor-painter. He used about 150 POWs from Daniel Field for about eighteen months at Oliver General Hospital. Buck, who knew no German, did not want the job until the army provided an interpreter. Speaking of this experience, Buck recalled that they "got along alright." He only had trouble with two of the men. "They were smart people….All were good workers."[176]

Camp Closure

In December 1944, the Southeastern Branch of the United States Disciplinary Barracks (Fort Leavenworth) assumed control of Camp Gordon's POW compound. The camp's fate was uncertain. The visiting inspector recommended that one thousand prisoners remain at the stockade. He reported that the post's commander had ordered a survey to determine the cost of erecting security around a one-thousand-man barracks in another section of the installation.[177]

Germany's Surrender Affects Treatment of POWs

When Germany surrendered on May 8, 1945, the treatment of POWs changed. Kohlhaas remarked, "Thereafter, conditions declined considerably due to orders, which called for a certain retaliation provoked by the horrible conditions discovered in the Nazi concentration camps in Eastern Europe." He explained how the U.S. Army cut rations:

> [T]here was no more fresh meat, there was no more oleo, there was no more milk, no butter and for instance; our wood cutting details had to go out to cut, clean out and stack three cords of wood a man on six slices of bread with mashed beans. That was their lunch....Everything was taken out of the PX. All we could buy was bootblack and razor blades. No more cookies, no more soft drinks, no more whatever else. It took the International Red Cross about half a year to change things a little bit, so we could buy milk at the PX which we loved.[178]

Occasionally, prisoners used their ingenuity to get food. "Some funny things happened," Kohlhaas remarked. He described a comical instance at Oliver General Hospital involving the POW kitchen work detail. Told not to eat anything save their six slices of bread and mashed beans, one morning members of a detail eyed a skillet of sausages. "[O]ne of the men went over…and grabbed a sausage and put it in his pocket and was not aware of the fact that he was trailing another twenty feet of sausages." The men started laughing. Fortunately, the American mess sergeant had a sense of humor and offered the prisoners breakfast.[179]

A POW working at a motor shop, "where there is nothing to eat," took an empty tool box with him. He "would walk over to an American mess hall where some German prisoners were working as a kitchen detail. He would park that tool box next to a refrigerator…and you would see that box be filled as soon as possible. Then he would walk up to the mess sergeant" with a monkey wrench and screw drivers in hand, telling the sergeant that he was there "to check on the pipes and wiring." After making "repairs," the prisoner would edge toward the refrigerator and ask the other POWs if the tool box was full yet. Then he would disappear with the tool box in hand and return to the motor shop for breakfast.[180]

While these incidents were humorous, they did not mask the serious situation. A Department of State representative visiting the Charleston, South Carolina camp in July 1945 reported that the food the POWs received needed better refrigeration. There was a lice outbreak and numerous prisoner complaints. The representative reported that "the physical condition as well as the morale of the prisoners seems to have deteriorated very much in recent weeks." These circumstances were widespread across America.[181]

Nearing War's End

In the closing days of World War II, uneasiness spread over Camp Gordon's POW compound. "None of us," Kohlhaas acknowledged, "had any idea of what to expect. We had come to experience the first genuine fear since being prisoners. The freedom we had behind barbed wire was the only freedom we'd known."[182]

Some attributed the low morale to the Reeducation Program, which intensified with the news of the concentration camps. Kohlhaas described the new atmosphere:

> *Security was strict, but sometimes—as in the case of Nazi activities— malfunctioning to the point that the very same people who had been sitting opposite the chapel entrance on a Sunday in order to take down the names of the prisoners attending Sunday services…[who] were to be punished in case of a final German victory were appointed leaders of the re-education program after the German Surrender in May 1945….They were still hoping for the secret weapon or whatnot.*[183]

Repatriation

When the Daniel Field camp closed in March 1946, Kohlhaas and the other remaining POWs began their repatriation. U.S. Army trucks took them to Camp Wheeler and to Fort Benning. Then they traveled by rail via Camp Forrest, Tennessee, onward to Camp Shanks, New York. The brief stops at the various posts enabled processing before repatriation.[184]

Kohlhaas recalled his odyssey home:

> *We sailed from Staten Island, N.Y., aboard the USS "Waycross," a Victory ship this time…[early in the morning] on March 21, 1946, and arrived at Antwerp, Belgium, after an extremely stormy crossing, on March 31. We disembarked on April 1 and were turned over to the British, who took us to a tent-camp near Brussels (Villevorde). By a mistake of the British bureaucracy I was discharged right there on April 24, 1946 and after an unbelievably adventurous Odyssey I crossed the German border in the disguise of a Belgium army-chaplain at 9:30 P.M. on July 10, 1946. But that would make a real novel.*[185]

The next day, Kohlhaas met Monseigneur Ferdinand Cammaert, "the Belgian Chief of Chaplains, who was supposed to return…[him] to British custody." He told the monseigneur that he planned to join the Benedictine monastery of Maria Laach. Monseigneur Cammaert, who was on his way to Maria Laach, volunteered to take a letter on Kohlhaas's behalf. "He would see to it that I would get to Maria Laach in due time. But that's the novel. Imagine the one prisoner out of 100,000 wanting to become a monk of Maria Laach meeting the one Belgian chaplain, who was going there at that very moment!" exclaimed Kohlhaas.[186]

Life After Camp Gordon

Kohlhaas fulfilled his dream, becoming a Benedictine priest at the Abbey of St. Hildegard in Rudesheim, Germany. Reflecting on the "general effect of…[his] POW experience," Kohlhaas, commented, "I shall be grateful for it to the end of my life. As you will have gathered from my record, I was a student of theology, and I made up my mind to join the Benedictine monastery of Maria Laach…right at Camp Gordon, Georgia."[187] "I hold

Georgia POW Camps in World War II

The white chains and posts enclose the burial grounds of the twenty-one German POWs buried at Fort Gordon. *From chronicle.augusta.com.*

only fond memories of Americans and my days as a German POW," Kohlhaas reflected in 1989.[188] Kohlhaas, silhouetted against twenty-one headstones in Fort Gordon's POW cemetery, ended his pilgrimage with a silent prayer.[189]

Aiken Branch Camp

The Aiken, South Carolina branch camp was activated on September 2, 1943. Before Aiken leased land for the camp, the Powder House Polo Field held the POWs. On January 21, 1944, Aiken mayor E.H. Wyman signed the land lease with owner Jack Roberts of Concord, North Carolina. The contract stipulated that Aiken would underwrite the site's rental costs and supply the camp with free water. Aiken County was to pay for the electricity.

The compound was located along Highway 19. A multi-strand barbed wire fence and elevated guard towers surrounded it. Two officers and forty enlisted American soldiers guarded the stockade. German POWs were held in Aiken from November 1943 to May 1946. The first prisoners to arrive were 250 Afrika Korps soldiers. By January 1945, Italian soldiers captured in Italy and in France arrived, raising the population to 620. Up to 5 men lived in each wooden-floor tent. The mess hall was a large wooden barracks. The POWs worked eight to ten hours daily, harvesting peanuts or peaches, cutting pulpwood or lumber, planting trees or working in a fertilizer factory.

The men received the usual wage of eighty cents a day in credit, which they could use at the camp's canteen.[190]

Former POW Wolfgang Peter made a return visit to Aiken. A glider pilot, he was drafted into the German army in the spring of 1944. Peter finished his training in southern France as a Luftwaffe ground soldier. Meanwhile, Operation Anvil, the Allied invasion of southern France, was underway. U.S. armor and mechanized units besieged Peter's unit until he and his comrades surrendered. They were now prisoners of war.[191]

Within a month, Peter was transferred from France to Naples, Italy. There he and other prisoners boarded a troop ship. They joined a convoy off North Africa destined for the United States. In late 1944, Peter arrived at the Aiken camp, where he was detained for eighteen months. He described the living conditions as "miserable." There were not enough showers and outdoor latrines. A secret memorandum sent in April 1945 to the provost marshal general confirmed the awful situation. An inspector warned that unless the circumstances improved, an epidemic might break out. Camp administrators kept problems like this and others from the general public. Many Americans thought that the prisoners' living conditions were as good as, if not superior to, their own, using the phrase "Frits Ritz" to describe their annoyance and frustration.[192]

After working briefly on a farm, the farmer's family invited Peter, other POWs in his detail and the family's neighbors to a barbecue. Hamer commented, "Not surprisingly Peter thought that this was one of the best days of his POW experience."[193] This fraternization violated the PMGO's regulations instructing employers to have as little contact as possible with the prisoners. All communication was to be work related. Farmers, other employers and the POWs commonly ignored the directive.[194]

On his return visit, Peter met with Margaret Holmes Noel, daughter of Charlie and Zilla Holmes. He remembered picking peaches as a seventeen-year-old in 1945 and 1946 on the Holmes farm near Johnston, South Carolina. He also cut lumber and picked cotton. Peter had never seen cotton before, but he quickly learned how to pick the lint. "I picked a hundred pounds a day."[195] He called it backbreaking work. He also "picked 25 boxes of peaches each day." Although Peter disliked cutting timber, he did his best. Mrs. Noel described seeing Peter after forty-five years: "You still look about the same....The more I looked at him...the more I remembered. He was about the youngest one we ever had, and I was younger than he was....He was just so young to be a soldier." Mrs. Noel said her mother was *so impressed with Wolfgang. She gave him and the others extra food. They were the best workers we ever had, before and after....My mother sent CARE packages to quite a few of them, and he was one of the special ones....She [Mrs. Holmes] wrote to Wolfgang and a lot of them....She talked about Wolfgang and the others a lot, because she never had a son of her own. If one of them (POWs) had a birthday, we always had a party. We always enjoyed each other so much.*[196]

Peter's opinion of the American guards mirrored those of some others. He thought they were "pleasant, although often naive and poorly educated." Many drank too much. On more than one occasion, a guard attending "Peter's work detail disappeared into the woods to drink the day away while the POWs worked. Sometimes Peter and his comrades had to search for their intoxicated guard at the end of the day before they could return to their camp." Luckily for most communities, this carelessness did not result in significant problems or escapes.[197]

In his spare time, Peter made drawings of the camp. He preferred the "Christmas scenes he drew of his tent and other camp facilities. He covered his tent with hand-painted decorations. A flap covered the tent's small door, allowing passage for pet cats. The POWs enjoyed playing soccer; performing theatrical productions, plays and concerts; watching movies; and taking night classes, among other pastimes.[198]

Local resident Jim Osborn recalled that the camp was "right in my backyard essentially."[199] Osborn and his father visited the camp on Sunday afternoons. The two became acquainted with the POWs and even traded with them. "One day a prisoner asked if he could make me a ring, but he'd need a half dollar to do it. Several weeks later, the prisoner brought me a ring."[200]

Another citizen, Dick Holstein, said that even with the passage of time and the distance separating them, he remained friends with Gunther Liebelt, who worked on the Holstein Farm near Monetta, South Carolina. "I remember him very well because he spoke English; he was the only one in the crew that did. Plus, he used to carry me around on his shoulders." In 1998, Liebelt located Holstein, who was eight years old when the two first met.[201]

When the POWs were released, Liebelt's group left Aiken, thinking that they would be repatriated directly to Germany. To their dismay, the men traveled to Scotland, where they worked for two more years. When Liebelt did return to East Germany, he learned that his parents had survived the war. But he also found "intolerable" conditions under Communism. Liebelt escaped, making his home in Stadthagen, a city in the north of West Germany. On February 25, 2012, he died at the age of ninety-one. His son, Hans-Dieter, and his family continued the correspondence with Holstein. In February 2015, Liebelt's family visited the Aiken POW campsite.[202]

Murder

Dr. Edward A. Freer of the Swiss Legation was at Camp Gordon a few days following a tragic incident. On April 6, 1944, Horst Günther was murdered at the Aiken camp. Günther was a twenty-four-year-old Afrika Korps corporal and a locksmith before the war. He was captured on May 9, 1943, in Tunisia. After Günther was transported to America, he was sent to the Aiken compound. An inquest determined that two Nazi POWs, Sergeant Erick Gauss and Private Rudolph Straub, strangled Günther, carried his body away and hanged it from a telephone pole to give the appearance of suicide. According to one report, Gauss and Straub thought that Günther had distributed food to the POWs inequitably. Another story stated that the POWs suspected Günther of having notified American authorities of a planned work stoppage; also, "he liked jazz music."[203]

Freer reported that Colonel Anderson got a confession. He applauded Anderson "for the manner in which…[he] and his assistants were administering the camp." State Department representative Charles C. Eberhardt, who accompanied Freer, agreed. He stated, "Colonel Anderson and his assistant deserve all commendation for their administration of this camp, grown so difficult in recent days."[204]

First Lieutenant Buckley (Advisory-Liaison Branch, Military Police Division, Fort Custer, Michigan) learned about the murder when he visited Camp Gordon in December 1944. He criticized Colonel Anderson's eight-hour delay in leaving Camp Gordon for Aiken.[205]

Radbert Kohlhaas thought that serious political factors were at play:

> Life at the PW-Camp was well regulated on the surface, but it could be dangerous underneath, at least for active church members; there was quite a strong undercurrent of Nazi persecution which led to outright murder in the spring of 1944. A plot aimed at our PW-priest in Cp. Gordon failed, but a prisoner was hanged in one of our branch camps at Aiken, S.C. The

killing was investigated by the FBI, the killers were found out and brought to justice after the war. Similar conditions seem to have prevailed in German PW-Camps all over the U.S.[206]

Krammer declared the Aiken murder was the "last of…a series of seven celebrated Nazi-inspired [political] murders." He concluded, "Günther was condemned by a midnight Kangaroo court." Hamer called it "shocking" and the "most bizarre case of German independence."[207]

Gauss and Straub (formerly a shoemaker) were tried at Fort McPherson, Georgia (near Atlanta), and received death sentences. Krammer described what came next: "Then came the normal flurry of diplomatic activity with Germany via Bern, to guarantee the rights of the condemned men, and, if necessary, to exchange the Germans for condemned Allied prisoners."[208] But when the war ended, so did the "threat to American prisoners in German hands," and so ended the diplomacy. The PMGO instructed authorities to proceed with the executions. President Truman concurred. The two, who had been transferred to the U.S. Army Disciplinary Barracks at Fort Leavenworth, Kansas, were hanged on July 14, 1945. Straub is alleged to have said just before his execution, "What I did was done as a German soldier under orders. If I had not done so, I would have been punished when I returned to Germany."[209] The army executed them in a warehouse elevator shaft that had been transformed into temporary gallows. Gauss and Straub were two of the fourteen German POWs the U.S. Army hanged in 1945 at Fort Leavenworth. All were buried at the fort's cemetery.[210]

Escapes

Another infamous event at the Aiken camp was a POW's attempted escapes. The *Aiken Standard* reported that sometime on the morning of Monday, January 24, 1944, Gurd Guztat sneaked away, undetected, from his twenty-five-man work detail. The men were cutting wood on Mr. Price's property, eight and a half miles southeast of Aiken. Nobody missed him until the American guards took a head count of prisoners during their lunch break. The newspaper described Guztat as "having blond hair, blue eyes and a fair complexion."[211]

The Aiken City Police Department, the Aiken County Sheriff's Office and the FBI began an extensive manhunt, setting up roadblocks and searching cars. Bloodhounds were brought in from Columbia, South Carolina. Forty-eight hours later, FBI agents found Guztat near the Aiken dump. He had startled some area black citizens. When arrested, "Gutzat was wearing German boots, blue POW pants, a short jacket, and a German raincoat."[212]

After the FBI questioned him, the agency disclosed that "Guztat had buried a cache of nine cans of German sardines, sixteen German candy bars and two Hershey chocolate bars….Some of the items were part of a Christmas care package sent by the German government to POWs and some items other prisoners had given to him." He had "traced a map of Aiken with all roads leading out of the city," using a swastika to mark the POW camp. Guztat intended to steal an airplane and fly to Germany! A newspaper article noted, "When arrested Guztat accepted his fate stoically." The FBI claimed that "his fanatical faith in the German cause seemed undimmed."[213] Within days, "an official order went out stipulating that POWs must wear only regulation clothing at all times."[214]

The U.S. Army transferred Guztat to Camp Gordon's POW stockade. He promised not to escape again. Nevertheless, on April 17, Guztat and three fellow prisoners ran away after "sawing the bars on a water culvert leading out of their compound." Within twenty-four hours, authorities had caught two of the fugitives "near the Colonial Club in Augusta." Gutzat and Hermann Mueller stole a MP's Ford. When it ran out of gas, they "commandeered a 1938 Chevrolet owned by an Augusta man." The two made it all the way to Columbia. On the loose for four days, Mueller went into a grocery store. "The female proprietor soon became suspicious, perhaps because of his accent or the absence of ration stamps.… [She] ordered a sailor who was in the store to hold Mueller while she contacted the authorities. As it turned out, the sailor was AWOL and both men were taken away." The following morning, Columbia police spotted Gutzat sleeping in a freight car with a beer bottle filled with milk.[215] That ended Guztat's exploits.

"Not surprisingly," Hamer wrote, "Army representatives who visited both

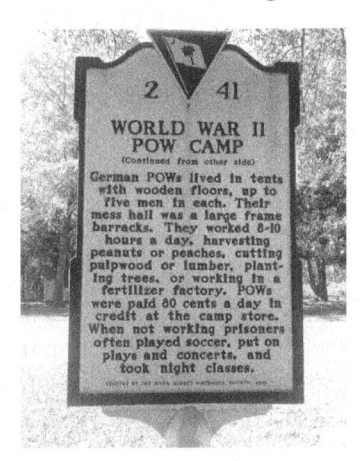

This historical marker is on the site of the Aiken, South Carolina POW branch camp once under Camp Gordon's management. Erected by the Aiken County Historical Society in 2008. *Courtesy Aiken County Historical Society, via waymarking.com.*

Gordon and Aiken during the first half of 1944 were unusually critical of what they saw. A lieutenant reported to his superiors that the staffs were composed of 'retread officers who were both unimpressive and unorganized.'" Furthermore, the enlisted soldiers "had no confidence in them."[216] The officer also disclosed "that an American sergeant of German extraction apparently upbraided a guard (also of German blood) who tried to extinguish the lights in a POW compound during a Christmas party held at Camp Gordon. 'I am drinking in here with my friends,' retorted the sergeant. 'What the hell kind of a German are you anyway?'"[217]

By the middle of 1944, Camp Gordon no longer managed the Aiken camp. Six months later, South Carolina was home to nine POW camps. In July 1945, each camp, except Croft, a base camp in its own right, was under the general management of Fort Jackson. The Aiken camp was closed on October 6, 1943.[218] A historical marker erected in front of the current healthcare center saved this intriguing aspect of Georgia's homefront during World War II from being lost and forgotten.[219]

Waynesboro Branch Camp

Before the War Department simplified the POW camp system, Camp Gordon's branch camps extended to North Carolina and Florida. The Waynesboro, Georgia branch camp was activated on June 13, 1944. The compound used its 249 German POWs to cut trees, load grain cars, clear pastures and harvest cotton. Patte found the "little camp…situated very close to a small cotton, tobacco and pecan town, so close even that it seems to be a part of the township.…You will find there, amidst pines and oaks, twenty-four tents and one little barracks for the German doctor attached to the camp, all the buildings are undecorated and of a very rugged appearance."[220]

Reidsville Branch Camp

In December 1944, Patte visited the Reidsville, Georgia compound. He wrote, "On this December day, the sun was shining brightly, and the temperature was so warm that I thought we were in May. On the sand, [forty-five] tents have been planted, of the usual type, brown, tan, dark olive." The executive officer introduced him to "a lanky, bony, red-haired spokesman and interpreter." Patte spent a few minutes "watching a football game played by teams of young men clad in gym shorts, body all bronzed and suntanned." The POWs wanted to learn exactly who was "the civilian in tweeds" who had left a red Hudson coupe at the stockade's gate.[221]

Chapter 4

CAMP STEWART

WORLD WAR II EXPANSION

The declaration of war increased the growth and improvement of Camp Stewart located near Savannah, Georgia. That meant enhancing antiaircraft artillery training; stationing a Women's Air Service Pilots (WASPs) detachment on post; adding a cook and bakers' school; and sectioning off areas on the cantonment for two POW compounds.[222]

ITALIAN SERVICE UNITS

On September 8, 1943, Italy surrendered to the Allies. The next month, Italy declared war on Germany. The Allies granted Italy cobelligerent status. That action resulted in the questionable status of more than 50,000 Italian POWs in the United States. The U.S. Army had to figure out what to do with them. The army's plan called for forming Italian Service Units (ISUs) comprising screened volunteers who were placed under Army Service Forces. In February 1944, the army took the first steps to organize the ISUs. Nearly 90 percent of Italian POWs joined ISUs. By October 1944, there were 195 ISUs filled with 954 officers and 33,898 enlisted men who did vital war-related work at sixty-six military installations. The

Italian service patch. *Courtesy of Jason Wetzel's private collection.*

units existed until October 1945. The ISUs "contributed materially to the successful conclusion of the war, releasing U.S. service personnel for overseas duties." Ordnance companies received training at the Atlanta Ordnance Depot.[223]

POW CAMPS

The War Department activated the POW compound at Camp Stewart on February 13, 1944, under the management of Camp Aliceville, Alabama. On about May 1, it was placed directly under Camp Stewart's supervision. Period maps show the complex was in multiple buildings on the post, close to the main gate. A 1945 POW compound was located in another area on the installation.[224] Jack Austin, a soldier with the 4406 Service Command Unit, recalled that there was a large sign posted facing the main road into the base that read:

> WARNING: MOTORISTS & PEDESTRIANS WILL NOT MOLEST OR PASS REMARKS TO OR ABOUT PRISONERS. TO DO SO WILL BE CAUSE FOR SEVERE DISCIPLINARY ACTION BY ORDER OF THE COMMANDING OFFICER.[225]

Dr. Rudolph Fischer of the Swiss Legation and State Department official Parker Buhrman made their first visit to the POW camp on July 3, 1944. The 540-by-230-foot compound held 250 Germans. There were four guard towers, but just two were manned regularly. The recreation

A U.S. Army colonel, camp commanding officer, is shown with captured German officers. Friendly cooperation by German officers was helpful to camp authorities in solving problems of morale and discipline among war prisoners. *Courtesy NARA collection.*

area, attached to the stockade, was about 60 by 100 feet. The one-story barracks were approximately 48 by 16 feet. Twelve to fourteen men lived in the fourteen preexisting barracks. The Germans had decorated the barracks' exterior. Buhrman reported that the camp had "individual flush toilets, wash basins, laundry tubs, and modern baths with running hot and cold water upon which there is no restriction." He believed that "the camp is unusually clean and orderly."[226]

The complex also contained "1 mess hall, 1 recreation building that housed the library, canteen, theater, chapel, and classroom; and

1 barrack housing the showers and latrines. The guard house…was an unheated trailer" without a stove, light or toilets.[227] The compound had a "dispensary or first aid station." Prisoners were treated at the post hospital in a "barred and locked" section typically used for army prisoners. The Germans objected to hospitalization in a "prison ward." The Swiss Legation was working with the hospital's commander to place sick prisoners in a "normal ward."[228]

The POWs in the "strictly [small] work camp" had jobs in the post machine shop, laundry, motor pool, salvage, stables and hospital bakery and labored "in other post maintenance details." Recreational activities included an outdoor field, the library, a weekly movie, a canteen, a choir and an orchestra.[229] Some prisoners took courses in English, history, geography and math. Fischer thought that the athletic field was too small. However, on Sundays the Germans could use the installation's sports field, where they played *faustball*. They used their homemade "bandstand near the fence along the main road…[where] on Sunday afternoons they would give a concert to the people parked along the road in their cars." Austin thought that the "band was really very good, and they had beautiful instruments. One such band was called Stille Nacht [Silent Night]."[230]

Buhrman ended his report with some broad observations. He thought the camp was "unusually well administered." The prisoners' morale was high, and their work was "satisfactory." "There was some indication of previous internal friction among the prisoners, but the camp administration appears to have been quite successful in removing the disturbing element." Although he did not specify the cause of the friction, it may have been Nazi versus anti-Nazi sentiments.[231] When Maurice Perret toured the German camp on July 4, 1944, there were 169 prisoners. The men wanted a German doctor. They had two radios for their amusement. Boxing was a new addition to the sports program.[232]

At the end of the year, Fischer and Eberhardt visited the camp. They found that the "German cook provides the prisoners with potatoes and more potatoes, as they desire; complete outfits of winter clothing have also been supplied recently." Eberhardt stated that Camp Stewart's commander had plans to relocate the POW compound to a "larger and better-adapted area." Installation of a "regulation-sized soccer field, etc.—is expected to be one of the first undertakings." Among the needed improvements were more books. The men wanted their own priest and preacher instead of having to rely on a post chaplain. They "appreciated that the fault [of the irregular mail] lay almost entirely in their invaded or surrounded Germany."[233]

After commenting on some common disciplinary problems, Eberhardt described one extraordinary situation: "There had recently been some rivalry among the prisoners...themselves which had resulted in a rough-and-tumble fight, when knives were also used but with no serious results.... Commanding Officer [Colonel William V. Ochs] considered it advisable to remove his No. one Spokesman (for the latter's own protection) to Turner Field [Georgia] until possible transfer of those who had provoked the attack. Although the valuable spokesman, who periodically visited the branch camps, wanted to return, Camp Commander Captain Howard E. Callahan thought otherwise."[234] Was this another Nazi versus anti-Nazi incident?

Field Service Officer Major Shannahan also visited in December 1944. He described an unreported "[i]ncident involving the camp spokesman and an undetermined number of other prisoners":

> *Spokesman was attacked when he attempted to quiet a boisterous group of prisoners....In defending himself, spokesman used a pen knife and wounded one of his assailants. Preliminary investigation reveals that prisoners have been purchasing rum from personnel at Camp Stewart with money they have found in clothing at salvage yard and in the laundry. It is recommended that a regulation be published allowing a camp commander to confiscate any money found in the possession of a prisoner after the prisoner has been initially searched. The money so confiscated to be deposited to the credit of the Treasurer of the United States. It is further recommended that adequate interpreter personnel be supplied to the base camp and its side camps.*[235]

This sounds like the same skirmish Eberhardt reported, but with some interesting, notable additions.

In February 1945, Captain Robert L. Kunzig, field liaison officer, made a visit to the camp. It then held 1,325 Germans, a significant increase. By then, the compound had been relocated; plans were in the works to improve the site and position the recreation area. The Intellectual Diversion (Reeducation) Program was "progressing excellently." The American officers were enthusiastic; Captain Callahan supported it "100%." None of the POWs were enrolled yet in correspondence courses, but they wanted a sponsoring university. A young prisoner was the director of studies. "Captain Kunzig reminded the assistant executive officer [Lieutenant Mason F. Richards] to be careful of the political background of this man [from Aachen], and he is being closely watched and his views studied."

The stockade lacked an acceptable reading room, although 80 percent of the prisoners used it. They were especially fond of Shakespeare, Dickens, Galsworthy, Twain and Poe and wanted books to be added for sale in the canteen. An American chaplain needed to be assigned to the camps since a "beautiful" chapel stood ready. For recreation, the compound had a day room, the canteen, several radios, a "fair record collection…[with an] electric turntable" and an exceptional seventeen-piece orchestra. Lieutenant Richards chose twice-weekly-shown films, which supported the Intellectual Diversion Program, and circulated them among the branch camps.

There was "no great segregation problem," indicating that the previously reported internal conflict perhaps was resolved or at least moderated. Kunzig thought the American guards' morale was "fair." Lieutenant Richards was beginning "orientation hours and is attempting to improve the situation." Kunzig determined that the overall anomalies were insufficient funds and transportation to the branch camps along with problematic procurement of "facilities and tools."[236]

OTHER POW COMPLEXES

A new POW complex began operating in February 1945. This compound included barracks (unknown number and capacity), a day room, a canteen, the camp spokesman's office, a classroom, an orchestra studio and a carpenter's workshop. The prisoners built an outdoor stage. A chapel was situated outside the complex. There was no recreation field yet. The POWs enjoyed a small beehive. Annotated 1943 maps show the boundaries of this camp.[237]

Another map illustrates a fenced section. The installation's engineer learned of circumstantial information suggesting this area did hold POWs. Likewise, hearsay suggests that the Civilian Conservation Camp (CCC) located to the southwest of the engineer's office housed one hundred Italian POWs.

Sometime after the war, a boundary street in the Department of Public Works region was renamed "Italy," but nobody knows exactly why. Since the known Italian POW camp was located nearby, conjecture has it that "Italy" Street may have been where the Twenty-Fifth Italian Dump Truck Company and the Tenth Italian Ordnance Materiel Acquisition Management Company were stationed.

Branch Camps

Chatham Army Air Field Branch Camp

On November 14, 1944, the PMGO announced that Camp Stewart's POW compound was to manage two new branch camps—one at Chatham Army Air Field (6.7 miles west-northwest of Savannah) and the other at Hunter Field (5.7 miles south-southwest of Savannah). The following month, Major Shannahan reported that Chatham Army Air Field camp was under construction. There were 125 prisoners already there, with another 125 expected soon. The barracks were prefabricated with connecting latrines. No laundry tubs existed. The labor program was "just being instituted and a little confusion exists, on the part of the Post Engineer, as to proper assignment of prisoners to details." Shannahan wrote, "One detail in particular was noted where 13 prisoners were being used to pour concrete, 6 prisoners could have been used to better advantage…details are moved throughout the area."[238] Jack Austin stated, "The prisoners were all enlisted men…so there was no problem about working them. If they had been officers, they would have to volunteer to work."[239]

Hunter Field Branch Camp

Hunter Field was a tent camp equipped with "latrine and kitchen buildings." Six Germans lived in each tent. Major Shannahan described the kitchen areas as unclean and unsanitary. The compound's commander promised action to remedy the conditions. The poor guard houses were like those at the base camp. He even found a "half filled bucket of excreta…there."

Shannahan believed that the POWs were "well utilized…[except for] overstaffing of some Engineer Projects." Camp Stewart's engineer and other officers thought that the Germans were doing a "good job." Hunter Field expected one hundred more prisoners on December 27, 1944. The base commanding general planned to request three hundred more POWs "to relieve American enlisted men from KP duties."[240]

Georgia POW Camps in World War II

475th Military Police Escort Guard Company

On August 21, 1945, the 475th Military Police Escort Guard Company was transferred to Camp Stewart. Its home station was at Fort Eustis, Virginia, a reception center for German POWs disembarking nearby at Norfolk. The MPs guarded the prisoners as they were transported to camps across the South. Typically, one or two crews escorted each train. At least one soldier recalled it as "dirty duty riding in non-air-conditioned troop sleepers, with their ill-ventilated 4-tiered bunks, behind oil- or coal-burning soot or cinder spewing locomotives." This time, the MP's job was to oversee POWs harvesting crops. One detail went to Statesboro and to Swainsboro. Each side camp had a medic along with an ambulance. One MP recalled:

> *I typed morning reports for the signature of the casual lieutenant who was the only commissioned officer at the side camp. I also typed...contracts for the farmers to sign hiring POW labor in harvesting peanuts. We had POW cooks and bakers and ate the same meals as the POWs. Outside the peanut farmers [sic] complaints about the too-small-size of stacks of peanut plants there was not much excitement at Swainsboro....The most excitement...occurred when a POW suffered a strangulated hernia and the medic, and I took him to several major Army installations in Georgia by ambulance before we found one with a hospital that would accept him. By mid-October the peanut harvest was completed, and Camp Swainsboro was about to close. POWs and personnel transferred to Statesboro which had more permanent facilities.*[241]

What a Building Tells Us

The last anecdote concerning POWs at Camp Stewart was their erection of Building 5019. This was "a single-story hollow-tile, wood and brick building located off of Hero Road, just south of the...Hinesville/Ft. Stewart wastewater treatment plant." It had a rectangular gabled roof. While it was "configured similar to other hollow-tile administrative buildings of the era...[the] brick quoins [masonry blocks] on the corners of the building and the windows...are framed with brick in a distinctive pattern. The building also features two windows per side as compared to the more typical single, centered windows found on most World War II mobilization buildings."

Since the building's measurements were metric, it provided further evidence that POWs built it. There are no extant records telling how the original building was used.[242]

Between November and December 1945, ISU soldiers were repatriated. According to Austin, "After the war was over we packed up everything and the prisoners and took all to Ft. Benning. After a few days we loaded the prisoners on trains and took them to Camp Shanks, New York to be returned to Germany." On July 24, 1946, the government inactivated Camp Stewart.[243] Regrettably, the complexes in two areas were bulldozed and revamped. Plus, woods have overtaken the former CCC camp used for Italian prisoners.

Chapter 5

FORT BENNING

POW Camp Establishment

The War Department's warning to the PMGO in late 1942 to anticipate nearly 30,000 Italian prisoners by February 1943 proved to be a conservative figure. In fact, by the end of 1943, almost 50,000 Italians were living on America's homefront. The Fourth Service Command (the noncombat arm of the Army Service Forces responsible for the southeastern states) feverishly sought additional commanders for new POW camps. One of those camps was at Fort Benning, located near Columbus, Georgia. The compound opened on September 8, 1943. At one time, it held 2,234 prisoners.[244] Colonel George M. Chescheir was the camp's commander. According to historian Antonio Thompson:

> *In all prisoner-of-war establishments, the treatment of captives is only as good as the men who implement policy. Accordingly, it is no accident of history that the operation of prison camps for German and Italian POWS by Louisville native George M. Chescheir exemplified military professionalism, mutual respect, and even lasting friendship between adversaries. Chescheir's leadership and character eased the burdens of those in his charge and, in his role as commander of POW facilities in Georgia (Fort Benning and its branch camps); northern Florida; and southeastern Alabama, hastened his nation's victory and its postwar reconciliation with European enemies.*[245]

Chescheir definitely did not fit the stereotypical image many Americans held of POW "keepers." He had extensive military experience. "In this emergency," wrote Thompson, "Chescheir was clearly able and available." When he assumed command in January 1943 of Fort Benning's recently constructed POW camp, no prisoners had arrived yet. He found two compounds, divided by barbed wire.[246]

LABOR SHORTAGE

The fact that no prisoners were in the state deeply concerned farmers. By July 1943, the *Macon Telegraph* was reporting, "With time rapidly approaching for harvesting the greatest peanut crop in the 24 counties making up the third congressional district, no prisoners have arrived…yet the hope of obtaining help is not very encouraging." The state had hoped to receive fifty POWs per county. Congressman Stephen Pace was not convinced that Georgia would receive any POWs. He sounded the alarm, telling his constituents:

> *The time is near when every man, woman, and child in the state, who is physically able and can possibly spare the time, must offer their services and go to the fields and help gather and save the abundant crop which the farmers have produced. Food is too important to let any of the crop waste in the fields. Our boys out on the battle lines of the world must be fed, our civilian workers must be sustained, and many of our bothers in arms must be provided for.*[247]

However, Italian POWs were on their way to Fort Benning.[248]

CAMP OPERATIONS: REPORTER'S PERSPECTIVE

Realizing that the prisoners were coming, a *Columbus Ledger* reporter wanted to write an article about the camp's operations. So, he "toured" the stockade as if he were an Italian POW. The inquisitive reporter first met with Colonel Chescheir, telling him that he "wanted the full POW experience and Chescheir promised to give him 'the works.'"[249] He spent the day "marching around camp filling out forms, getting his POW uniform, and learning about his job and barracks assignment." Chescheir let him know that he and his staff "had been very careful in picking...[the] complement of U.S. Army men in the camp." They were from a "score of nationalities" and had "been learning the language for months, and it has been amazing how rapidly they have mastered it." Chescheir praised them: "I cannot too highly compliment them."[250]

Chescheir guaranteed the curious reporter that "these prisoners...are not going to be lions or animals in a cage." The reporter concluded that "to an Italian prisoner of war fresh from the heat and horror of North Africa...[Fort Benning] will be a paradise." He "left with a strange thought in...mind—that if the Italian army, its rank and file, knew just what was in store for them in the prison camps over here, [they] would surrender, unconditionally today."[251]

POWs Arrive

The *Macon Telegraph* informed local citizens on August 28, 1943, about the transfer of several hundred Italian POWs from Camp Wheeler to Fort Benning and to Albany, Georgia. They were needed "to help speed up the agricultural program."[252] One month later, more than 2,900 Italian prisoners streamed into the camp. Chescheir described the influx of prisoners and their initial reactions: "The first group of prisoners...had been fired upon by Nazis in Sicily."[253]

With a copy of the Geneva Convention in hand, some instruction from the PMGO and from the Army Service Forces, Chescheir and his staff set about managing the two compounds. By the middle of September, little progress had been made on camp preparations. The prisoners did have sleeping quarters, but almost everything else was incomplete.[254]

Inspections, 1943

On September 26, 1943, inspector Andre Vulliet from the YMCA's War Prisoners Aid Division visited the compound. He wrote that it had "a most pleasant aspect. Its high pine trees, left untouched inside the enclosure, contribute their light and shadow effects to the beauty of the camp and provide plenty of shaded areas, so rarely found in camps." Chescheir wanted Vulliet to observe the camp in its unfinished state and interact with the POWs. He urged Vulliet to talk with Gaetano Fascina, the Italian senior ranking noncommissioned officer. Fascina told Vulliet that Chescheir had formed a "bond of firmness, compassion, and cooperation with the Italians." The result was comparative tranquility.[255]

Vulliet spent five days observing the day-to-day schedule and the in-processing of POWs. He thought the newcomers' reactions were humorous, noticing that "they would alternately proclaim that they would return home to their mothers and then ask the guards for cigarettes." He saw Chescheir meeting the prisoners soon after their arrival and promising them descent treatment. The colonel made a point to salute each work detail as it departed. As a rule, he promoted good relations between the POWs and the American staff. Vulliet asked the POWs what they thought of Chescheir, finding their answers very revealing. Several asked him if the commander was *"veramente fantastic"* (really fantastic) or whether he was following a propaganda line, because "if he had in mind to make them all love America, he could not do it in any better way." Vulliet returned numerous times; he and the colonel became trustworthy friends.[256]

Chescheir told Vulliet that he intended to meet the Geneva Convention's stipulations, providing "intellectual diversion and recreation." Vulliet discovered Chescheir had set in motion

> the groundwork for an enlightened camp culture. The library, for instance, while consisting of only a "small building" with no books, already had a staff of five Italians who eagerly anticipated the arrival of reading materials. Carlo Stefani, a marathon runner for the Italian 1932 Olympic team, had been appointed head of the Athletics Committee, and he was assisted by both a former ski champion and a former member of the Italian National Soccer team.[257]

Vulliet recommended that two musicians head a music department. The only POW-owned instrument was one guitar; there was no sheet music. The prisoners owned several records but not a record player. Chescheir informed Vulliet that the stockade was trying to get one. Until then, he let the prisoners use his personal "phonograph for 'concerts' played over the camp loudspeaker."[258]

Later summarizing his observations, Vulliet wrote that "running a camp is a give-and-take proposition in which work and good-will seem to be the two factors of a bargain." Vulliet knew that his modest words had a larger

Georgia POW Camps in World War II

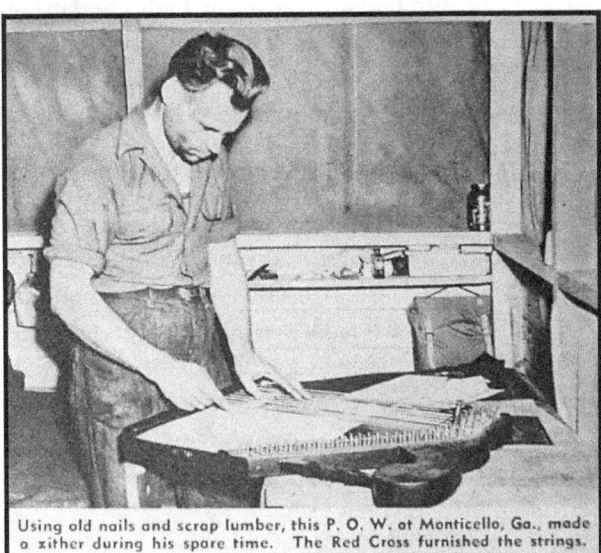

Above: Fort Benning's commander, Colonel Chescheir, met the Geneva Convention's stipulations of providing "intellectual diversion and recreation" comparable to this scene of POWs in Texas. *Courtesy NARA collection.*

Left: German POW makes musical instrument with scrap material. *Courtesy NARA collection.*

Using old nails and scrap lumber, this P. O. W. at Monticello, Ga., made a zither during his spare time. The Red Cross furnished the strings.

inference concerning the complexities of America's POW program along with the uncertain, sensitive condition POWs posed. He thought under the circumstances that "Americans'…best assets…are their own genuine qualities; their generosity, strength and roughness [which are] as likely to impress prisoners as any propaganda or indoctrinate plan."[259]

Chescheir ensured that the POWs received the "utmost in humane treatment" while demanding respect and orderliness from his American soldiers and from the prisoners. The Swiss Legation team of George Bonetti and R.W. Roth, along with State Department officials Charles Eberhardt and Parker Buhrman, visited the stockade from October 7 to October 15, 1943. They reported that the forty-acre camp was located about ten miles from Fort Benning. It was "sufficiently removed from the United States Army activities…to give it a satisfactory…isolation aspect" and no "interference" with its operation.[260]

The stockade was built like a "standard theater of operation construction." There were two divided "compounds, and the [adjoining uncompleted] hospital unit….No. 1 compound, which quarters about 1500 prisoners, was originally constructed to house an infantry battalion. The [15] hutments… are two storied theater of operation construction." The second compound's buildings were standard "one story, 20 x 120 and provide[d] quarters for about 50 men each." The POWs had "ample…showers and wash basins and hot and cold running water." The camp had an "especially high standard of sanitary order." The compounds held 2,949 Italians. The only complaints had to do with personal items taken from them upon incarceration without any receipt and the fact that the items had not been returned.[261]

The inspectors wrote that the stockade was "especially well disciplined and ordered. Not only in its equipment but also in the general morale of the prisoners. The prisoners obviously respect the Camp Commander and are satisfied with the general disciplinary administration of the camp." Apparently that admiration extended to Fort Benning's commander, as the team observed "no indication…of any friction or interference" between Chescheir and the installation commander.[262] As with other camp commanders, Chescheir, obviously, encountered challenges in controlling prisoners. Thompson thought that Chescheir overcame the obstacles using his interpersonal skills and some luck.[263]

Reporting on the American guards, the team stated:

> *The guard companies in this camp have the appearance of being somewhat better trained than in most camps….It is especially noticeable that the non-commissioned officers, particularly the sergeants, are older and more experienced than are usually found in Prisoner of War Camps. They undoubtedly have the respect of the prisoners and it is perhaps through the influence of the camp's personnel that the camp presents such a fine aspect….There was only one complaint to make and that was that there was nothing to complain about.*[264]

Georgia POW Camps in World War II

A camp welfare officer and chaplain provided recreational activities. The prisoners played volleyball, *bocci* (a ball sport) and table tennis, along with indoor games like checkers, chess and cards. They organized theatrical performances. The POWs had oil paints, water colors and musical instruments. They organized schools with classes in English. In addition to the *New York Times*, they read the *Columbus Ledger* and an Italian paper, *Progresso Italo-Americana*. Inspectors observed, "The Camp Administration places no restriction on their subscribing to standard American publications." The prisoners monitored the war through the *New York Times*, *Life* and *Time*, as well as other sources.[265]

A favorite pastime was going to the camp's canteen, where the prisoners bought candy, soft drinks, area produce, cigarettes and toiletries. Prices spanned from five cents for candy bars to thirty-five cents for a cigar or shaving cream. The War Department supplied the POWs with a "nonnegotiable camp script" to purchase items. Script or chit denominations were in one, five, ten and twenty-five cents. The canteen used at least two types of chits. Evidently, there was more than one canteen. As of October 1943, none stocked beer.[266]

POWs enjoying recreation with their "pal." *Courtesy NARA collection.*

POWs even used the installation's cafeteria on some posts. This sharply contrasted to the practice afforded African American soldiers. Retired Tuskegee airman Lieutenant Colonel Charles Dryden recalled that he and his companions saw "German prisoners of war, readily identifiable by the letters PW painted on the backs of their fatigues in white paint, going into the 'White' side of the post exchange cafeteria and WE COULD NOT!…WE WERE INSULTED AND HUMILIATED IN OUR OWN NATIVE LAND!"[267]

MEDICAL TREATMENT

POWs had to complete a medical treatment form, recording past and present diseases and operations. Each Fort Benning compound had a POW medic-staffed dispensary. The dispensary was the initial treatment for the ill or injured. The medics dispensed rudimentary medicines and dressed less serious wounds; some sutured small cuts. They were not authorized to do critical surgery. All serious and acute medical issues and emergencies were referred to the post clinic or hospital.

At the time of the Swiss Legation's first visit, Fort Benning's Martin Army Hospital serviced critically ill prisoners. Hospital doctors examined Sergeant Alex Pydd and found that he was suffering from serious headaches. In June 1944, the camp surgeon sent a transfer request to the PMGO. After detailing the sergeant's prewar injury, the doctor diagnosed post-concussion syndrome, adding that Benning's hot climate exacerbated Pydd's headaches. The PMGO granted the request to send Pydd to a cooler climate at Michigan's Fort Custer POW camp. A two-hundred-bed hospital with a dental unit (six dental chairs and one Italian dentist) for the POWs was under construction.[268]

On March 21, 1944, Colonel Cheschier requested the transfer of two of the Italian medical officers to another camp because they were "actively engaged in organizing Fascist groups within this Prisoner of War camp and persuading enlisted prisoners not to sign the Application for Service in Italian Service Units." Less than a month later, the two officers were transferred to the branch camp at Monticello, Georgia. Cheschier learned that "Italian medical officer replacements were unavailable. "While he got rid of one serious problem, the commander may have created a new one by not having any Italian doctors to treat his POW population."[269]

Georgia POW Camps in World War II

Labor

Thompson claimed that one of the areas in which Chescheir's "humanity shone was his use of work as an ameliorating tool, both on and off the grounds of Fort Benning." The commander knew that some of the POWs did not want to work when they first arrived at the camp. But when they learned work was obligatory and they would be paid, the prisoners changed their minds.[270]

They worked on the post to erect a building, painted, mowed grass, washed vehicles and harvested peanuts and cotton for local farmers. The farmers, who contracted POW laborers from the government, paid the government for their work; the government paid the prisoners, meaning at the war's end prisoners could return home with the money.

The War Department released safe work guidelines and the rights of POWs in the event of accidents. Accidents did happen, like with the two Italians who suffered grave injuries. A third prisoner died in a work-related incident when the truck carrying a load of sand went under an overpass; the bridge struck the three men riding on back of the truck. One died shortly after his arrival at the hospital; the other two had critical injuries including skull fractures.[271]

In October 1943, the Swiss Legation team found 500 POWs assigned without pay to work details, while about 1,800 assigned to other details received the customary pay. The inspectors stated that 250 prisoners living in an Oneonta, Alabama, tent camp picked tomatoes. Some details cut pulp wood, built roads, practiced soil conservation and cooked in bakeries."[272]

Using prisoners as laborers had problems like fair wages (guaranteed by the Geneva Convention) and competition with civilian laborers who

Poultry processing by POWs. *Courtesy NARA collection.*

often were paid less. In April 1944, friction came to Fort Benning when Congressman Pace and President of the Columbus Central Labor Union Howard Anthony levied charges against Fort Benning commander Brigadier General William H. Hobson and Colonel Chescheir. Pace and Anthony charged that the POWs took jobs from civilian workers. Anthony noted that "it is certainly not right that Italian prisoners, who had the opportunity to kill our own soldiers, should take work from our citizens." Commander of the Fourth Service Command Major General Frederick E. Uhl released a statement: "[I]n no case where there was available civilian help was a prisoner of war being used." Most of the prisoners were unaware of these labor issues.[273]

Religious Freedom

Chescheir avidly supported the rights of POWs to religious freedom, sanctioned by the Geneva Convention. The Italians, however, arrived without a priest; there was no chapel. The solution was to reassign a Catholic priest, Roderick MacEachen, from the post to the stockade. When Father (Captain) MacEachen first saw the Italians, he thought, "As [the POWs] descended from the trains, they were a pitiable multitude of broken ragged, almost bare-foot, pale, weary, silent, scarce lifting their eyes from the earth… it was the most pitiable sight, it seemed, that I had ever witnessed."[274]

Even in their poor condition, the POWs surrounded Father MacEachen, requesting to receive communion. They wanted to "thank God for bringing [them, as they said,] *salvi* and *sani* during our twenty-four long days of travel…to thank Him for having brought us to America where we already have experienced the best of treatment—these good clean clothes, the good food, the kindness of American Officers and men."[275]

Their faith astounded Father MacEachen. By the next Saturday, the prisoners had created an area to celebrate Mass, complete with an altar. Just a few missed the Mass due to illness, injury or mandatory duty. It disturbed Father MacEachen when he learned that the Army Public Relations Office intended to record "this momentous occasion, but he forged ahead, conducting the ceremony alone and running out of wafers before he ran out of POWs. He had to perform a second Mass when the additional one hundred wafers arrived. To his amazement, 'all those eight hundred men remained for this second Mass.'"[276]

Georgia POW Camps in World War II

An American army chaplain discusses theology with POWs. More than half of the POWs attend church services, March 11, 1944. *Courtesy NARA collection.*

About three thousand Italian POWs gather for a Christmas Mass in Fort Benning, Georgia, on December 20, 1943. *Courtesy NARA collection.*

The Star of Hope, symbolizing the faith of Italian POWS at Fort Benning, Georgia, was dedicated at their compound by Chaplain Frank Thompson, chief of chaplains. The prisoners built the concrete monument in honor of Thompson. Many of the POWs were artisans. At center is Chaplain Thompson, with Colonel George Cheschier, commanding officer of the POW camp, on his left and Captain Roderick MacEachen, Catholic chaplain for the Italian POWs, on his right, December 1944. *Courtesy of Fort Benning historic preservation specialist Edward Howard.*

Fourth Service Command chief of chaplains Colonel Ralph W. Rodgers likened U.S. Army chaplains to pioneer preachers who rode horses between towns. World War II homefront chaplains were "jeep-riding Circuit chaplain[s]." After the Germans arrived, a Catholic and Lutheran German POW chaplain rode with Father MacEachem to the southwestern Georgia branch camps at Americus, Bainbridge, Fargo, Moody Army Airfield Field and Turner Field. Branch camps tested the ability of chaplains to serve such an extensive region.[277]

Some Italian POWs displayed their gratitude to Chescheir for their sound treatment by creating a semi-permanent symbol. They painted and assembled rocks, exemplifying the "American and Italian flags linked together," with "U.S.A. written in big letters, made of small colored pebbles at the entrance to Compound No. 1."[278]

ITALIAN POWs CONFLICTED

After the government of Marshal Pietro Badoglio signed an armistice with the Allies on September 8, 1943, the U.S. Army organized Italian Service Units [ISUs], "quasi-military group[s] made up of Italian POW volunteers who aided the American military in noncombat roles."[279] As the PMGO required, Chescheir informed the prisoners about the ISU choice during an International Red Cross Committee's visit. Dr. Marc Pete said that Chescheir told the prisoners joining an ISU was voluntary; he did not try to influence their decision. Pete thought this reflected the mutual respect existing between the commander and the POWs.

The prisoners faced a dilemma. They could cooperate with America or side with Mussolini's Fascist republic. They were divided on what to do. Armando Boscolo thought the decision he and others faced was complex. If he changed sides, that meant being untrue to himself while some of his countrymen still fought the Allies. He believed that "Americans were 'grossly mistaken' and 'speaking in bad faith [if they] said that the non-collaborationists were all Fascists.'"[280]

Louis Keefer claimed in *Italian Prisoners of War in America, 1942–1946: Captives or Allies?* (1992) that American army personnel thought the choice was simple: "help the Americans and leave the camp or refuse and stay behind the barbed wire for the duration of the war." The sometime violent friction between Italian POWs did not happen at Fort Benning. This may have been due to the "nonconfrontational atmosphere" Chescheir fostered.[281]

About 35 percent of Italian POWs in America rejected joining an ISU. American officials isolated the more die-hard and possibly violent members of this group from the others. About 27 percent (less than 1 percent at Fort Benning) were "hard-core fascists…[who] jeered the collaborators with cries of 'traitor.'" Pete believed the formerly cooperative Gaetano Fascina "was particularly obdurate and stubborn in this matter…[and] seemed to have influenced many fellow prisoners against signing."[282] Chescheir was upset with Fascina and two others who were behind much of the resistance. Vulliet later wrote to Chescheir:

> *You must not let that thing, neither the fact that this is a bloody war, make even a dent in the belief that you have done the right thing all along and that you must continue to do so…that irrespective of what your prisoners reaction [is] to a form to sign, you have done more for your country and certainly more for the future of a better world (if there can ever be one) than anyone I know….Salvatori* [one of the resistant] *talked about the form to whoever was ready to listen….He talked to me about it till he was hoarse….* [Y]*ou cannot ask Italians to sign something as vital as that form and expect them not to talk about it.*[283]

Francesco Panucci characterized the feeling of those who chose to join an ISU: "It is my wish to fight for Beautiful America and with all my pride I am willing to offer all my energies and all my strength with the sacrifice of my life disdaining every danger to attain the Victory that cannot fail."[284]

Chescheir thought the positive results of Italians joining ISUs proved his defense of using Italian POW labor even when confronted with objections

Italian Service Unit (ISU) party. *Courtesy NARA collection.*

from area citizens and labor unions. On April 13, 1944, he notified the unions that there was no cause for alarm because "it may not be long before there are no Italian prisoners at Fort Benning...there will not be an Italian prisoner at the post who has not signified his intentions about Germany and who will not have signed papers stating he will fight against the Nazis."[285] On May 6, 1944, Panucci wrote to Chescheir:

> [A]*s my country has pledged to collaborate with Great America I shall do all efforts to contribute specially to drive out the criminal enemy and be enabled to breathe some pure air and to see again that new peaceful life of civilization, which all Peoples need....I beg you to extend my sincerest and most cordial wishes to the Dear and Heroic American Fighters, who are fighting...to liberate the oppressed Peoples from the barbarous enemy.*[286]

Chescheir received similar letters from other former POWs. They were filled with respect for Chescheir and expressions of gratitude for his fair treatment. On July 20, 1944, Supply Sergeant Carlo De Stefano, a member of the Second Italian Engineer Regiment, avowed in his letter to Chescheir, "I shall never forget to have found in this Land far away from home, a person like you, who was able to understand us and make us forget our grief at certain moments."[287]

Germans Arrive

The last Italian prisoner left on May 18, 1944. With the Italians gone, a "horde" of German POWs arrived. Area residents read in the *Columbus Enquirer*, "Germans Now at Benning." Most were transferred from Alabama's Camp Opelika. Later, they came directly from Europe. By the time of Perret's visit in September 1945, the stockade held 4,894 Germans. Their work shirts, inscribed in large letters with "PW," were a familiar sight in Georgia. The Germans had the use of the now-constructed POW hospital where their doctors and dentists worked.[288]

Education Program

"With the addition of 600 Nazi prisoners captured in Norway," a new educational program began. POWs took courses in English, mathematics, engineering and pre-med. They enrolled in correspondence courses offered at several universities. The Germans paid for the courses. Before the courses began, the military censored them.[289]

Perret commented on the camp's "very extensive program of studies." There were five groups of classes. They ranged from an intermediate program with several subjects like English and history to a baccalaureate preparation program with different language choices; first-semester university-level courses in medicine, law, Catholic theology and correspondence courses; ten free courses (e.g., electrotechnics); and a business school (e.g., commercial arithmetic, business correspondence). One group of POWs wanted to take teachers' training. Director of Studies Alfred Krestchmer organized courses in the work detachments.[290]

The Camp Opelika prisoners brought with them "1,200 books for light reading and 1,250 'soldatenbriefe' [soldiers' letters]." These were divided between the base camp and the work detachments. Benning's spokesman requested books from the German Red Cross, especially medical and technical books. However, they ended up at Camp Opelika.[291]

Recreation

In addition to reading, the Germans enjoyed seeing motion pictures, listening to classical music radio concerts and performances by the camp's orchestra and chorus and watching vaudeville shows. The prisoners had two "good football fields and several tennis courts." On Sundays, there were "about 10 football games." There were championship games. They liked gymnastics, using a POW-made "apparatus." Among the other sports were handball, *faustball*, ping-pong and wrestling. A priest and a pastor, both POWs, provided religious services in the base camp. Both traveled biweekly to the work detachments, except for the one in Atlanta.[292]

Like American soldiers, the German POWs regularly received mail. However, some Italian prisoners had waited more than two years to hear from their families. When the Germans controlled Italy, they "tightened up on outgoing mail...and not more than 41 letters from Italian families were ever received by Italian captives at Benning."[293]

Labor

Perret reported that "all the privates and some of the noncommissioned officers" worked in the installation's "kitchens, the mess halls, the officers' club, the garages, the supply depots, repair shops, etc."[294] But "[e]ven for the seemingly Midas-touched Chescheir, getting the Germans to avoid trouble by productive work created new difficulties." The small American staff limited the size of work details, hindering crop harvesting. The concerned War Department reduced the number of guards required on a detail. The fact that German officers still did not have to work, as stipulated in the Geneva Convention, chaffed Chescheir. He wrote to Vulliet, "[V]ery few [officers] have applied for any full-time job. This, of course, will mean that time will hang heavy over their hands, and they will be unhappy in their idleness."[295]

Chescheir pointed out to Vulliet his distinction between prisoners taken during and following the Allied invasion of France in June 1944: "I was struck with the difference [between] the quality of these prisoners and the smart, intelligent men of the Afrika Korps. The [new] men looked like they were the left-overs after good troops had been culled out." Of the most recent POWs, 378 were members of defeated Soviet units who had defected to the Germans. They hated the Wehrmacht and were very "outspoken in their hatred of the Germans." To avoid friction, Chescheir transferred the Russians.[296] These recent arrivals encouraged him. Chescheir told Vulliet that the "quality of the German soldier now has dropped to such a point that once we crash through the sturdily defended crust which surrounds Germany…the peace will come quickly."[297]

POW CAMP SYSTEM EXPANSION

The throng of inbound German prisoners and the need to juxtapose them with farms and work details meant a quick extension of camps throughout Georgia. In July 1944, the base camp assumed control from the Eastern Flying Training Command of four branch camps in southern Georgia. The Albany, Bainbridge, Moultrie and Valdosta camps employed one thousand POWs in agricultural jobs.[298] Still, the number of available American guards was a problem. Fort Benning executive officer Major Clarence T. Johnson announced, "Until guard strength is increased the 500 German prisoners from the Normandy beachhead will not be available for labor outside the post"—unwelcome news for Columbus farmers.[299]

By the spring of 1945, the base stockade managed the following nine branch camps: Atlanta, Albany, Americus, Axson, Bainbridge, Fargo, Moultrie, Thomasville and Valdosta.[300] Usually branch camps held fewer than 1,000 captives and frequently just 100 to 250. Prisoners worked as "seasonal agricultural labor and then returned along with their American commanding officers and MP escorts to their base camp." Several camps remained operational throughout the war, serving as semi-permanent sites for nonseasonal work and as places to accommodate the base camp's surplus POW population.[301]

Like the Italian POWs, the government used the rising population of Germans in Georgia to harvest peaches, peanuts and tomatoes; can fruits; and work in lumber production. By March 1945, the Fourth Service Command claimed that fifty thousand POWs worked in its seven-state region. The command projected by the summer that another twenty thousand prisoners would join the command's labor force. Although the command's prisoner allotment was increased in May to sixty-five thousand, that was still not enough to fill farmers' labor needs.

Georgia POW Camps in World War II

POWs working on lumber production. *Courtesy NARA collection.*

The Fourth Service Command was the country's top employer of POWs in the logging and sawmill industry. These jobs could be dangerous, and prisoners, most of whom knew little if anything about the work, could refuse to do them. "Few guards or prisoners had any experience in logging beyond some pamphlets or possibly training films. And the POWs had to learn lumber skills from employers and supervisors who all too often could only speak English." This explains the comparatively higher number of injuries and deaths among prisoners working in lumbering than in other types of labor. Former POW Horst Blumenberg said that "after a few days, he termed the job 'real work' and happily resumed his job on post."[302]

Reeducation Program

Unlike other camp commanders, Chescheir played an influential role in shaping Fort Benning's Reeducation Program. He began a "camp-operated university staffed by qualified POWs, guards, officials, and some civilians." His staff ran a groundbreaking and robust program designed to "reeducate his German prisoners in the ways of American democracy." Prisoners enrolled in classes on "democracy, American government, and…[began their] preparation…for a future role in postwar Germany."[303]

Chescheir's version of POW reeducation drew national attention because of its inventive approaches to foster a positive view of America in the minds of German POWs. The *Louisville Courier-Journal* and the International YMCA praised Fort Benning's program as a model. Other camps tried to copy it, "particularly those being designed strictly for reeducation purposes."[304] Nearly all the camp's German prisoners signed a pledge or oath repudiating Nazism. Numerous POWs in thirteen branch camps across Georgia and

Alabama did the same. "Better-connected U.S. Army officials...co-opted... and developed" Chescheir's "University of Democracy." As noted in another chapter, the Fort Benning model was the prototype for the U.S. Army's Reeducation Program.[305]

A few of Fort Benning's POWs were in camps under management of Chescheir's former assistant executive officer, Captain Myrvin C. Clark. In September 1945, he told Chescheir (who had retired a month before) that "the leading P.W.'s always ask about you and made such favorable and flattering statements and remarks about you, that I would be afraid to put them in writing!!" Clark acknowledged, "It was impossible to fully realize the full strength that you gave to our Program, until after you were gone."[306]

In his retirement, Chescheir continued to support the Reeducation Program. In January 1946, Fort Benning commander Brigadier General Hobson wrote to Chescheir, "You and Clark especially merit high praise for the educational program which you put over for our German P.W.'s, and I cannot thank you both enough for the success you made of your experiment." In short, Chescheir was critical in shaping the War Department's Reeducation Program.[307] The base camp closed on June 26, 1946.[308]

BAINBRIDGE ARMY AIR FIELD BRANCH CAMP

The Bainbridge Army Airfield (BAAF), under the command of Colonel Mills S. Savage, was "home" to several hundred German POWs. The camp, eight miles south of Bainbridge, was activated on August 28, 1943. It was on the northwest corner of the main air field. The POW camp commander was Lieutenant Robert R. Pige.

On July 6, 1944, Dr. Rudolph Fischer of the Swiss Legation visited the compound. He described it as "very well situated on slightly sloping sandy, loamy land in the midst of a pine forest." In May, the tent camp was made permanent. One irregular-sized compound was "approximately 260 feet by 275 feet." The screened tents were "16 feet by 16 feet...[with] wooden floors....[They had]...steel cots and cotton comforters for mattresses." Six men lived in each tent. A single barbed wire fence enclosed the camp, which had the "usual guard towers."[309]

The German population included 28 noncommissioned officers and 219 other enlisted soldiers. The POWs had no complaints about the camp or of their treatment before arriving at BAAF from a side camp in Opelika, Alabama.[310] Fischer thought that the drainage system was "not altogether satisfactory." The camp "has all the aspects of a purely temporary installation. The tents appear to be old and are leaky. The sewage system and toilets are of the field type with sewage pits which frequently…are allowed to become filled before additional pits are provided." The "shower baths [are] adequate…but there are no wash tubs for washing clothing." The prisoners had "no mess hall or recreation building." Fischer considered the camp to be "the most primitive installation" he had seen, not measuring "up to the usual standards of United States military installations and other prisoner of war camps and is regarded as unsatisfactory as a permanent camp."[311]

The BAAF's station hospital serviced the POWs. The prisoners were in "unusually good" health. Two were hospitalized "in a normal hospital ward." The compound had a "dispensary tent…equipped with emergency first-aid equipment."[312]

The number of POWs and the fact that this was a work camp meant "limited" recreational events. Fischer learned that the army intended to "fence an area adjacent to the camp" for recreation. "In the meantime," Fischer wrote, "the prisoners are permitted to use the unfenced area under guard four days weekly. They are also permitted to enjoy swimming in a nearby creek weekly."[313]

"The prisoners are not supplied with reading material, newspapers, or magazines. The religious activities at the post are limited by such services as may be held by the post chaplain who does not speak German. Some effort should be made," Fischer recommended, "to obtain religious services for the prisoners by a German speaking Lutheran pastor and a German speaking Catholic priest."[314]

About 95 percent of the POWs worked in details around the area, particularly in lumbering, logging and in peanut planting and harvesting. They earned on average about twenty dollars per month. The POWs had a small "fairly well supplied" canteen. The prisoners cooked and served their food rations. The outdoor kitchen "[c]onsists of fire pits over which all cooking is done in the open." Fischer described the "kitchen and cooking facilities [as] unusually primitive."[315]

Fischer applauded the POW camp commander "for the excellent morale and working spirit of the prisoners." He added, "This is a work camp unit which is not employed on the Bainbridge Army Air Field post but uses the Bainbridge Army Air Field post as a base of operation. As such there are indications that the administration of the Bainbridge Army Air Field is not primarily concerned with the prisoner of war camp; in fact it may be regarded as more of a burden than an asset."[316]

Fischer thought that the camp perhaps could be "considered satisfactory as an emergency temporary prisoner of war field unit." Its inadequacies juxtaposed against the positive morale of the POWS, he believed, were due to the commander's "efforts to provide some extra recreation for his prisoners such as allowing them to attend the post theater occasionally and taking them to swim in the nearby creek." On the other hand, Fischer found "the usual morale building factors such as providing a satisfactory athletic or recreation field in the camp, encouraging schools and providing adequate religious services, have not been fully utilized."[317] Fischer understood that some improvements were on the way, like allowing POW subscriptions to newspapers and magazines. He reiterated his overall assessment: "It certainly does not measure up to the standards of any other camp seen up to the present time.…The principle problem in this camp is to provide permanent quarters for the prisoners."[318]

Personal Reflections

After seventy-three years, Faye Beazly remembers clearly her first encounter with German POWs. In 1945, she was nine years old when her father, Edgar Heard, contracted with the government to hire prisoners from the BAAF POW camp to work on his farm near Bainbridge. Standing at a gate, Faye saw a guard drive the POWs in a converted school bus onto her father's property. The American staff sergeant spoke to her in an unfamiliar English dialect. The probable northern way of talking was strange to Faye. Her younger brother, Ed, was five years old when he rode along with the POWs on his father's "old wood body" truck to the fields. Their father drove with the guard seated beside him. Ed and Faye recalled that several POWs would lift Ed up, so he could see where they were going as they traveled between the fields. Ed and Faye told about the "fat, lazy" MP who escorted the prisoners to the fields. The guard sat with Ed in the shade, spitting and "pissing" in his helmet. Ed believed that the guard's weapon was "primary for show." Ed was not afraid of these strange-speaking men. To them he was "just an aggravating kid." The men showed Ed pictures of their families. He looked on and took "an interest in them." Ed noticed one POW with a loaf of bread under his arm, leading him to think they might have stopped along the way to the field. Ed's grandfather and one prisoner, who cleaned the courthouse, became good friends.

Faye watched as the Germans hoed peanuts. Reading from her father's records, Faye said the POWs were paid eleven cents per stack of peanuts. Between November and December 1945, they harvested corn. Ed believed that his father had a positive view of the POW laborers. Ed experienced no "hostility from them," and "no prisoner wanted to escape." He later thought that "there must have been some kind of screening of POWs to let them out of the camp....They kept the bad ones on base."[319]

Moody Army Air Field and Fargo Branch Camps

In late 1943, the first German POWs arrived at Moody Air Force Base, located northeast of Valdosta, Georgia. They were housed on parade ground buildings "near the motor pool." POW Camp commander Lieutenant Edward T. Lillis was in charge of the 315th Military Police Escort Guard Company. The MPs' quarters were "in the same area, outside the prison stockade."[320]

On November 22, 1943, the *Valdosta Times* reported on an upcoming meeting between Moody's Army Air Forces Pilot School representatives and Valdosta and Lowndes County officials about farmers using the prisoners. The *Atlanta Constitution*'s story on the Valdosta POWs read, "There are... [pulpwood] producers in and around Valdosta who have been making shipments weekly in excess of 200 carloads, because of available manpower from farms. Production is expected to soar even higher...it [is] being planned to put a number of German war prisoners from Moody Field into the woods...and things will move smoothly unless the shipments should cause a shortage in transportation."[321]

Like other farmers on the homefront, Harley Langdale of Valdosta had difficulty locating capable workers. When Langdale learned that he could contract with the federal government to hire German POWs to chop his timber, sow seedlings and clear land, he jumped at the opportunity. Langdale commented, "Some people were afraid of them....They thought some would get away. But we never did have any serious incidents." The prisoners Langdale hired were from Moody Army Air Field and from Fargo, a remote Okefenokee Swamp city. The prisoners planted several of the azaleas still thriving at the base. Prison Camp Road north of Fargo is evidence of the camp.

Georgia POW Camps in World War II

Walter and Herman Schroer, Elias M. Knight and Lewis Bauknight employed Moody's POWs. The Schroer family, who owned a bedding plant farm south of Ray City, hired more than one hundred prisoners to "pull and bundle the plants." Knight and Bauknight hired six to eight POWs every week to crop tobacco. In Lowndes and adjacent counties, prisoners "worked sugar cane, peanuts, and especially timber."[322]

Judge W.D. Knight was age ten when he first spied Moody's POW camp. Later he described his experience:

It was 1943 or 1944....My Daddy, [E.M. "Hun" Knight], had a farm located three miles south of Moody....On this farm lived Lewis and Loudell Bauknight..."tenant farmers."...My Daddy and Lewis received permission from the military authorities to work a group of these prisoners on our farm "cropping" tobacco. Lewis would go to Moody...early each morning in his old pickup truck and get the prisoners and transport them back to our farm....As I recall the prisoners would sit in the back of the truck and the MP (armed guard) would sit in front with Lewis. There would usually be six or eight prisoners working each time and they would bring their lunch which had been prepared in the "mess" at Moody....Each group would have one or two who could speak English and they would receive instructions from Lewis as to how to "crop" the tobacco and translate it on to the other prisoners. When they first began to work they wanted to "crop" all the leaves off the tobacco stalk and had to be told to only "crop" three leaves from each stalk. They were dressed in military clothes (brown) with a large "PW" on their backs. They all had military issue shoes and were real neat with short haircuts and most of them had blonde hair....I was...very impressed by this entire matter.

As I recall, my daddy had to pay each prisoner twenty-five or fifty cents per day as the military didn't want people to say we were using slave labor on the farms. Each time they came, Lewis' wife, Loudell...would prepare a huge farm dinner for all of us who worked at the barn. She would always give them some of that food and they very quickly began to like it, and the same group wanted to come back to our farm for each tobacco gathering which was once each week during the summer months.[323]

The POWs fascinated others too. These peculiar-sounding men were enemies who had fought "the native sons of South Georgia." Residents thought of them as "Hitler's 'supermen'...they were the economic salvation of the region, in a time when the available farm labor had all been recruited

Georgia POW Camps in World War II

for the war effort." Residents remembered gazing at "truckloads of German POWs being transported around the region under military guard, to serve as laborers on the farms and timber lands of the Wiregrass."[324]

In a December 6, 1943 op/ed titled "Heil Roosevelt," the *Valdosta Times* commented on the myth and facts of Moody's POWs:

> *The appearance of German prisoners at work in various places about this section has been creating quite a stir lately. Crowds have flocked to these spots to get a view of the Germans, anxious to see what they look like... only to find that they look just about like the Americans they see on the street every day...exploding in their minds any ideas they may have had about Hitler's race of supermen. It seems there's been a false impression made by the rumors going the rounds that the Nazi prisoners are not such good workers. Reports coming in from the pulpwood operators and others employing the prisoners indicate that the prisoners are catching on speedily to jobs which they have never done, and which they have never seen done.*
>
> *One pulpwood operator, S.M. Hemingway, is quick in telling you that the German prisoners of war are the happiest bunch of fellows he ever saw...and that they are easy to guard, since the last thing they seem to have on their minds is the idea of leaving three squares daily, comfortable living quarters and the regular pay they receive...only for a chance to escape to their own bomb-ridden country where they would be again sent into battle to face death. Their chances of getting back are nil, anyhow. Mr. Hemingway says that while the Germans are entirely "green" when it comes to cutting pulpwood, they are good workers, and learning fast. He also states that they are witty and enjoy a good joke as well as the next fellow.*
>
> *This writer visited a few of them at work at the Nat Smith brick warehouse one afternoon...where they were hard at work unloading fertilizer from boxcars. They were in high spirits. One of the prisoners, while waiting to load the wheelbarrows, had drawn on the side of the car, in the dust of the fertilizer, an image of President Roosevelt. Probably they wanted someone's picture to heil.*[325]

South Georgians recalled the influence the POWs had on them and the "positive cultural interchange that occurred, even under difficult war-time conditions." Audrey Peters, an employee who worked at Moody Field, kept a wooden jewelry box one of the prisoners made for her. On the bottom, he carved, "Gerhard Todte, Moody Field 1.9.1945." She added, "They were nice people....Of course, we didn't fraternize with them. I tried to locate him, but I couldn't. I wanted to see how he was doing and thank him for the box." Georgians like Langdale, who chaired Langdale Company (a large timber company), believed that the POWs "won people over....I got the impression they were glad to be over here....I didn't see any animosity toward us at all."[326]

On a visit to Fargo in 1999, Heinz Roehrs, a former POW, reflected, "A prison camp can't be very good because you are fenced in....You have no freedom. But we thought it was better to be a prisoner in America than Russia. We got the same food that the American Army got." Roehrs said that 250 POWs worked in the forest near Homerville, less than thirty miles north of Fargo.

Renate Milner, a German-born historian in Valdosta, discovered, "The young women from the area...remember they were good looking and didn't spit because they didn't chew tobacco." The government, she continued, "classified them as unskilled laborers, but in reality, they were very skilled—carpenters, mechanics and goldsmiths....They were pulled into the military at 16 or 17, but by then, they had already been trained in technical schools. Everybody knows about the people who got a Purple Heart, but the POWs are kind of forgotten. You don't give medals to soldiers who surrendered to the enemy. The German internees are still remembered for their skills and hard work." Walter Rommeswinkel had worked as a hospital orderly in Thomasville, Georgia. His wanted to make a return visit to "fulfill...a lifelong dream." Unfortunately, Rommeswinkel died five months before his planned return. Milner observed, "Those WWII veterans are dying by the minute....They have a history and it needs to be preserved. As young kids, they went to war. By the time they got home, they had to rebuild Germany."[327] The Fort Benning POW base camp closed on June 25, 1946.[328]

Chapter 6

CAMP WHEELER

POW Camp Establishment

In 1940, the U.S. Army reopened Camp Wheeler on 14,394 acres of its World War I site.[329] The POW camp was activated on April 13, 1943.[330] The next month, the *Macon Telegraph* announced that Bibb County authorities were considering using the prisoners to repair roads. However, the War Department said the POWs were not allowed to do that work.[331]

Inspection

In June 1943, Mr. Ben Adams reported on his visit to the base compound. The barracks were "clean and in good order." Since it was Sunday, the only work the prisoners were required to do was to prepare meals and maintain their quarters. Adams described the kitchen's operation:

> One of the most interesting places visited was a kitchen and dining hall. Let it be said here that the Italians held in the camps do not waste anything. However, they don't like some of the things we Americans count as good and they prefer to prepare their own food and serve it when they like it. There are U.S. Army mess sergeants in charge of the kitchens. All of the

cooking is done by Italians. One man is head cook but on the day of my visit he had plenty of help. There were twelve men assisting him and each one appeared most willing to do anything he could to prepare the food.[332]

Adams observed prisoners preparing dough:

At least six men were kneading dough in large metal pans and with such vigor that they were wet with perspiration. Getting a big batch of dough worked up to suit Italian war prisoners is no small undertaking. The prisoners complain that we Americans don't bake good bread and they prefer to make up their dough and bake it in a form to their taste. The dough the men were working on had a large amount of white potatoes boiled and mashed in the flour.... After working the dough for a long time...then comes the rolling in which eight or ten men take part. The dough is...cut into small pieces. These are run by hand over a grater...and roll off like a wafer curled up.[333]

The American mess sergeant said that the POWs disliked butter and lard; they did not eat much meat. He added they "like spaghetti and macaroni and make these to suit their taste from the flour provided." The POWs had a "sweet tooth," so they used a lot of sugar, cooking oil, vinegar and black pepper. "They eat Georgia cane syrup for breakfast." When Adams explored the camp, "the men look fat and healthy and are said to be not so ravenously hungry as they were upon arrival." He commented on how the prisoners decorated the mess hall and barracks with a "little flower pot on either side of the door, and between some of the buildings are vegetable gardens showing good care." These gardens were products of the enlisted men's resourcefulness.

Using army-issued coupon books worth three dollars per month, prisoners bought "soft drinks, combs, Vaseline, hair tonic, cigarettes, and other small items" in the canteen. The army's monthly spending limit for each POW was thirteen dollars (ten dollars in earnings and three dollars from the government).[334]

When asked about his experience on entering a POW camp, Adams replied:

[T]he first gate swing[s] open under the watchful eye of an armed American soldier. You get through the first gate and then you are halted between two high wire fences. In a high tower nearby (one at each corner of the enclosure), are more soldiers...pass through another gate into an

POWs gathered around a radio. *Courtesy of Georgia State Library Digital Collection.*

> *enclosure where there is a tool house....Another high gate opens, and you are inside the internment camp with an unknown number of war prisoners dressed mostly in pants and sleeveless under shirts. Some still wear the uniforms they wore in battle while others wear fatigue cloths. The Italians at Macon are all young men and look strong and physically sturdy. They are on the average, smaller than American soldiers and some look a bit on the Nordic side....Music is to be heard in many of the barracks. In one building there was an artist at work with his paint brushes. He had painted a country scene on his large canvas tacked on the walls of the building.*[335]

LABOR

By July 1943, Georgia farmers in the Third Congressional District had become awfully anxious about the scarcity of labor. Congressman Stephen Pace painted a gloomy picture, calling "every man, woman, and child in the state, who is physically able and can possibly spare the time… [to] offer their services and go to the fields and help gather and save the abundant crop."[336]

Major Earl L. Edwards, the assistant director of the PMGO's POW Division, toured the camp on September 4, 1943. There were 2,206 Italian prisoners; 750 were at side camps harvesting peanuts. The POWs carried boxed lunches with them to agricultural details. Local farmers provided transportation to the fields. Others had jobs in the post laundry, on-camp engineer projects and cleaning up a large lumber pile. There were 142 contracts for POW labor. In fact, there were not enough prisoners to satisfy the labor demands. During bad weather, the Italians kept busy working in shoe repair, tailoring and carpentry.[337]

Facilities

Edwards described how the "Theater of Operations type barracks" were arranged in accordance with the standard design for this sized camp. The barracks, "covered with white asbestos board," had "black tar paper roofs." They measured twenty by two hundred feet and held fifty prisoners. Edwards observed cramped quarters when considering each prisoner was allowed forty square feet. That meant the interior barracks' capacity was forty-four. The complex had the required sanitation facilities along with two infirmaries. However, there was no medical staff. POWs with serious illnesses received treatment at the post hospital. There was an ongoing effort to acquire four POW doctors. Although the food rations were "adapted to Italian tastes," their monetary valued equaled those of American soldiers.

Seventy-one American soldiers were attached to the camp, seven of whom had training and other duties. Edwards noted that the two companies were "efficient except for the fact that many were not physically fit." The customary octagonal guard towers and "non-graduated hog wire" surrounded the complex. Each two-manned guard tower had "a standard slide table as a mount for a machine gun." White stakes six feet inside the inner fence marked the "deadline" beyond which POWs were not allowed. Except for the visitors building, the nearest building was thirty-six feet away from the inner fence, creating "a clear field of fire from all sides." The commanding officer depicted the POWs' treatment

POWs at Macon and Dublin camps admire pin-ups, Georgia, 1945. *Courtesy of Georgia State Library Digital Collection.*

as "firm and fair but never trust them." He did not venture into the compound nor did he speak with the prisoners "to maintain...[their] respect...and avoid any familiarity which would lessen his complete control."[338]

RECREATION

The post and the PMGO provided the POWs with some games and sports equipment. A sixteen-piece POW orchestra and a choir served as entertainment. The lack of facilities prevented movies. Edwards's office had equipped a workshop with "CCC power equipment." The camp's appearance was "fair." Because of the color of the barracks and the fact that the fenceposts are unpainted, the camp's general appearance depended on "the vegetation and development by the prisoners." But the soil prevented most vegetation, and POW gardens were "almost impossible because of

Italian prisoners at Camp Wheeler tend a vegetable garden, 1943. *Courtesy of Georgia State Library Digital Collection.*

the heavy erosion." The prisoners spent most of their time on "agricultural details," leaving little time for camp beautification.

Edwards recommended that four enlisted men be assigned to each POW company. The headquarters detachment needed sixty-four enlisted soldiers. Furthermore, he advised:

> *Some arrangement should be effected* [sic] *to avoid the difficulties of the…*[POW] *camp commander* [Lieutenant Colonel Ralph E. Patterson] *while serving under the jurisdiction of a post commander who has no great interest in…*[POW] *problems or the administration of a…*[POW] *camp. Greatest difficulty is experienced in the shortage of personnel and the caliber of officers and men assigned to the…camp. The Post Commander has effected any required reduction in personnel by cutting the allowance to the…camp and has assigned to that camp those officers and men who were not qualified to perform duties elsewhere on the Post.*[339]

Edwards also suggested, "There should be a minimum daily wage for picking cotton since the prisoners will not be able to clear eighty cents a day on piece work. The Commanding Officer is of the opinion that farmers are not paying the real going wage. In that section of Georgia, most of the farmers allot so many acres to negro employees and perhaps cows in addition to the wages paid. As a result, instead of $1.00 per day, these negro employees actually receive…$2.00 per day."[340]

REJOICING

Five days after Edwards's visit, local residents read in the September 9, 1943 edition of the *Macon Telegraph* "War Prisoners Grin at Italy's Capitulation." They learned that "Italian prisoners of war at Camp Wheeler yesterday greeted with wide grins the news that their homeland capitulated to the Allied nations and left no doubt that they were glad Italy was out of the conflict." A camp spokesman said, "Their only concern now is that Germany may 'punish' the Italian people by bombing Italian territory."[341]

1943 LABOR

In November 1943, the newspaper ran Adams's story, "Captive Italians May Farm Here." He wrote, "All labor outside the camp is voluntary. The Italians are said to be willing workers and the officer in charge said farmers had reported satisfaction over their employment." Middle Georgia's farmers, fruit packers and sawmill operators especially needed POW laborers. Another article, "War Prisoners May Be Used to Cut Wood," was welcome news to many.[342]

1943 FACILITIES

For two days in December 1943, Captain Edward Shannahan from the PMGO's POW Division inspected the compound. There were two thousand Italian POWs, including two officers who lived in quarters separate from the enlisted men. Shannahan reported that the camp had "a very pleasing appearance inasmuch as the barracks are all painted white and much work has been done by the individual prisoners to make their surroundings more home-like. A large log chapel was under construction." He approved of the sanitary conditions, noting the kitchen's use of a "dish-sterilizer." The prisoners had the authorized number of latrines and washtubs.[343]

Guards

Unlike Edwards, Shannahan commented favorably on the American guards in the four guard towers. He found them "alert." The 356th and the 357th Military Police Escort Guard (MPEG) Companies enforced security measures like "challenging" Shannahan when he got within thirty feet of a tower, conducting daily inspections of the barbed wire and driving weekly around the compound to ensure there were no tunnels. Each guard tower now had three mounted machine guns. The MPEG companies were receiving some training. Patterson planned to "erect a guard tower on the firing range…to instruct all guards…[on how to correctly fire] from the towers." Shannahan thought that the guards' attitude toward the POWs was outstanding. However, he noted a few cases of fraternization.[344]

The local War Manpower Commission representative and the regional director disagreed over using POWs to build a housing project. Meanwhile, Patterson expected to get many labor contracts for the next harvest season. The prisoners used a new field bakery to bake their own bread. Their vegetable garden bore about $2,500 of produce. Two prisoners suffering from mental health issues were recommended for transfer to a hospital in New York.

Recreational Improvements

Recreation improved with the showing of motion pictures. The PMGO continued to provide recreation kits and supplies along with those from the War Prisoners' Aid and the National Catholic Welfare Association. The camp commander planned to use canteen proceeds rather than the

Georgia POW Camps in World War II

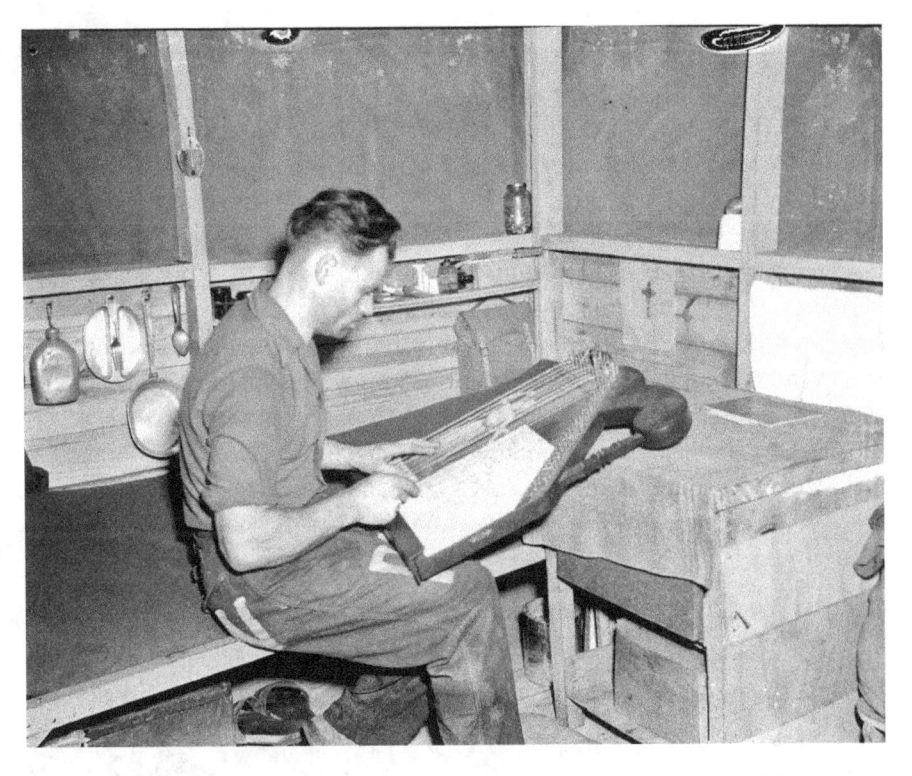

POW with lyre, Macon and Dublin, Georgia, 1945. *Courtesy of Georgia State Library Digital Collection.*

"allotment of 15…cents per prisoner for [future purchases of] recreation aids." By Shannahan's visit, the POWs had a "well-organized theatrical program." The base camp and the Charleston, South Carolina camp each had an orchestra. The base compound had two recreation rooms furnished with PMGO-supplied furniture and some prisoner-crafted small items. The prisoners had built "tennis courts, soccer fields, boccie [*sic*] alleys and boxing rings within the compounds." Each compound had a "well equipped" carpentry, cobbler, barber and tailor shop. Also, a librarian in the compounds staffed the small library. The POWs wanted the librarians to be paid from the canteen's dividends.[345]

Georgia POW Camps in World War II

Two Side Camps

There were 299 Italians at the Charleston camp and another 249 at the Jessup, Georgia side camp. Camp Stewart, Georgia, provided rations for the Jessup facility; Fort Moultrie, South Carolina, serviced the Charleston camp. These camps had makeshift latrines. "On work details, the men utilize straddle trenches surrounded by latrine screens." A medical officer periodically inspected the camps, ensuring compliance with U.S. Army standards. Two MPEG company officers and forty-four guards policed the Jessup camp compared to the Charleston camp's security of two officers and sixty-five enlisted MPEG company soldiers from Fort Benning. In July 1944, the PMGO notified the commanding officer of the Camp Gordon POW facility that the branch camps at Aiken and Charleston, South Carolina, and at the Wilmington, North Carolina camp were being transferred to other base camps.[346]

POW canteen, or recreation area, Dublin, Georgia. *Courtesy of Georgia State Library Digital Collection.*

COMPLAINTS

Shannahan mentioned the camp spokesman's complaint about the treatment of the Italian prisoners, now co-belligerents. He complained that camp officials were not treating the prisoners in accordance with a letter from Italian prime minister Marshal Peter Badoglio. Specifically, they were "still marching the prisoners to work under guard and confining them at night to the stockade." The spokesman said that a "labor commissioner" had told him the prisoners "would be paroled and that they would be given the same privileges American enlisted men are given" like allowing noncommissioned officers to stay out all night and allowing privates to remain out until 11:00 p.m.[347]

Shannahan learned from Patterson that the so-called labor commissioner actually was Captain Paul A. Neuland, chief of the PMGO's Field Service Branch. He had toured the camp in an effort to separate the Fascists from the rest of the POWs. Shannahan found out the "complaint resolved itself into a request from the spokesman that women be made available to the prisoners of war." Well, Shannahan informed the spokesman that he "had been misinformed…no such policy was expected to be put into effect at the present time." Shannahan did tell the spokesman about the "possibilities of limited parole." The spokesman may have taken some comfort from this. He wanted to let the PMG know how much he appreciated his "care and thoughtful attention" toward the prisoners and for the POWs' plentiful food supply.[348]

ASSESSMENT OF COMMANDER

Distinct again from Edwards, Shannahan wrote that Patterson "impressed… [him] as being very desirous of running an excellently-managed camp." But the commander did not "want to be responsible for the actions of any…[POW]…placed on limited parole," nor did he like that "system… [because] of an incident which occurred when he had prisoners at a… Camp Gordon, Georgia [side camp]. Two…prisoners escaped and planned to attack a girl they had been watching." Fortunately, the two were caught before they could carry out their plot. Patterson went on to tell Shannahan that he felt POWs on limited parole would be problematic as the men "attempt[ed] to satisfy their physical needs."[349]

1944 Conditions

The following December 1944, Shannahan paid another visit to Camp Wheeler's stockade. He found 2,558 prisoners. Since his last inspection, the Italians had built an outdoor theater. They had planted trees and shrubbery in both compounds, but the German POWs had destroyed them. The barracks were "dirty and unkempt." There was no "regularity of dress." Patterson told Shannahan about his idea of reducing the number of guards around the complex, the number of guards in the towers during the day and the number of guards on work details. This seems a little at odds with Shannahan's observation about the camp's "poor" discipline and courtesy, agreeing with remarks he had heard from Dr. Fischer and from Mr. Eberhardt. Shannahan brought the matter up to Patterson and to the new post commander, Colonel Carlos Brewer, who promised action. However, Shannahan thought that "the policy of…[Patterson] seems to be to side step any imposition of disciplinary measures on the prisoners." Patterson had asked Dr. Fischer to help enforce a no-singing-outside-the-stockade policy.[350]

Evidently, even more startling to Shannahan was Patterson's habit of letting the German POWs try several other prisoners "who were guilty of a disorder—after the 'trial' he examined the findings of the 'court' and found that their sentence was fair, he then had the guilty prisoners confined." Shannahan told Patterson this was not a War Department practice.

The educational program included thirty-five classes in subjects ranging from English to Greek, Russian, stenography and chemistry. The theater used to show movies was too small, causing a film to be shown ten times before all the POWs had a chance to see it.

Shannahan observed that only 804 prisoners were employed outside the stockade; 83 of them worked on private contracts. He had confidence that Brewer would see to it that more prisoners worked. Shannahan, Patterson and other camp officers met to discuss some new work projects, like paving the major dirt road into the compound, removing brush from post ranges and manning the fire department.

Shannahan investigated the spokesman's complaints of insufficient dental care, medical treatment, classrooms and recreation. He found them unsupported. In the event Patterson did not "show better initiative, imagination and a better system of organization," Shannahan recommended "that he be either retired or assigned to another job where he will not have contact with prisoners of war." Brewer agreed.[351]

1945 Conditions

On March 7, 1945, Major Neuland reported on Captain Robert L. Kunzig's visit in February. By then, the base camp and its five branches held 3,250 Germans. The population increase reflected Camp Wheeler's assumption of Camp Gordon's POW facilities. Kunzig discussed the Intellectual Diversion Program with Post Executive Officer Colonel Carl A. Flon, and with the stockade's executive officer, Major Anselm Hendrickson. Camp Gordon's assistant executive officer, Captain Richard J. Moran, was transferred to Wheeler, where he was doing a "phenomenal" job with the program. In just three weeks, Moran wrote to "all universities offering correspondence courses mentioned in Prisoner of War circulars." Each replied. Courses were to begin soon. The POWs were happy to hear that Emory University was the sponsor. The forty-year-old director of studies was "sincerely interested in aiding the education of his fellow soldiers." The Germans wanted to buy their own textbooks and were ordering them through Moran. Neuland reported, "Education is well under way at Camp Wheeler."[352]

The library had 1,700 books. When added to the branch camps' libraries, the total volumes rose to 5,500. About 85 percent of the prisoners throughout Wheeler's satellite network used the books on a rotational basis. The POWs were planning a camp magazine. The lower quality of the available films perhaps explained the prisoners' "poor" interest in watching them once a week. Moran anxiously awaited the start of the PMGO's film circuit. The 16-piece orchestra played regularly and was among the 141 musical instruments across Wheeler's camp system. Because the Germans expressed an interest in art, Moran was ordering art books "displaying the best of art of this nation for study by the...[POWs]."[353] Apparently, this was another part of the Intellectual Diversion Program.

Moran was convinced that the camp spokesman, formerly an "Olympic diving champion," was a Nazi, "but no difficulties have developed as yet," added Neuland. "A close watch is being kept on his activities and statements." Continuing his findings on segregation, Neuland wrote, "Forty prisoners have been transferred for subversive activities in the past week. Captain Moran is keenly aware that segregation is the keynote to the successful carrying out of the Intellectual Diversion Program and is cooperating closely with the intelligence officer. They work together, hand and glove." He was pleased with the guards, stating they were going to take some orientation training. The guards had "their own library, reading room, canteen, radios, photographs, etc." They could watch the post's movies but transporting them two miles was a problem.[354]

In January 1945, Karl Nehfischer fled from a work detail at the Southern Crate and Veneer Company. Evidently, he caught a train to Grovania, about thirty-five miles south of Macon. There he approached Mrs. Grover Watson, who became suspicious. With the assistance of Mrs. Watson's daughter, Mrs. Dorothy Waston Goumas, and area residents, military police arrested Nehfischer. They escorted him back to Camp Wheeler.[355]

In December 1945, Camp Wheeler's Public Relations Office announced the transfer of almost 3,000 POWs to other installations as the "first step in their return to Germany." That left 1,950. Patterson claimed the prisoners' contribution to central Georgia's economy was "$3,500,000." He elaborated:

> *German POWs under the direction of Camp Wheeler's POW camp made more than $750,000 for the United States government in the past year and at the same time saved the War Department an equal sum. In their free time prisoners prepared themselves to carry democracy back to their homeland. Since May 1944, only Germans have been located in the base camp…and in the eight branch camps in central Georgia. The largest number of Germans stationed in the Wheeler camp and its branches was 4,700. The prisoners filled 3,500 separate contracts with farmers and producers in the Georgia area in addition to working in camps. The contracts varied in value from $8 to $36,000. The pay for that work—an estimated $2,000,000—was forwarded to the U.S. Treasury. To hire civilians to take the place of prisoners at Wheeler would mean the Army hiring 1,000 extra men a day. The value of the men, if they had received wages mechanics, typewriter experts, tailors, and laborers, would have varied from $2 to $12 per man per day….Now only the Daniels* [Daniel] *Field and the Dublin branches remain open.*[356]

A Guard's Story

"There are no ordinary lives," said Ken Burns of those who served in a global cataclysm so momentous that the filmmaker simply entitled his 2007 documentary *The War*. "Funny how people can get along when they're not shooting at each other." The realization struck Ted Lesniak not long after he started guarding German soldiers at a POW camp in Georgia.[357]

Georgia POW Camps in World War II

In October 2011, Ted Lesniak, then eighty-five, sat for an interview with Brian Albrecht. Lesniak began telling his story with his draft into the army in 1944, shortly after his high school graduation. "I was the angry guy in basic training....We all reached the conclusion it was either kill or be killed. That was the bottom line." Lesniak started his service in the U.S. Army as a "military policeman but found that his 140-pound physique put him at a decided disadvantage in trying to subdue larger, sometimes inebriated GIs, so he asked for a transfer to POW guard duty."[358]

When he arrived at Camp Wheeler, Lesniak had reservations about his new duty of guarding roughly two thousand Afrika Korps soldiers. He said that "a more accurate description of his role was protecting, rather than guarding." "You were there to protect them from crazy civilians if somebody wanted to come and kill a Nazi." He came to realize that he and the POWs "shared more than a barbed wire enclosure."[359]

Lesniak spent most of his time supervising POWs while they worked in farm fields. He recalled because of the manpower shortage, "the farmers just loved them to death, they were such good workers....The remarkable thing was that they all knew what to do. I didn't have to do anything. Just stay out of the way." From a truck cab as he read, wrote letters or slept, he guarded the prisoners. Lesniak "stuck his carbine ammo in his pocket and left instructions to be awakened if anyone saw another Army vehicle approaching." None of the prisoners tried to escape. "As an English-speaking POW told Lesniak, 'We're not going anywhere. We're not going to swim across the ocean to go home.'" The prisoners received a dollar a day, which they spent in the canteen on "cigarettes, recreational equipment, musical instruments and anything else that helped pass the time in camp."[360]

The prisoners continued their "strict military discipline; marching wherever they went and snapping off stiff-armed *Sieg Heil* salutes during soccer games." They thought American soldiers were "too casual, which they regarded as a character flaw of all Americans." Lesniak remembered they would "hash over strategies of the war. The Germans steadfastly believed they were going to win, to the point where they'd quiz him about his hometown; asking for geographic, manufacturing and other details." Lesniak believed they were thinking, "If we ever take over, we'll want to know these things."[361]

The Germans realized that events were quite different when new prisoners arrived toward the end of the war. Lesniak recollected that these were the "last-ditch remnants of the German army—either very young or very old, beaten, battered, half-starved, 'looking like hell' and smelling

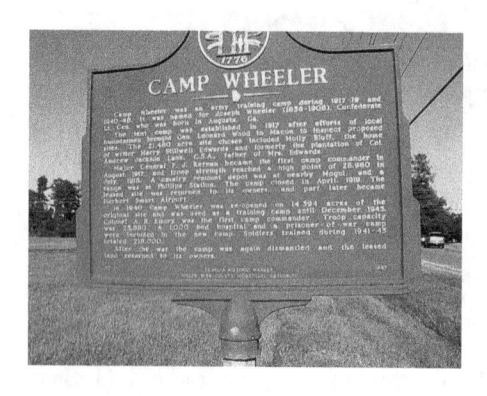

Camp Wheeler Historical Marker, Bibb County, Georgia, erected in 1987. *Courtesy Georgia Historical Society.*

even worse." After receiving "hot showers and fresh clothing," they were "confronted with the typical culinary largesse of a GI mess hall," bringing them "to tears." One of them yelled, "Are we in heaven, or what?" After Germany's surrender, the "Afrika Korps soldiers volunteered 'to a man' to fight with Americans against Japan." The commander told the POWs to assemble, telling them, "To fight for America is a privilege. The privilege is granted to citizens only. You guys are not citizens; therefore, you cannot fight for America." Irate, they replied, "We're the best soldiers in the world, and you're going to turn us down?" Since many did not want to be repatriated, they asked Lesniak how to become American citizens. Lesniak thought this "was sad, in a way."[362]

After the war, Lesniak returned to Cleveland with the "wooden suitcase made for him by one of the POWs using materials purloined from various work sites—a common practice, as guards looked the other way." That now "battered wooden case" means:

> [W]hen...[Lesniak] *pulls it out and remembers...*[he] *realizes that those who had to battle the Germans or lost loved ones in the war might not appreciate the sentimental attachment packed in that suitcase. He knows how the dark memories can linger. One of his brothers served in the Marines during the war and always refused to talk about the experience—except once, after a few drinks, when he remembered the days he spent on Iwo Jima, trapped under enemy fire in a foxhole with a dead buddy. But to Lesniak, the war also represented a time when enemies could peacefully co-exist; perhaps not as friends, but as fellow soldiers.*[363]

As Lesniak concluded, "Once you got to know them, they became people, just like you and me."[364]

Georgia POW Camps in World War II

Branch Camps

Camp Wheeler's public relations officer, Colonel J.A. Muldrow, announced in late August 1943 that the PMGO had approved a branch camp in Dublin, Georgia, and one at Albany, Georgia's Turner Field, previously known as Air Corps Advanced Flying School Albany. The Dublin camp was located at the fairgrounds. The U.S. Army planned to transfer hundreds of prisoners to Dublin and Albany to harvest peanuts. The camps were situated near the fields, reducing travel expenses and saving tires for cars. County agents and agricultural authorities were responsible for farm work assignments. In fact, County Agent Harry A. Edge of Laurens and several members of the Farm Labor Advisory Committee had lobbied for POW laborers. Camp Wheeler intelligence officer Captain Henry J. Boudreaux, who reported to Colonel Patterson, controlled one hundred prisoners. Albany's Turner Field expected the arrival of three hundred POWs on August 28, 1943. They were housed on Camp Wheeler.[365]

In addition to Dublin and Albany, branch camps were located at Monticello, Ashburn, Waynesboro and Daniel Field. The army established seasonal work camps or detachments at Griffin, Sandersville, Fitzgerald and Hawkinsville, Georgia. Together, they held at least 4,700 prisoners. Most worked on farms or in sawmills while others labored as mechanics, typewriter experts and tailors.[366]

Monticello

Major Shannahan included in his December 1944 report his visits to several branch camps, including the one at Monticello, Georgia, in Jasper County. The camp was activated on June 1, 1944, and located on the Wilburn farm grounds (now the Jasper Middle School). When Shannahan reached Monticello, there were 250 German POWs living in the "winterized tent camp"—5 to 7 men slept in each of the thirty-five tents (including those for the guards). He thought the Germans "had done an outstanding job of beautification…by…adding…vine covered rustic porches on the rear of the tents…and numerous flower gardens." They used contractor-donated "scrap lumber" to shape the tents' floors and "installed windows and built enclosures on the tents front to serve as wind breaks and a place for wood storage."[367]

The compound had a mess hall, a latrine and a recreation area. About one company of guards provided security. There were no fences; no POWs tried to escape. One resident recalled, "[T]hey were all glad to be here instead of on the Russian front. My good friend, C.T. Pope…an MP… told me about transporting our troops over to France and then loading out German prisoners to bring home on the same ship. When loading, he said the Army furnished him an empty shotgun but even that was not needed as hundreds of the prisoners rushed to the ship to board and leave, they were happy to leave Europe."[368]

Two Germans in the camp treated those with non-critical illnesses. The camp's ambulance transported more seriously ill prisoners to Camp Wheeler. An American doctor visited the compound three times a week, monitoring the Germans' work. The camp's commanding officer told Shannahan that there was enough work to keep the POWs occupied throughout the winter. The main types of work included "pulpwood cutting, cutting lumber and general farm work (pruning trees and pulling corn)."[369] Townspeople also hired them to pick peaches. The hourly wage was twenty cents per hour for tree pruning and corn pulling and forty cents per hour for saw filing. Shannahan spoke to Patterson about the variation in wages and his apparent objection. Patterson said that it was the Fourth Service Command's policy for pulpwood contractors to pay POWs twenty cents per hour.[370]

Evidently, Shannahan was unconvinced. Remember that he already had issues with Patterson's abilities. The lumber cutting contract required POWs earn forty cents per hour. The contractor was paying the Germans on the "hourly basis until the prisoners were fully trained and a task [production rate] could be established." Now that they were experienced, the contractor wanted a task to be created for him to pay the POWs on another basis. Since no task was set for civilians until a more accurate production rate was determined, Shannahan recommended referring the matter to the War Production Board. The Germans knew the suggested task. Shannahan thought this helped explain the POWs' lower productivity. The branch camp commander thought the U.S. Army Service Commands should consider setting tasks for each state. Shannahan supported that recommendation, thinking it "would be especially helpful in woods operations." He noted in this area of America the hourly wage apparently was "$1.60 per day (approx., in a few cases it is higher) as the wage rate for…[POW] labor."[371]

Again, Shannahan conducted his own investigation. He "stopped along the road and asked negro laborers on different types of work how much they are payed, particularly pulp and lumber cutters, in no case was the figure less than 35…[cents] per hour."[372] So, the POWs were paid less.

Marilyn May Allen, daughter of a lumberman in Jackson, Georgia, kept letters her father received from former prisoners who had worked for him. They told stories about their release in France and desire to return to America. The camp was closed on November 17, 1945, ending an intriguing episode in Monticello's history.[373]

Dublin

To fill the agricultural labor scarcity, in 1943 State Senator Herschel Lovett, County Agent Harry Edge and Emergency Farm Labor Assistant Walter B. Daniel turned to Milledgeville's Congressman Carl Vinson. Their answer: locate a prisoner of war camp in Dublin. Vinson reached out to Colonel I.B. Summers of the Prisoner of War Division. Summers informed Vinson that placing a POW camp in the area was problematic because the U.S. Army simply lacked qualified prison guards. Determinedly, Vinson contacted Colonel Patterson, who seconded Colonel Summers's misgivings. Farm Labor Advisory Committee representatives (including Bob Hodges, Wade Dominy, C.L. Thigpen, R.T. Gilder, H.W. Dozier, Frank Clark, D.W. Allgood and A.O. Hadden) persistently urged Vinson to try harder. Finally, Vinson won out when the U.S. Army approved sending some of Camp Wheeler's POWs to Dublin. The Corps of Engineers and the Quartermaster Corps finished the camp in just three days. It was located on the timeworn Twelfth District Fairgrounds, where in 1940 Olympic champion Jesse Owens had competed.

On August 26, 1943, the first POWs reached Dublin. Captain Henry J. Bordeaux supervised this group of about two hundred Italians. The prisoners arrived in time to help harvest and stack peanuts in Laurens County and in surrounding counties. They also chopped cotton.[374] The nearby, recently completed naval airfield quickly started handling the airmail into the Dublin compound. Civic and church groups hosted parties for the guards, cooked meals and entertained them at the local service center. The soldiers showed their appreciation when a young woman critically needed a blood transfusion. Her friends contacted Dublin POW Camp Commander Colonel S.L. Irwin. Ten minutes later, soldiers stood ready at the hospital; each gave a blood transfusion and returned later for another one. Almost all the POW camp's

250 guards answered the call of Lehman P. Keen, chairman of the Third War Bond Drive.

The POWs adapted well to the South, singing "Dixie" after a long day in the fields. Almost every Sunday, they marched from the camp to the Catholic church on Church Street as they sang hymns. Most of the residents did not dislike the POWs. Some parked their cars outside the compound to hear the prisoners singing and to smell their food. Wrightsville native Janice W. Williams remembered watching a truck full of Germans passing through Johnson County: "One man stood in the back of the truck facing the front as their leader. I would watch them go through and they were strong, healthy men. Someone said they didn't want to escape because they were out of the war and well fed."[375]

One day, while Oliver Bennett worked at the Naval Hospital's paint shop, he saw a POW, S. Pretscher, sketching a female image on a piece of cardboard. Bennett was awestruck. He asked Pretscher to paint a picture for him. Bennett got the canvas material and the paint. Pretscher worked on the painting in his makeshift tent/studio. Pretscher painted a German country scene and gave it to Bennett. The two became friends, continuing their relationship after the war.[376]

POW artwork. German POW S. Pretscher painted this German country scene for Oliver Bennet of Dublin. *From Pieces of Our Past, http://dublinlaurenscountygeorgia.blogspot.com.*

Georgia POW Camps in World War II

By October 1943, Dublin and the nearby areas did not need so many farm laborers. Accordingly, the U.S. Army planned to relocate the Dublin camp, but not before the Fourth Service Command decided to keep the camp open into November. In the third week of October, Captain Jennings moved 250 of the 500 POWs. Soon the camp closed for the winter.

In June 1944, German POWs returned to Dublin. That summer was problematic. A tree on Snellgrove plantation fell, killing one prisoner while he worked with Robert Cullens's pulpwood crew. Then, on July 4, three prisoners, (Josef Damer, Jeorge Fries and Willi Pape) escaped from a work detail at Warner Callan's farm near Scott, Georgia. Their getaway lasted one day. Various residents thought that the men simply were lost in the woods, not trying to flee. Nonetheless, the camp commander set up stern disciplinary procedures. The Germans reacted with a sit-down strike, refusing to work. By summer's end, the tension had lessened to the point that the guards had time to play baseball, basketball and football games against the U.S. Navy at the new naval hospital.

When Major Shannahan visited the camp in December 1944, he found the tents did not compare to those in the Monticello camp. The POWs were busy building a "large combination recreation building, mess hall and

Dublin, Georgia POW barracks ruins in 1995. *From Pieces of Our Past, http://dublinlaurenscountygeorgia.blogspot.com.*

classroom" with lumber salvaged from the naval hospital and from window glass and other materials donated by contractors. That left little time for tent maintenance. The 250 prisoners worked on "pulpwood, stacking lumber, turpentine, raking pine trees and general farm work." They attended religious services in the camp and were allowed "once or twice a month…to attend a church located approximately 3 blocks [away]."[377]

Shannahan reported the satellite camp's "serious health situation." Rats had been running rampant in the city. Three people had died of typhus. The extermination efforts drove the rats into the stockade. The rats "burrowed under tent floors…to gain access to the…interior." Shannahan suggested calling in the state health department and using "iron left over from the recreation building to rat proof…[the] food storage tents." The commander ruled out using cyanide, fearing it would get into the food and "also kill some of the animals in the vicinity."[378] What happened is unclear.

POWs returned one more summer to harvest crops. The camp closed on December 24, 1945. The lone barracks at the corner of Troup Street stood silent testimony to this long-forgotten piece of Dublin's homefront during World War II—until its recent demolition.[379]

Dublin's Carl Vinson VA Hospital

In January 2016, Carl Vinson Veterans' Administration (VA) Medical Center's public affairs chief, Frank Jordon, made a remarkable discovery, adding to the history of POWs in Georgia. Using the light from his cellphone, Jordon made his way into a little obscure room in Building 4 of the hospital's basement. He found "against one wall…four concrete cubicles, about 5 feet wide by 10 feet long, with open fronts. The fronts were once cell bars." Jordon examined each cubicle's walls. "On the wall of the last cubicle…is an etching about the size of a half dollar coin. It faintly bleeds through paint that an overzealous contractor put on the walls a few years ago. It's a swastika." Jordon explained that a German POW in that cell drew the Nazi symbol.[380]

The U.S. Navy opened the facility in 1945 to treat injured Americans returning from the Pacific Theater. Coming as a surprise to most, the hospital also was a "mini-prisoner of war camp." Jordan thought that the hospital retained about six POWs. Originally, the hospital used the cells "as a brig for sailors." Jordon learned that "at one time…the walls were covered in graffiti

Georgia POW Camps in World War II

Left: Frank Jordon uses his cellphone's light to discover a cell with a swastika on the wall. *Courtesy of Jason Voorhees.*

Right: Former prison cell bars are used in a machine shop. *Courtesy of Jason Voorhees, jvorhees@macon.com.*

written in German, clearly from POWs. Unfortunately…a contractor…took it upon himself to paint the walls. 'Our folks…ran down to stop him, but it was too late.'"[381]

Jordon learned most of this story from local people. They told him at first the Germans were held in the cells, carefully guarded. Later, some stayed in hospital rooms and "roamed the hospital somewhat freely." Jordan explained, "It very quickly evolved into a very casual type thing."[382]

Although local historian Scott Thompson was unaware of the hospital's POWs, he conjectured that they may have been sent there to work. The cell bars are still at the hospital, but someone moved them to another building for use in a tool storage area. Jordon wants the bars reattached to the cells "to commemorate that part of the hospital's history." Regrettably, the POW camp's last standing barracks was bulldozed. Only the cells remain (now without the bars) as evidence of POWs in Dublin's VA hospital.[383]

Chapter 7

FORT OGLETHORPE

Camp Establishment

On March 20, 1944, the Fourth Service Command announced the forthcoming stationing of a "considerable number of Prisoners of War" on Fort Oglethorpe located in Catoosa County, Georgia. The post's executive officer and the engineer were to "plan, allocate and supervise" employing POWs in jobs on the installation. In accordance with the Geneva Convention, the prisoners could not work for personal use; they were to work under armed guard(s) in groups ranging from six to twenty, and they were not to be employed as replacements for civilian employees. The stockade opened two days later as a branch camp of Tennessee's Camp Forrest.[384] It could detain at least three hundred prisoners. On May 1, 1944, the branch camp was "transferred to Fort Oglethorpe as a permanent prisoner of war camp unit branch camp."[385]

City council member Harold Silcox recalled how frequently a POW "would wander away on his return to camp after a workday and would come knocking at the family's back door. My mother would invite the prisoner in and would seat him at the table with the family. After we all had enjoyed a nice meal together, she would call the military police (MP) to come get their missing prisoner."[386]

Inspections 1944

Around July 13, 1944, Fischer and Buhrman made the initial official visit to the permanent camp. Fischer was impressed with the camp's administration.[387] By the following month, the compound held 197 POWs. All but two (sick) worked in twenty areas on the post, such as the shoe repair shop, on roads and grounds, ditching details, in the tent repair shop, in the bakery, on agricultural projects and sawing scrap wood.

In October 1944, Eberhardt reported that he found the prisoners "enjoying the same rights and privileges as the American soldiers, as to meals, barracks, bathing and latrine service." This was the first time Eberhardt had seen "wash rooms and toilets on the second story of any… POW barracks." He imagined Fort Oglethorpe's POW camp "reflect[ed] as near an approach to contentment as men behind wires can feel."[388]

The stockade's infirmary provided first aid, while the post hospital serviced the prisoners' more serious medical needs. The arrival of a German doctor and surgeon was on the horizon. The POWs used the "ample" sports field daily. Eberhardt learned that the POWs watched motion pictures twice a week. Although educational classes were "making some progress," the lack of books hindered the program. After D-Day, the prisoners had refused to attend religious services, but attendance was improving, especially with the new German Lutheran pastor along with the Catholic priest.[389]

During the harvest season, the POWs gathered peaches and completed silage storage. A farmer, who said he spoke for himself and others, told Eberhardt that he was "so well pleased [with the POWs' work] that he hoped he could secure the same grade of labor for next year's crop." The prisoners received the "usual three dollars per month against canteen coupons, plus 80 cents per day when employed in a pay status. The average monthly earnings…[were]…about $23.00." The POWs built an indoor sports center using their wages.[390]

Eberhardt noted the exceptional consideration and cooperation between the prisoners and the American guards (three officers and forty enlisted men). Both groups treated each other as soldiers; the guards had "more than ordinary training and/or experience in their lines." He praised the camp's commander and his staff for their compliance with the Geneva Convention. Like Fischer, Eberhardt thought that the camp was "usually well administered."[391]

Patte toured the compound on November 8, 1944. In his customary style, he expressively wrote:

> *Camp Oglethorpe is very far from having a severe aspect. It is built in a pretty region a few miles from Chattanooga. There, in the northern section, an area was set apart to be the Prisoner of War Section. Towers, barbed wires as usual. But nothing gloomy about them. Facing the gates, outside the compound small dark green barracks form the camp headquarters. Petunias, pink and rose, are blooming, and contribute, with the very clear atmosphere, to giving the visitor a cheerful welcome. The near-by trees, lawns and flowers-on the other side of the wire-help to make the general appearance of this small camp quite agreeable.*[392]

Patte described the camp's above-average physical features. There was a sizeable mess hall. But the "play room," equipped with a "gramophone, radio, ping-pong table, and an attempt at 'interior decoration' was too small." The German chaplain had his own room. The POWs watched movies (contracted from a Georgian company) in "an old shed."[393]

Patte lunched with the prisoners, fifty-four of whom had arrived the previous day from France. The POWs had a favorable impression of the camp. They wanted to work and looked forward to their assignment to detachments. When Patte saw a detachment leave the camp, he thought work along with the chaplain's spiritual support "would be…the best remedy to their worries."[394]

Patte wrote positively about the camp spokesman's appearance, his effective management skills, the respect he had from the other prisoners and his good teamwork with the interpreter. But "[t]here is a draw-back: They seem to have no imagination whatsoever!" He thought this explained the dismal activities program along with the American commander's disposition. By the next month, Captain Curtis T. Burch was the new commander. Patte wondered if the prisoners cared. He asked himself: "Question of climate? Question of difficult readaptation [*sic*] to a life without danger after having been for years in the front lines? Perhaps—But in my opinion, there is, first of all, a lack of dynamic and intelligent leadership, among the POWs."[395] However, when he visited on December 6 while on the way to another camp, he found the prisoners with candy and nuts they had bought in town and busily decorating ten Red Cross–donated trees.[396]

Inspection 1945

In late January 1945, Major Neuland described Captain William F. Raugust's visit to the stockade in early January. There were 238 detainees. Raugust discussed the "Intellectual Diversion" program with Fort Oglethorpe executive officer Lieutenant Colonel Horace Fredericks and with POW camp commander Captain Burch. They gave Second Lieutenant Thomas A. MacWilliams, assistant executive officer, "a free hand to carry it out." The program was progressing well.[397]

Meanwhile, the educational curriculum was still in a "preliminary stage." It included eleven courses with about twenty prisoners in each class. Raugust recommended offering courses in geography and American history and building a classroom in an idle barracks. The textbooks and visual aids were adequate. Although the director of studies (a POW) had good managerial skills, Raugust believed that his dubious "political background" meant he required "careful supervision—he should not be the interpreter."[398]

A POW is reading a book in the library corner of the POW clubroom. One POW library had more than five hundred books. German-language books predominated, with a few books in English for those POWs learning the language. *Courtesy NARA collection.*

The compound had "no separate library or reading room," even though there were about 312 books. This was a big improvement since Eberhardt's visit. Raugust proposed constructing a library room in another vacant barracks. There were enough newspapers and magazines. The POWs wanted "musicals, adventure, westerns, travelogs [sic], and historical" films. There was insufficient interest to begin a camp newspaper.[399]

The indoor and outdoor recreational equipment was ample. Thirty artists and painters exhibited their works in the barracks. The POWs sang after the seven-piece orchestra performed. Raugust advised forming a chorus and "theater group" along with a POW-built stage, since "sufficient talent" existed. He added American personnel should supervise all programs.

In December 1945, fourteen "trouble makers" who were "believed to be Nazis" were sent to Oklahoma's Camp Alva. Consequently, Raugust recommended keeping thorough files on those POWs "who are likely to interfere with the Intellectual Diversion Program."[400]

Neuland described the American guards' "general appearance, attitude and morale...[as] good in spite of the fact that they consider the work to be very monotonous. Their recreational facilities are excellent. Raugust suggested that regular orientation lectures based on the War Department circulars be prepared for the Guard Personnel. He recommended that courses in German be offered."[401]

By February 1945, the number of German prisoners had risen to 246. German Red Cross posters decorated the recreation barracks. The new library had 356 books, including novels, technical books and *soldentenbriefs*, which mainly came from the POWs' families. About 160 POWs took courses like elementary and advanced English, algebra, chemistry, accounting, physics, geometry, mechanical drawing and calligraphy. Some prisoners had contacted American universities, expecting to enroll in correspondence courses. "A gang," wrote Patte, "will soon begin farm work; at first the men will prune fruit trees and plant straw berries."[402]

Effects of Germany's Surrender

On his May 8, 1945, visit, Patte discovered "a decline in educational classes. The program majors are football, quiet games and movies." Revealingly, he ended the brief report stating, "A lack of initiative for leisure time activities is noted, which is certainly due in good part to the circumstances of war in Germany, which affect here seemingly more than in other camps."[403] Germany had surrendered the day before.

During his September trip, Patte reported that the new camp spokesman had created "a real and cooperative 'esprit-de-corps.'" Continuing, he articulately wrote:

> *The compound is very well kept, with lawns and flowers, the day-room with a small canteen attached is attractive; the small soccer-field has been flattened and a sort of hangar...is used for movies and entertainments....* [There is a] *broadcasting system...; good concerts are given every day, partly with our own records, and a "News Service," in German, controlled by the Camp authorities, is also given every night through the headquarters.*
>
> *Here, as in other camps in the south, the high temperature is not inducive to serious summertime study. English classes seem to be the only successful ones. Soccer and football championships create great interest....* [A] *camp paper is issued weekly with comments and articles on the facts of the day, on current events in the world and on American way of living.*[404]

Patte talked to the new pastor, whom he had met before. The pastor told him about the "spiritual needs" at Battey General Hospital in Rome, Georgia. Patte asked to visit that camp.[405]

Battey General Hospital in Rome, Georgia. *Courtesy NARA collection.*

Georgia POW Camps in World War II

Three months after Germany's surrender, Captain Alexander Lakes, POW Special Projects Division, toured the Fort Oglethorpe camp. He cited the following non-compliances with Special Projects Division policies and recommendations: (1) None of the authorized "educational films" had been shown; (2) "No classes...in American civics, history and geography" existed; (3) The library needed more approved books and "Text books on basic American subjects"; (4) Acceptable "Magazines of orientation value" should be ordered; (5) "The Prisoner of War magazine...does not contain definite democratic or anti-Nazi Material, and...[tends] to stress German subjects. Every effort should be made to publish this newspaper in conformance with the reorientation program"; and (6) "The PA system should be used...[to] broadcast...daily news, lectures, and any other orientation material of value to the program."[406]

Six months following Germany's capitulation, the stockade's liaison officer, Captain Lyle Dawson, reported there were 302 POWs working on the post. He did not think the military's use of the work program was "entirely satisfactory." Nonetheless, he expected improvements.[407]

Dawson learned that plans were beginning for the transition from POW laborers to civilians. There were no private work contracts. Still, camp officials accepted certifications from two Georgia contractors (Crandall Timber and Lumber Company for twenty POWs and Chatsworth Lumber Company for another twenty) and from J. Quintis Shepherd dairy farming (three POWs) in Chattanooga, Tennessee. Camp authorities continued allocating POW laborers like fifty for industrial jobs outside Fort Oglethorpe and ten in Tennessee. There were no allotments in either state for agricultural jobs, whereas in 1944 seventy-five to one hundred POWs worked in agriculture. Camp administrators instructed a Rossville, Georgia U.S. Employment Service (USES) representative to determine if labor companies needed "saw filers, brush cutters or any other hourly labor...and if so to prepare proper certifications." The agent thought the lumber companies were unaware of their "obligation to train and properly supervise" the prisoners, adding that he would correct that. One month after Dawson's trip, the Fort Oglethorpe base camp closed on December 16, 1945.[408]

BATTEY GENERAL HOSPITAL BRANCH CAMP

The branch camp at Battey General Hospital was activated on June 6, 1945. In August 1945, Captain Dawson stated the maximum prisoner strength was 250. Like the base camp, the hospital was working to replace POW laborers and American enlisted soldiers with civilians. Dawson recommended completing personnel files, improving supervision and changing "mess employment so prisoners will work [a] full day."[409]

On September 18, 1945, Patte described his trip to Battey. He met with the facility's commander, Captain Raber, "a wounded returnee from the Pacific Theatre." Patte also saw the camp spokesman, whom he had first greeted at Alabama's Camp Aliceville. The recreational and social activities program included "movies twice a week and English classes, worship services on Sundays. There are a few individual books available, and a few soccer balls, a ping-pong table but no balls; there is no radio, phonograph, nor musical instruments." So, Patte left "some equipment and materials." "Faces were beaming," he noted, "when I was able to produce one electric record-player, a splendid collection of records, some ping-pong balls, tennis balls, soccer balls, one color set and two wood-carving sets. I promised…some important shipments with chess-men and boards, guitar, badminton and shuttlecocks and mouth-organs."[410]

Patte discovered that Camp Oglethorpe's pastor "had delegated his spiritual responsibility to a young German YMCA member." He assured the "strong looking, keen-eyed, unostentatious, clean cut lad" of the YMCA's support. He commented, "We could talk at length and freely…of the religious problems in camp, of the place of the YMCA in tomorrow's Germany." Two months later, on November 19, 1945, Battey closed.[411]

Chapter 8

THE PRISONER OF WAR STORY IN GEORGIA NEWSPAPERS

HEADLINES

"Enemy Alien Camp Started Near Macon"
—*Macon Telegraph and News*, November 17, 1942, 1

"Allied Mercy Leaflets Lead Axis Fighters to Surrender"
—*Macon Telegraph and News*, April 18, 1943, 10

"80-cents-a-day Wage Planned for Prisoners"
—*Macon Telegraph*, May 13, 1943, 5

"FDR Confirms Prisoners Due to Aid Farmers"
—*Macon Telegraph*, May 15, 1943, 6

"Italian War Prisoners Here Seem Cheerful but Stick to Roman Salute for Officers"
—*Macon Telegraph*, June 14, 1943, 1

"Nazi Prisoners Prefer 'Jazz'"
—*Macon Telegraph*, July 1, 1943, 7

"Peanut Farmers Face Serious Labor Shortage"
—*Macon Telegraph*, July 15, 1943, 2

Georgia POW Camps in World War II

"Question: Why are the faces of prisoners of war always turned away from the camera?"
—*Macon Telegraph*, July 20, 1943, 3

"Prisoners to Harvest Peanut Crop—Hundreds Moving to Goober Fields"
—*Macon Telegraph*, August 28, 1943, 1

"Italians at Fort Benning Available for Farmers"
—*Sunday Ledger-Enquirer*, August 29, 1943, 1

"War Prisoners Refuse to Do Harvesting Work"
—*Macon Telegraph*, September 2, 1943, 2

"German Prisoners"
—*Macon Telegraph*, September 2, 1943, 2

"War Prisoners Grin at Italy's Capitulation"
—*Macon Telegraph*, September 9, 1943, 10

"Savannah Seeking War Prisoners for Pulpwood Duties"
—*Columbus Enquirer*, October 30, 1943, 8

"Liner Torpedoed 800 Lives Lost"
—*Sunday Ledger-Enquirer*, February 20, 1944, 3

"Nazi War Prisoners Obedient American Officer Declares"
—*Macon Telegraph and News*, April 16, 1944, 2

"Escaped Nazi Seized in South Carolina"
—*Macon Telegraph*, April 24, 1944, 3

"Italian Prisoners Offered Chance to Volunteer for Non-Combat Duty: Most at Fort Benning Accept"
—*Sunday Ledger-Enquirer*, May 7, 1944, 1

"German War Prisoners Working at McRae Mill"
—*Macon Telegraph*, June 28, 1944, 3

Georgia POW Camps in World War II

"Four Prisoner Camps Come Under Benning"
—*Columbus Enquirer*, July 26, 1944, 2

"German Prisoners Are Not Available"
—*Macon Telegraph*, July 28, 1944, 2

"Congress Probing POW 'Coddling'"
—*Sunday Ledger-Enquirer*, August 20, 1944, 1

"Toombs Farmers Face Crisis in Securing Adequate Labor"
—*Macon Telegraph and News*, August 27, 1944, 3

"Nazis Treat US Prisoners Well, Post Officer States"
—*Columbus Enquirer*, September 6, 1944, 10

"War Prisoners Not 'Coddled' in U.S. Camps"
—*Macon Telegraph and News*, October 8, 1944, 20

"Army Chaplains Re-Enact Pioneer Preachers' Role"
—*Columbus Enquirer*, December 22, 1944, 17

"Midville Ships Pulpwood Cars"
—*Macon Telegraph and News*, May 27, 1945, 3

"War Prisoners Ready to Aid in Harvesting"
—*Macon Telegraph and News*, August 19, 1945, 12

"Nearly 3,000 Germans Leave Wheeler; Work in Area Valued at $3,500,000"
—*Macon Telegraph*, December 25, 1945, 14

Articles

"Enemy Alien Camp Started Near Macon"
A Contract has been let and work is now under way on some 125 buildings designed to house "several thousand" enemy aliens. The concentration camp project is being built on a "large tract" of land which extends southward from a mile south of Franklinton. The H.W. Beers Company holds the contract for construction of the giant camp.
—Bob Fackelman, *Macon Telegraph and News*, November 17, 1942

"Allied Mercy Leaflets Lead Axis Fighters to Surrender"
Psychological warfare today is paying big dividends for the Allies as the battle for Tunisia roars to its climax.

Mercy leaflets promising fair treatment to captured German and Italian soldiers has resulted in a steadily increasing number of surrenders by the enemy.

Some of the leaflets are fired by artillery guns, while others are delivered to enemy troops by a method which must remain secret. But regardless of how they are delivered, they have proven almost as effective in some instances as bombs, bullets, and bayonets. Axis troops have come running to the American lines frantically waving yellow-covered tissue-weight leaflets which constitute their ticket to safety.

One side of the leaflet reads: "You are surrounded." The other says: "Good for one safe passage through the Allied lines."

But one would have to be deaf and blind not to note the fervor which many enemy soldiers have been surrendering. They tear into the cuffs and seams of their tattered uniforms to extricate the yellow tickets to freedom which they have so carefully hidden from their own commanders.

Time and again they ask how things are going on other world battle fronts and even in other battle sectors in Tunisia. It is painfully apparent that the Nazi propagandists have succeeded in keeping them in complete ignorance of German military disaster on the Russian front and the great Allied air offensive over Germany itself.

Utter amazement crosses the faces of German prisoners when they are assured by their American captors they will not be bayoneted.

The effectiveness of Nazi propaganda among German troops is evident in the small percentage of German prisoners taken as compared to the Italians, but the Italians are not necessarily inferior to the Germans as fighting men.

Georgia POW Camps in World War II

Batches of Italian soldiers have approached our lines shouting: "Take us to America! All we want is to work in peace. To hell with Mussolini." Invariably they bring their mess kits with them, a sure sign they are here to stay.

—Michael Chinigo (with American Forces in Tunisia), *Macon Telegraph and News*, April 18, 1943

"80-Cents-a-Day Wage Planned for Prisoners"

POW enlisted men were paid 80 cents per day for farm and factory work. This was "in addition to the 10 cents daily given to them at prison camps for the purchase of small luxuries." The Geneva Convention prohibited POWs from defense work. POW "officers who may not be required to work outside prison camps are paid $20, $30, or $40 per month, depending on rank, in addition to their keep." As of May 1943, there were 20,000 POWs in the county "but that number will probably be swelled considerably by Italian and German soldiers captured in Tunisia."

—*Macon Telegraph*, May 13, 1943

"FDR Confirms Prisoners Due to Aid Farmers"

"President Roosevelt declared Friday that many of the 175,000 German and Italian prisoners captured in Tunisia will be brought to the United States...." Two problems confronted the Allies with regard to keeping the prisoners in North Africa: providing for their security and feeding them. The POWs "would be ferried across the Atlantic aboard the very transport and cargo ships which took the soldiers abroad to smash the Axis in North Africa." The POWs "will be used in farm work."

—*Macon Telegraph*, May 15, 1943

"Italian War Prisoners Here Seem Cheerful but Stick to Roman Salute for Officers"

Mr. Adams reported on his visit to the Macon POW Camp Wheeler. "All barracks visited were clean and in good order. The visit was made on Sunday when the men were all in the enclosure as none of them are required to work outside on Sunday and carry on only such work as is required to prepare their meals and look after quarters."

"One of the most interesting places visited was a kitchen and dining hall."

"Let it be said here that the Italians held in the camps do not waste anything. However, they don't like some of the things we Americans count as good and they prefer to prepare their own food and serve it when they like it."

"There are U.S. Army mess sergeants in charge of the kitchens. All of the cooking is done by Italians. One man is head cook but on the day of my visit he had plenty of help. There were twelve men assisting him and each one appeared most willing to do anything he could to prepare the food."

"At least six men were kneading dough in large metal pans and with such vigor that they were wet with perspiration. Getting a big batch of dough worked up to suit Italian war prisoners is no small undertaking. The prisoners complain that we Americans don't bake good bread and they prefer to make up their dough and bake it in a form to their taste. The dough the men were working on had a large amount of white potatoes boiled and mashed in the flour. The mess sergeant says they prefer it that way. After working the dough for a longtime a large counter or table is covered with dry flour and then comes the rolling in which eight or ten men take part. The dough is rolled into long strips and cut into small pieces. These are run by hand over a grater very lightly and roll off like a wafer curled up. I was told this was cooked like a dumpling."

"The Italians do not care for butter or lard and are not big meat eaters, says the sergeant. Save every bit of the grease from pork or sausage and this is used in their cooking."

"Oh yes they like spaghetti and macaroni, and make these to suit their taste from the flour provided. How about a cereal? Oh no, not like you and I take them. The prisoners eat cereal, but not with milk and cream. They take a small individual serving, like those served in army mess halls, and empty the package into a bowl with a rich soup made with every kind of vegetable they can get."

"They have a sweet tooth, says the sergeant, who when questioned, admitted they don't like some things we eat but go strong for sugar, cooking oil, vinegar, and black pepper. They eat Georgia cane syrup for breakfast but don't want their sausage until the midday meal."

"When the prisoners first arrived, they showed the need for food. Nothing was left on the plates, white chinaware, except a few bones. At this time the men look fat and healthy and are said to be not so ravenously hungry as they were upon arrival."

"The young man who cuts the meat for the mess hall was butcher in his home town in Italy. He knows how, said the mess sergeant."

"Almost every mess hall and barracks have little flower pots on either side of the door, and between some of the buildings are vegetable gardens showing good care." The gardens were done on the enlisted men's initiative and were not required by their officers.

"There is a canteen in the compound where the prisoners may get soft drinks, combs, Vaseline, hair tonic, cigarettes, and other small items. Each man is given a book of coupons by the army that entitles him to buy $3 worth of merchandise a month. In addition, when he works on one of the labor projects outside the camp he receives 80 cents per day. However, he is not allowed to spend more than $13 per month, which means $10 of his earned money and $3 given by the government."

"All labor outside the camp is voluntary."

"The Italians are said to be willing workers and the officer in charge said farmers had reported satisfaction over their employment." Officers in charge said the demand for workers is greater than the available supply of POWs.

The War Department said there were 36,688 POWs in 21 prison camps in America as of June 1943. "These included 22,110 Germans, 14,516 Italians, and 62 Japanese. Officers at Camp Wheeler said there were no Germans or Japanese held here."

Farmers in middle Georgia, fruit packers and sawmill operators were seeking POW labor. Bibb County commissioners were told that no POW labor would be used on county roads.

"There is one point that is confusing..." concerning the 80 cents per day paid to POWs. The employer "must pay an agreed upon wage scale for the type of work." "The difference between what he pays and the 80 cents the prisoner gets goes into the United States Treasury."

What was it like to enter a POW camp? "...watch the first gate swing open under the watchful eye of an armed American soldier. You get through the first gate and then you are halted between two high wire fences. In a high tower nearby (one at each corner of the enclosure), are more soldiers." "...pass through another gate into an enclosure where there is a tool house (here every tool used by the prisoners working in the camp must be checked in carefully after each detail is relieved). Another high gate opens and you are inside the internment camp with an unknown number of war prisoners dressed mostly in pants and sleeveless under shirts. Some still wear the uniforms they wore in battle while others wear fatigue clothes."

"The Italians at Macon are all young men and look strong and physically sturdy. They are on the average, smaller than American soldiers and some look a bit on the Nordic side instead of the Latin. This is impressed on one when he sees a blond or a redhead, and there are a few here."

"Music is to be heard in many of the barracks. In one building there was an artist at work with his paint brushes. He had painted a country scene on his large canvas tacked on the walls of the building."

—Ben E. Adams (passed by Army Censors), *Macon Telegraph,* June 14, 1943

Georgia POW Camps in World War II

"Nazi Prisoners Prefer 'Jazz'"
Camp Blanding, Florida [a branch POW camp commanded from Georgia]—American jazz music and corn flakes are particularly popular with German prisoners of war interned here, says Capt. Ralph E. Lewis, in command of the compound where they are quartered.

"One of them told me he thought Germany should have a corn flake factory after the war," Capt. Lewis said.

"All other American foods—the prisoners receive US Army rations—are popular with the Germans with one exception—they heartily dislike sweet potatoes," Lewis declared.

"The prison compound here is being used only for the present as a reception center for German captives. Prisoners are kept here only temporarily and are transferred to work camps as needed."

—*Macon Telegraph*, July 1, 1943

"Peanut Farmers Face Serious Labor Shortage"
"War Prisoners May Be Used in Some Areas"
Americus, Georgia—"With time rapidly approaching for harvesting the greatest peanut crop in the 24 counties making up the third congressional district, no prisoners have arrived....yet the hope of obtaining help is not very encouraging. Congressman Stephen Pace said that none of the many thousands of Mexican laborers that come to this country will be distributed in Georgia, but will go mainly to the far west farm areas."

The wish for harvest labor was that 50 POWs could be allotted per county. Pace said, "There is not a surplus supply of farm labor at any place in the United States. This means that we have practically no hope of having workers brought into Georgia from other parts of the nation."

Pace said, "Neither is the prospect so good as to war prisoners. There are no Jap or German war prisoners in Georgia and it is not likely that any will be stationed in Georgia. Very few farmers would want to work with them anyway. There are now only 21,000 Italian prisoners in the entire United States. Of these only about 15,000 are available for farm work. Of these 1,015 are at Camp Wheeler near Macon. A prison camp has been constructed at Fort Benning and is ready for occupancy, but no prisoners have arrived there yet. As the prisoners are only allowed to be away from the camp for 10 hours, their work must be confined to within 25 or 30 miles of the camp."

Pace said, "...farmers must depend...on local help..." for the harvest. "The time is near when every man, woman, and child in the state, who is physically able and can possibly spare the time, must offer their services and go to the fields and help gather and save the abundant crop which the farmers have produced. Food is too important to let any of the crop waste in the fields. Our boys out on the battle lines of the world must be fed, our civilian workers must be sustained, and many of our brothers in arms must be provided for."

—*Macon Telegraph,* July 15, 1943

"QUESTION: WHY ARE THE FACES OF PRISONERS OF WAR ALWAYS TURNED AWAY FROM THE CAMERA?"
The War Department said that the publication of photographs showing recognizable features of prisoners of war is not permissible under conditions of existing international agreements.

—*Macon Telegraph,* July 20, 1943

"ITALIANS AT FORT BENNING AVAILABLE FOR FARMERS—500 PRISONERS OF WAR TO HELP HARVEST CROPS IN THIS AREA"
Over 500 Italian POWs were put to work to harvest crops in a 35 to 40-mile radius of Americus, Georgia. The temporary POW camp near Americus was located at the Southern Field, Army Air School. The Seventh Armored Division's 48th Armored Regiment provided guards at the Americus location camp and eight other POW camps in Georgia during the harvest season.

During the harvest season POWs were used at the following Georgia locations: 500 in Dublin under Capt. D. D. Jennings; 250 in Swainsboro under Maj. E.L. Henderson; 500 in Sylvania under Capt. J.C. Kennedy; 250 in Fitzgerald under L.N. Garrett; 250 in Albany under Capt. R.E. Madden; 250 in Bainbridge under Capt. H.S. Forrester; 250 in Moultrie under Capt. T.E. Kyle.

The Americus camp also used German POWs from Alabama POW camps in Anniston and Opelika.

"War Department policy will not allow spectators to gather to watch the men being taken out in trucks to work, nor, will spectators be allowed to watch the men at work, it was pointed out."

—*Sunday Ledger-Enquirer,* August 29, 1943

"PRISONERS TO HARVEST PEANUT CROP—HUNDREDS MOVING TO GOOBER FIELDS"
Hundreds of prisoners of war are being moved into the Georgia peanut belt to assist in harvesting the crop, it was disclosed last night.

Georgia POW Camps in World War II

Branch prison camps were authorized for Dublin and Turner Field in Albany, Georgia. Col. J.A. Muldrow revealed through the Public Relations Office at Camp Wheeler. These camps will house prisoners near fields in which they will work and thus reduce the transportation costs and save tires and cars.

Assignment of farm work will be under the direction of county agents and agricultural officials.

Capt. Henry J. Boudreaux, an Intelligence officer at Camp Wheeler, is in charge of a detail of 100 prisoners to be used in harvesting peanuts. The camp is being established at the fairgrounds in Dublin. Capt. Boudreaux is working under Col. R.E. Patterson, war prison commander.

The contingent of prisoners to work in the Dublin area was obtained through the efforts of County Agent Harry A, Edge of Laurens and Walter B. Daniel, Bob Hodges, Wade Dominy, TC Waldrep, D.I. Parker, J.L. Allen, M.F. Beall, Dennis Rawls, C.L. Thigpen, R.T. Gilder, H.W. Dozier, Frank Clark, D.W. Allgood, and Oswell Hadden, members of the farm labor advisory committee.

Three hundred prisoners are scheduled to reach Turner Field today to begin work in the peanut fields. These prisoners will be housed on the military reservation.

It is understood that a similar number of men will be sent to Americus for work on farms. These prisoners will be available to farmers in Calhoun, Worth, Lee, Baker, and Dougherty counties.

J.C. Richardson, county agent for Dougherty county, said farmers must sign contracts with the government for the use of prisoners who will work in units of 20 men, under a non-commissioned officer.

Several hundred POWs from Camp Wheeler were transferred to Fort Benning and Albany "to help speed up the agricultural program in those areas."

—*Macon Telegraph*, August 28, 1943

"War Prisoners Refuse to Do Harvesting Work"
Fitzgerald Georgia—"More than 250 war prisoners assigned to this section to harvest crops refused to work today," County Agent Henry Harden of Ben Hill County, said.

Harden said the prisoners had worked Monday and Tuesday harvesting peanuts on farms in the adjoining counties...."18 to 20 prisoners had refused to harvest peanuts on a farm because of sand spurs—small weeds with sharp thorns—and that prisoner non-commissioned officers refused to order their men back into the fields. The prisoners obey their non-coms implicitly," he said.

"Meanwhile in Atlanta, the Fourth Service Command announced work on ten temporary camps to house more than 3,900 prisoners in South Carolina and Alabama, starting tomorrow." These POWs would do farm work in those states.

POWs from the Fitzgerald camp worked in Ben Hill, Irwin, Wilcox, and Turner counties. "Harden said farmers in those counties had no complaints, but are 'very patient and hopeful because we need the work.'"

Under the Geneva Convention war prisoners cannot be forced to do work other than housekeeping duties involved in maintaining their own living quarters. They cannot be assigned to work directly connected with the war effort, but are usually used in agricultural labor.

There were no other reports of POWs refusing to work. At Avera, Georgia Camp Gordon authorities said two POWs escaped while working on a farm.

"The Fourth Service Command said camps in South Carolina will be located in Aiken, Barnwell, Bamberg, and Hampton. Alabama camps will be in Andalusia, Geneva, Enterprise, Daleville, Dothan, and Troy." The majority of POWS were assigned to Alabama camps.

—*Macon Telegraph*, September 2, 1943

"GERMAN PRISONERS"

Edison, Georgia—Several farmers here are using German prisoners of war to help harvest their peanut crops, with their arrival today. One of Edison's farmers, J.H. Sheppard, states that he is very much pleased with the work being done on his farm by the prisoners.

—*Macon Telegraph*, September 2, 1943

"WAR PRISONERS GRIN AT ITALY'S CAPITULATION"

Italian prisoners of war at Camp Wheeler yesterday greeted with wide grins the news that their homeland capitulated to the Allied nations and left no doubt that they were glad Italy was out of the conflict. The captured Italians were almost unanimous in cheering news of the surrender.

"Practically all the prisoners grinned widely when they heard the news over radio stations permitted in their quarters," a spokesman said. "Their only concern now is that Germany may 'punish' the Italian people by bombing Italian territory."

—*Macon Telegraph*, September 9, 1943

Georgia POW Camps in World War II

"Savannah Seeking War Prisoners for Pulpwood Duties"
Savannah, Georgia—Representatives of the pulpwood industry met with government agents in the office of the area director of the war manpower commission, Harvey Enroe, Jr., seeking 250 POWs for the pulpwood industry near Savannah.

—Columbus Enquirer, October 30, 1943

"Liner Torpedoed 800 Lives Lost"
Vancouver, Canada—The journey of POWs from the combat zone to POW camps in Allied countries was hazardous. The British ocean liner *Empress of Canada* (21,500 tons) was torpedoed on March 9, 1944, by an Italian submarine off Freetown, West Africa. The ship was transporting allied "troops, navy personnel, Italian prisoners of war, and Greek and Polish refugees." Close to 800 people were rescued; however, of the 800 lives lost "most were Italian Prisoners of War."

—Sunday Ledger-Enquirer, February 20, 1944

"Nazi War Prisoners Obedient American Officer Declares"
Fort McClellan, Alabama—Discipline among German prisoners of war here—former members of the Afrika Korps—is no problem, an American officer said today.

There have been no escapes from 2,736 prisoners quartered here and at side camps. The Germans want to work and perform well. Visiting newspapermen saw the Germans making cement blocks, repairing automobiles, planting crops and performing other work. The cement workers, clad in blue denim, swung their shovels as vigorously as any free Americans. The prisoners appeared sturdy and healthy.

A group of prisoners in a garage were servicing non-combat vehicles. The American in charge said they were efficient after learning their tasks. No case of sabotage had occurred.

Lightly guarded prisoners planted onion sets at a farm. The camp plans to farm 65 acres with prison labor to raise food for the post. All German prisoners are given 30 cents per day for canteen purchases. Those that work on projects other than their own maintenance receive 80 cents daily in canteen script.

Canteens are similar to those of American soldiers. Popular items include the army 3.2 beer, orange drinks, chocolate, cigars and cigarettes. Their taste in smoking runs to better brands. Profits from the canteen go the prisons welfare fund.

Georgia POW Camps in World War II

Prisoners' morale is good, American officers said. Prisoners can employ their energies in many ways including working outside, beautifying their own camp, decorating their quarters, using power tools in the wood working shop, painting, music, dramatics, and sports.

There is a regular flow of mail and parcels from Germany. Mail requires from 90 days to four months since it follows devious world routes. Currently about 1,000 letters arrive daily. Parcels include food such as pumpernickel.

American authorities carefully observe the Geneva Convention for treatment of prisoners to insure like treatment of American prisoners. Germany quickly applies restraints parallel to those imposed here. Recently German prisoners were instructed not to sing Nazi songs outside their camps. The Germans promptly prohibited American prisoners from singing the Star-Spangled Banner and God Bless America.

—*Macon Telegraph and News*, April 16, 1944

"Escaped Nazi Seized in South Carolina"
Atlanta, Georgia—Capture in Columbia, SC of the last of four German prisoners of war who escaped from Camp Gordon internment camp near Augusta, Ga, was announced today.

Two of the four men Josef Lisinski and Heinz Stolte were captured near Augusta shortly after they escaped last Monday night. Herman Mueller, 22, was picked up on a Columbia street Friday.

—*Macon Telegraph*, April 24, 1944

"Italian Prisoners Offered Chance to Volunteer for Non-Combat Duty: Most at Fort Benning Accept"
Washington DC—Italian POWs were offered a chance to serve in non-combat support services under American officers. This allowed "thousands" of American soldiers to be released for combat. Of the 3,000 Italians POWs at Fort Benning 90% volunteered. As of April 1, 1944, there were 50,136 Italian POWs in the United States.

—*Sunday Ledger-Enquirer*, May 7, 1944, via AP Washington

"German War Prisoners Working at McRae Mill"
McRae, Georgia—Twenty German prisoners of war have been working every day for the past two weeks at the Shepherd Lumber Mill, stacking lumber.

Georgia POW Camps in World War II

The prisoners are brought here every morning from the prison camp at Dublin, in equipment belonging to the lumber mill and returned every night. Two government guards stand watch over them as they work.

—*Macon Telegraph*, June 28, 1944

"Four Prisoner Camps Come Under Benning"
Four branch camps in Southern Georgia came under the command of Fort Benning. The camps located at Albany, Bainbridge, Moultrie and Valdosta were formally commanded by the Eastern Flying Training Command.

All four camps have a total of 1,000 Nazi prisoners of war employed in critical agricultural projects to help alleviate manpower shortages.

—*Columbus Enquirer*, July 26, 1944, 2

"German Prisoners Are Not Available"
Fort Benning—Until guard strength is increased the 500 German prisoners from the Normandy beachhead will not be available for labor outside the post. Maj. Clarence T. Johnson, Fort Benning executive officer, announced yesterday.

Farmers in the Columbus area had hoped to utilize the prisoners for farm work.

Four branch camps, controlled by the Eastern Flying Training Command, now reported to the Fort Benning base camp: Albany, Bainbridge, Moultrie and Valdosta.

—*Macon Telegraph*, July 28, 1944

"Congress Probing POW 'Coddling'"
Washington DC—Congress sent investigators to Pennsylvania and Kentucky to investigate reports "that Axis prisoners are being coddled and treated like heroes."

—*Sunday Ledger-Enquirer*, August 20, 1944

"Toombs Farmers Face Crisis in Securing Adequate Labor"
Vidalia, Georgia—"Toombs county farmers have planted and cultivated the most valuable food and feed crop in the history of agriculture in this area. The early fall onion crop was handled, and the tobacco crop has been brought in and sold. Cotton, sweet potatoes, peanuts, and feed crops for winter remains to be gathered, no farmer seeming to know how the labor shortage is to be met."

Georgia POW Camps in World War II

Without labor to bring in the crops large losses were predicted. "Farmers expect to work long hours daily in the harvesting operations, will make use of all available man, woman, and child power and some large farmers in the lower part of the county have contracted for German prisoners to come from nearby camps in Tattnall county and do what they can to bring in this season's harvest from the fields."

"With all agencies working to relieve the manpower shortage in this section, it is quite likely that the farmer and his own family will bear the heaviest part of the burden of harvesting by working long hours daily during the next three months."

—*Macon Telegraph and News*, August 27, 1944

"Nazis Treat US Prisoners Well, Post Officer States"
In response to questioning by Kiwanians of American prisoners in Germany, Col George Chescheir, POW camp commander at Benning, said he had occasion to talk with authorities closely associated with the issue and said that the Americans were treated exceptionally well.

"The food is not quite as good as we feed German prisoners," he stated, "but it is better than food served to the average German civilian. Any loss in diet is made up of Red Cross parcels, and the Germans are trying to live up to the Geneva convention."

"Scant knowledge is available regarding American prisoners in Japan," he said, "and it is definitely not enough [information] to be comfortable."

German POWs at Fort Benning are divided on their opinion of the Allied progress in the war, according to Col Chescheir. Generally, the German enlisted POWs are happy with allied advances and look forward to the end of the war. The POW German officers are less enthusiastic with the progress. POWs follow the war by reading the New York Times, and the magazines Life and Time, from the POW camp library.

Col Chescheir recounted the POW experience at Fort Benning as follows:

"The first group of prisoners received at Benning were Italians who had been fired upon by Nazis in Sicily." He said prisoners are a burden to troops in the field and are rushed to the rear with nothing but their clothes on their back and a few items that can be carried in their pockets. Col Chescheir said, "Consequently, when they arrive in the states they are in horrible condition, physically and otherwise. After thorough physical examinations, the prisoners are given new clothing and put on a good American diet which in turn clears up skin eruptions within a week. Some of the prisoners are so hungry for sweets that they scoop up handfuls of sugar from the bowls on the table."

The first week or so that they are here, they are rather disillusioned, and are unable to comprehend why they are being treated so fairly. As a result, they wander around, never lifting their eyes from the ground. But after a week of this new life, their attitudes change as they are organized into companies, and permitted to do their own work under the supervision of their American guards.

By September 1944, only a few Italian prisoners remained at Benning. After the fall of Mussolini "98% of Italian prisoners volunteered and were accepted for every line of duty except for combat."

With the addition of 600 Nazi prisoners captured in Norway seven weeks ago [July 14, 1944], a new program is in operation at the camp with English, mathematics, engineering and pre-medical courses being taught. Very recently the government has allowed the prisoners to enroll in correspondence courses with various universities throughout the country. The prisoners pay for these courses with their own funds and each lesson is censored by military officials before it is turned over to them.

Sports are greatly enjoyed at the prisoner of war camps, Col Chescheir explained. At the present time there are two former Olympic champions who direct soccer, baseball, and other athletics.

A great many of the prisoners attend religious services on Sunday. A Catholic priest and a Lutheran minister are among the captives and they direct services at the Benning camp and at six side camps that are located between Americus and Florida.

Upon arrival, prisoners are opposed to work, however, when they learn that work is compulsory in order to increase their monthly allowance of $3, which is used wholly for personal items, they react differently.

Laborers are paid 80 cents a day, and can "up" their pay to an amount of $1.20 for overtime work. When they are bound out to factories and other private enterprises, the prevailing labor wage is charged, and all arrangements are made through the War Manpower Commission. The captives are not paid in actual cash, but instead are compensated with canteen coupons which may be spent at the post exchanges with the POW camp.

A certain amount of work is set out for them each day, and they are obliged to complete the task before they can cease working. Most of the prisoners dislike the intense heat that prevails during the afternoons, and hasten to complete their work before the wave sets in by 1 PM, the commander reported.

Georgia POW Camps in World War II

Discussing mail call for POWs, Col. Chescheir explained that German mail comes through quite regularly while some of the Italian prisoners had not heard from their families in over two years. "When the Germans were controlling Italy, they really tightened up on outgoing mail" he said, "and not more than 41 letters from Italian families were ever received by Italian captives at Benning."

In relation to the possibility of prisoner escapes, it was reported that up until June 1 [1944], only 338 prisoners had escaped from all prison camps in the country. Fifty percent of these prisoners were captured within a few hours, while 35% were gone only a few days. Here at the Benning camp there were no escapes among the Italian prisoners, and only two Germans have escaped to date. Because of the immensity of the reservation, the splendid work of the FBI, and the adequate guard system, there is little opportunity for prisoners to escape, the Col. emphasized.

—*Columbus Enquirer,* September 6, 1944, 10

"WAR PRISONERS NOT 'CODDLED' IN U.S. CAMPS"
The House Military Affairs Committee's investigation concluded that POWs were not "coddled." Committee chairman, Andrew J. May (D-Ky) ordered investigations after receiving complaints that in some cases German and Italian prisoners were being treated as heroes and given undue freedom.

The committee's Chief Investigator H. Ralph Burton addressed "numerous" complaints that war prisoners, particularly Italian ones, were better housed and fed here than American troops stationed abroad. Other complaints came from American soldiers who charged that Italian prisoners were accorded privileges and treatment better than that to be expected by war prisoners—including the "dating" of American girls.

—*Macon Telegraph and News,* October 8, 1944

"ARMY CHAPLAINS RE-ENACT PIONEER PREACHERS' ROLE"
US Army Chaplains are modern day circuit-riders reenacting pioneer preachers who rode on horseback from town to town, said Chaplain (Colonel) Ralph W. Rodgers, chief of chaplains, Fourth Service Command, Fort Benning.

The difference from pioneer times is that Army chaplains ride in jeeps instead of horses and their congregations are German prisoners held in base camps throughout the seven southeastern states. The chaplains do this to meet the Geneva Convention's mandate to provide religious services for POWs.

Georgia POW Camps in World War II

An example of a modern jeep-riding circuit chaplain is Fort Benning's Captain Roderick MacEachem. At Fort Benning there are two German POW chaplains, Catholic and Lutheran. They ride with Captain MacEachem to POW branch camps at Americus, Bainbridge, Fargo, Moody Field, and Turner Field, all in southwestern Georgia.

There are sometimes six or seven branch camps attached to a main base camp, like Fort Benning. This allows the army to get the maximum productive work from POWs by having the labor source near the farms and log mills. But this is a challenge for chaplains to cover a large geographic area like southwestern Georgia.

—Columbus Enquirer, December 22, 1944, 17

"Midville Ships Pulpwood Cars"

Midville, Georgia—More than 250 cars of pulp wood have been shipped from Midville in the past few months. German prisoners of war have taken care of the labor problem in handling the logs. Largest shippers are JJ Kennedy, EL Scott, and CJ Belt.

—Macon Telegraph and News, May 27, 1945

"War Prisoners Ready to Aid in Harvesting"

Hawkinsville, Georgia—The Pulaski County fairgrounds has been transformed into a camp with many rows of tents being placed on the enclosure of the racetrack to take care of the German prisoners who arrived to assist the farmers in harvesting the peanut crop.

Four hundred prisoners have already arrived, with more expected later. About forty army trucks and other equipment will arrive at the camp in a few days. The camp is under strict military rule. The officer's headquarters are on the opposite side of the racetrack. There will be about six officers and 60 guards. Capt. Gamble is the commanding officer in charge.

A high barbed wire fence has been erected around the tents where the prisoners will be quartered. Lights and water have been connected, furnished by the city. Farmers will furnish transportation to the various farms, while the government will furnish food and clothing. They will be paid on the basis of the number of stacks. Poles have already been erected in the fields.

For this harvest POWs worked in Pulaski, Bleckley, Wilcox, Dooley, Houston, and Dodge counties.

The farmers in Pulaski County who contracted for POW labor were: CL Bennett; TD Little; Marshall Saxon; JF Hart; LA Blount; DH Simmons; FB Calhoun; Julian Holder; JK Wilcox; HT Fleeman; James Conner; JD

Georgia POW Camps in World War II

Nelson; LG McKinney; OM Newsome; RW Lancaster; Oliver Daniel; JB Miller; Ira Mays; SW Smith; JC Wilcox; TE Wood; PE Bennett; William Lampkin; DT Sparrow; JM McKinney; Pete Watson; SJ Harden; WG Miller; Better Farms No. 42; DF Jones; JD Barrs; RH Mays; WF Daniel; JH Busbee; CR Foster; Howard Coody; EL Jennings; Alf Nelson; Nick Cabero; David Clarke; Elmer Treisch; HM Martin; SM Stewart; Archie Sloan; JW Poole; JJ Woods; Parsons farm; Bob Massee; AL Mashburn; Grady Nelson; VR Franklin; EO Richardson; Emmett Holland; WB Horton; FH Grantham; VC Mullis; JF Sparrow.

—Macon Telegraph and News, August 19, 1945

"Nearly 3,000 Germans Leave Wheeler; Work in Area Valued at $3,500,000"

First Step on Return to Germany—Nearly 3,000 German prisoners of war have been shipped from Camp Wheeler to other military posts, according to an announcement made by the Camp Wheeler Public Relations Office. This is the prisoners' first step in their return to Germany.

Lt. Col. R. E. Patterson of Boone, Iowa, commander of the Wheeler POW camp, said the Germans at Camp Wheeler did $3,500,000* worth of work in central Georgia.

German POWs under the direction of Camp Wheeler's POW camp made more than $750,000 for the United States government in the past year and at the same time saved the War Department an equal sum. In their free time prisoners prepared themselves to carry democracy back to their homeland.

Since May 1944, only Germans have been located in the base camp Wheeler and in the eight branch camps in central Georgia. The largest number of Germans stationed in the Wheeler Camp and its branches was 4,700. As of December 1945, only 1,950 remained.

The prisoners filled 3,500 separate contracts with farmers and producers in the Georgia area in addition to working in camps. The contracts varied in value from $8 to $36,000. The pay for that work—an estimated $2,000,000—was forwarded to the U.S. Treasury.

To hire civilians to take the place of prisoners at Wheeler would mean the Army hiring 1,000 extra men a day. The value of the men, if they had received wages as mechanics, typewriter experts, tailors, and laborers, would have varied from $2 to $12 per man per day.

Camp Wheeler commanded branch camps in Monticello, Ashburn, Waynesboro, Daniels Field, and Dublin. Work camps for seasonal duties

Georgia POW Camps in World War II

were established at Griffin, Sandersville, Fitzgerald, and Hawkinsville. Now only the Daniels Field and the Dublin branches remain open.

Southern farmers still want private employment of prisoners of war beyond March 2, 1946. Sawmill and pulpwood labor shortages could use the prisoners too, they claim. But present War Department plans, as announced by War Secretary Patterson, call for shipment of all prisoners to their homeland by February 1956, and this will result in the closing of the existing central Georgia camps in the near future.

—*Macon Telegraph*, December 25, 1945

Chapter 9

DAILY LIFE FOR PRISONERS OF WAR

The following gallery is a general overview of what daily life was like for most POWs. The POW experience began with their capture on the battlefield and continued through their transport to America, the prison camp experience and the eventual return to their homeland. U.S. Army original photographs are from the National Archives, unless otherwise noted. They illustrate the POW experience. Captions are taken from the back of each original image.

GEORGIA POW CAMPS IN WORLD WAR II

CAPTURE

Above: Recently captured German soldiers in North Africa, June 3, 1943, soon to be POWs in America. *Courtesy NARA collection.*

Opposite: Vanquished in battle, an officer of the German Afrika Korps jokes with an American navy officer, *center*, and American Coast Guard officer, *right*, shortly before he and other prisoners were brought to America on a Coast Guard manned ship, August 5, 1943. *Courtesy NARA collection.*

Georgia POW Camps in World War II

GEORGIA POW CAMPS IN WORLD WAR II

VOYAGE TO AMERICA AND ARRIVAL

POWs arrive in Boston, Massachusetts, 1944. *Courtesy NARA collection.*

Georgia POW Camps in World War II

November 27, 1944: Hundreds of German soldiers, captured in the Allied drive through France and into Germany, jam the deck of a U.S. troop transport headed for America. Two U.S. Coast Guardsmen stand guard over the prisoners. They are but a small contingent of the 691,989 Germans who surrendered between June 6, 1944, and November 21, 1944. *Courtesy NARA collection.*

Georgia POW Camps in World War II

Above: Each POW's clothing and property are searched, and weapons and propaganda are confiscated. Certain items of equipment are picked up for comparison with, and possible improvement of, American equipment. Each man's valuables are placed in a paper bag, which is returned to him before he entrains. Boston, Massachusetts, 1944. *Courtesy NARA collection.*

Opposite, top: Italian POWs officers read instructions printed in English, German and Italian. In-processing, Boston, Massachusetts, 1944. *Courtesy NARA collection.*

Opposite, bottom: Processing of POWs upon their arrival in Boston. An American interpreter instructs the POWs, 1944. *Courtesy NARA collection.*

Georgia POW Camps in World War II

These POW officers have just had their valuables returned to them. In-processing, Boston, Massachusetts, 1944. *Courtesy NARA collection.*

In-Processing

The Iron Cross, Second Class, is being removed from a POW's blouse. POWs were allowed to retain their medals but not display them. In-processing, Boston, Massachusetts, 1944. Note that this restriction was not enforced at all POW camps.

Georgia POW Camps in World War II

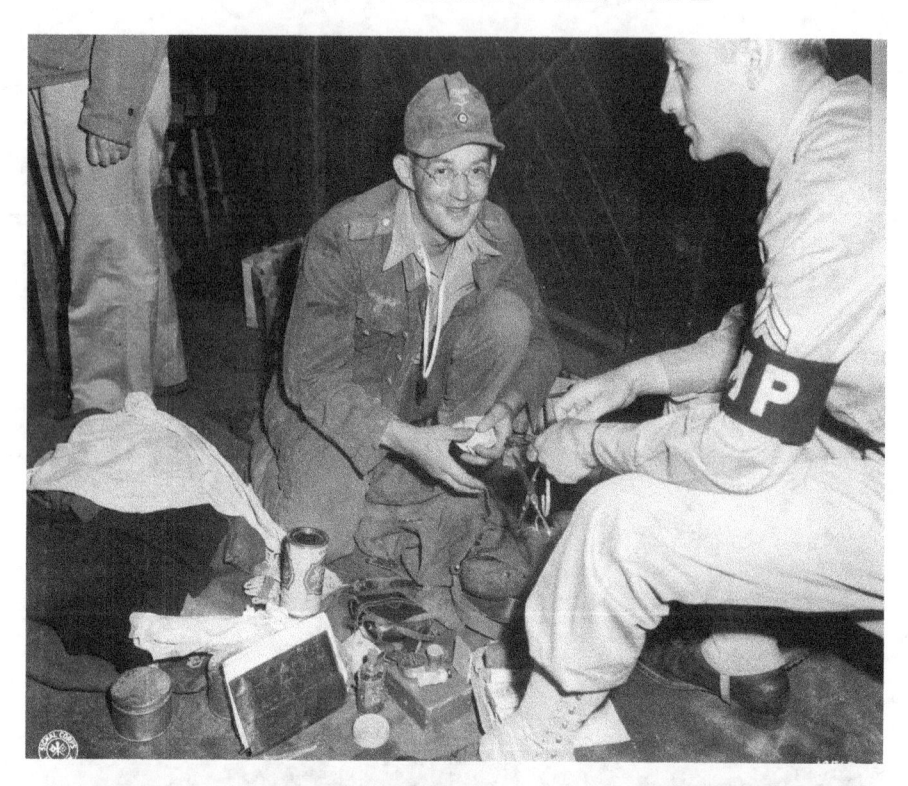

Georgia POW Camps in World War II

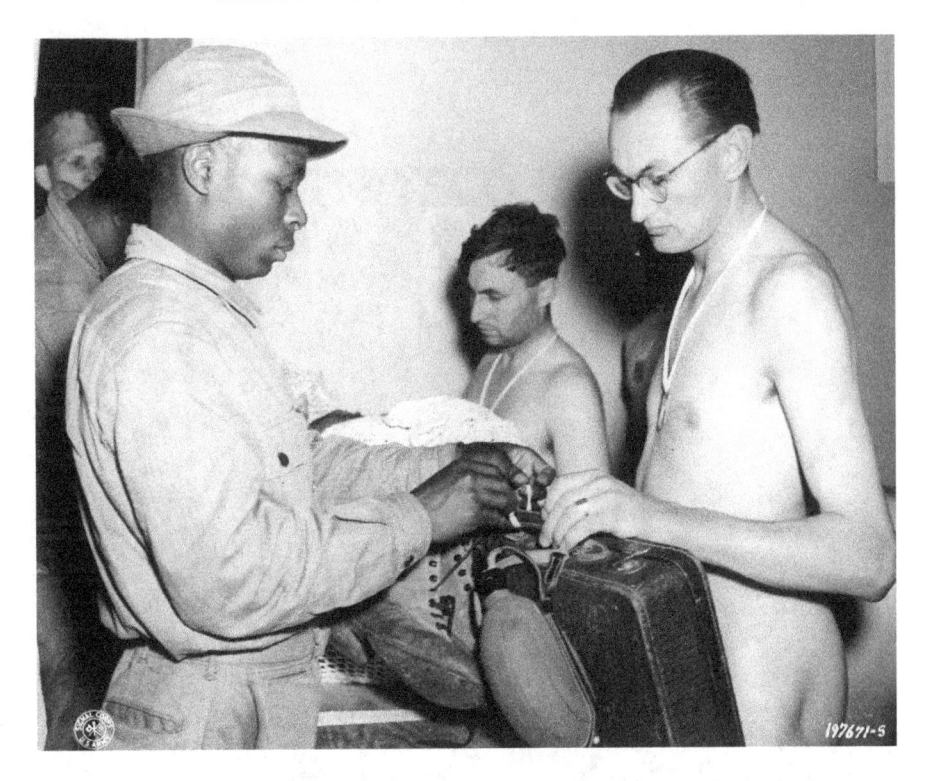

Above: Clothing, blankets and similar items are placed in a large net bag for fumigation. Shown here, leather goods were handled separately. Boston, Massachusetts, 1944. *Courtesy NARA collection.*

Opposite, top: A POW unpacks his personal belongings on the dock for inspection by an MP. Boston, Massachusetts, 1944. *Courtesy NARA collection.*

Opposite, bottom: POWs, after passing through showers and being sprayed with disinfectant, wrap themselves in blankets until steam fumigation of clothing has been completed. Here, the bags containing their clothing are being handed back to them. Boston, Massachusetts, 1944. *Courtesy NARA collection.*

Leather suitcases, shoes and other items not suitable for steam fumigation were sprayed with chemicals. Boston, Massachusetts, 1944. *Courtesy NARA collection.*

Georgia POW Camps in World War II

Leaving for Prison Camp

Processing complete, these POWs are boarding a train to their permanent POW camp. Boston, Massachusetts, 1944. *Courtesy NARA collection.*

Georgia POW Camps in World War II

Barracks

Georgia POW Camps in World War II

Above: Many POW buildings and barracks were voluntarily improved on by prisoners. *Courtesy NARA collection.*

Opposite, top: A general view inside the POW stockade. *Courtesy NARA collection.*

Opposite, bottom: View of a main street in the POW barracks area. *Courtesy NARA collection.*

Georgia POW Camps in World War II

POW camps resembled little towns with well-kept lawns and wide, clean streets. Here German POWs are walking down one of the camp's main streets. *Courtesy NARA collection.*

A standard war prison barracks, living quarters of prisoners. Prisoners kept the barracks and areas surrounding them spotlessly clean. *Courtesy NARA collection.*

Georgia POW Camps in World War II

View of the barracks interior. *Courtesy NARA collection.*

POW barracks sleeping quarters. *Courtesy NARA collection.*

Food

German POW preparing food in the camp kitchen. *Courtesy NARA collection.*

Georgia POW Camps in World War II

Above: These German POWs are cleaning sweet peppers in preparation for cooking and canning in a cannery. *Courtesy NARA collection.*

Right: German tastes dictate camp menus. A prisoner cook is preparing to serve frankfurters in the camp mess kitchen. *Courtesy NARA collection.*

Georgia POW Camps in World War II

Above: POW mess hall. *Courtesy NARA collection.*

Opposite, top: General view of a prison mess hall during the midday meal. *Courtesy NARA collection.*

Opposite, bottom: One war prisoner is shown serving meat to another. Most servings are invariably a surprise to new arrivals. One man shed tears of amazement at getting an entire pork chop. *Courtesy NARA collection.*

Georgia POW Camps in World War II

Georgia POW Camps in World War II

Georgia POW Camps in World War II

Above: POWs in their mess hall. *Courtesy NARA collection.*

Opposite: Prison mess hall. *Courtesy NARA collection.*

Medical

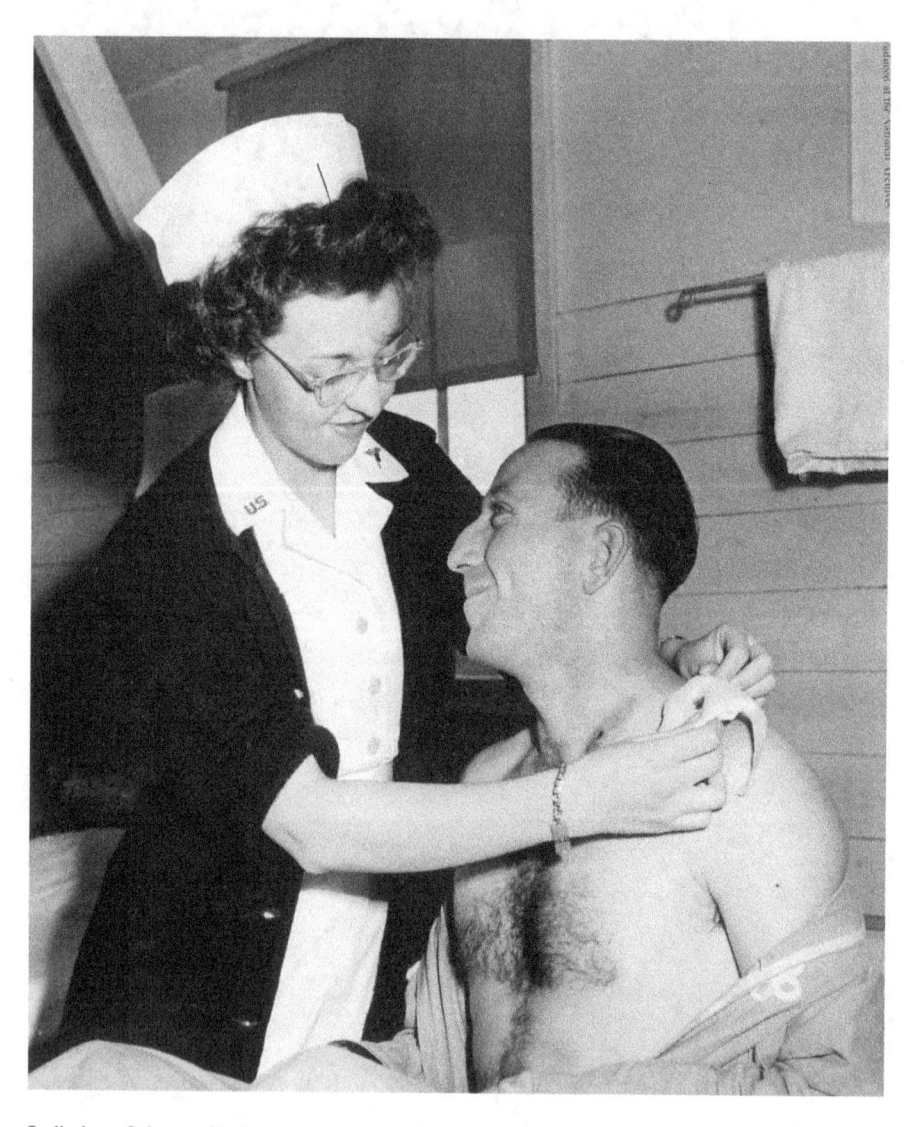

Indictive of the medical care given war prisoners is this picture of an American nurse changing a shoulder dressing on one of her POW patients. *Courtesy NARA collection.*

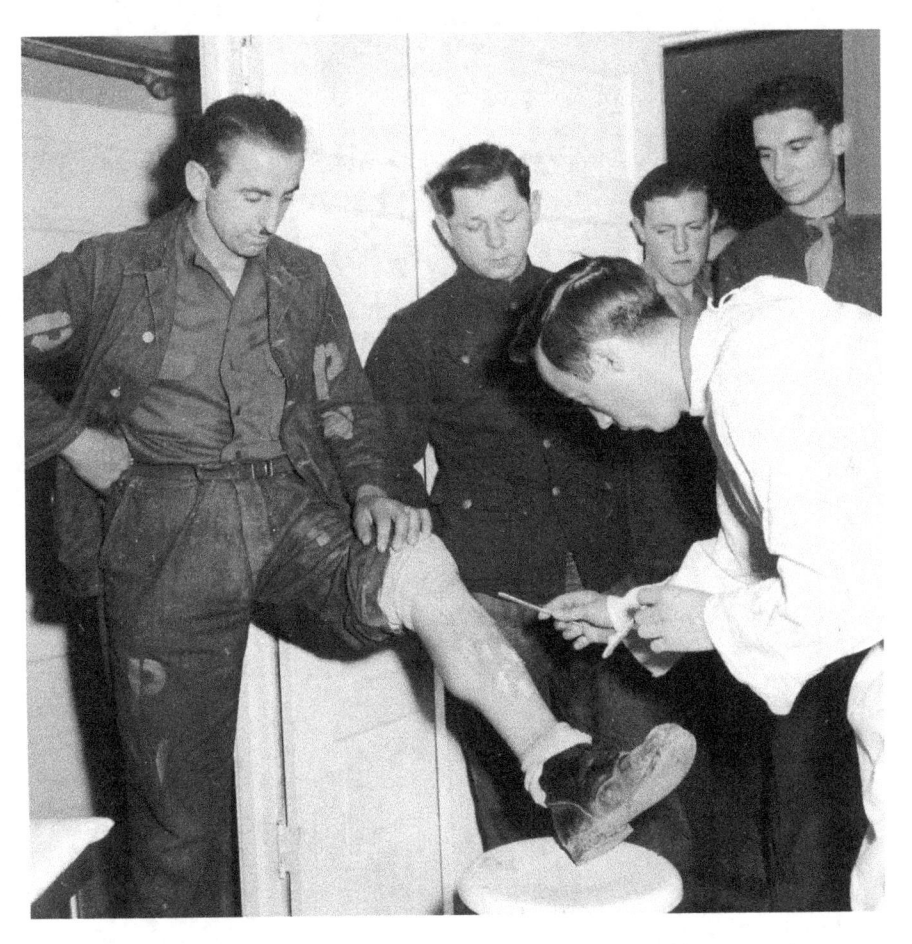

An American doctor is shown dressing sores, developed during the African campaign, on the leg of a German war prisoner. The picture was taken in the camp's medical dispensary. *Courtesy NARA collection.*

Georgia POW Camps in World War II

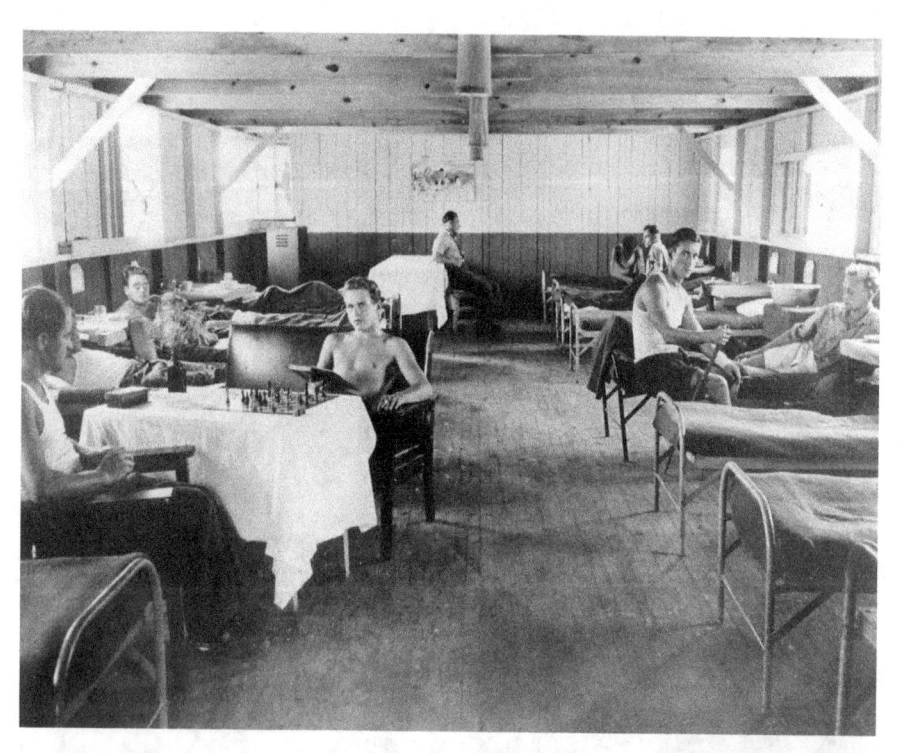

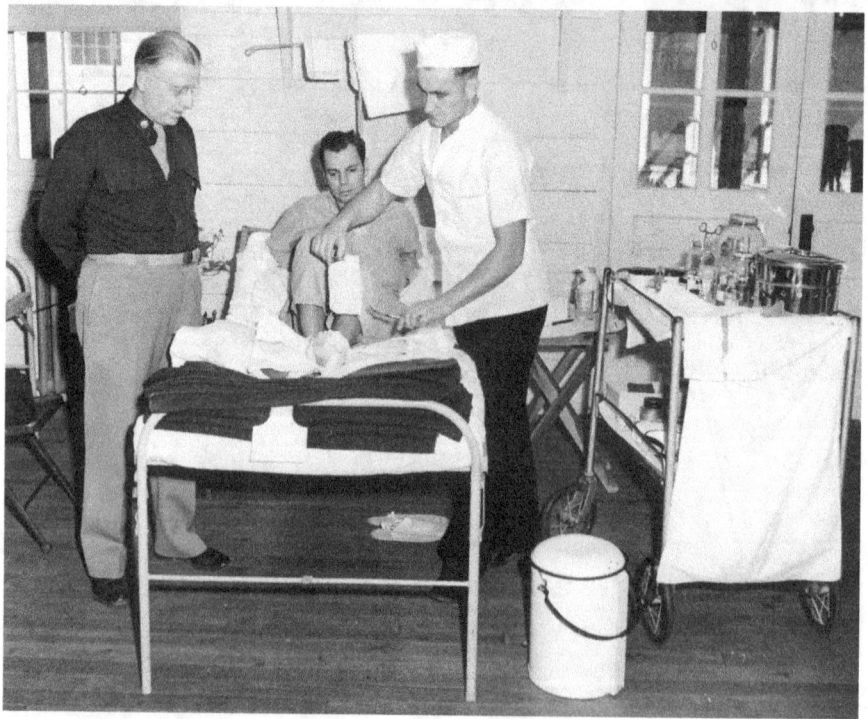

Georgia POW Camps in World War II

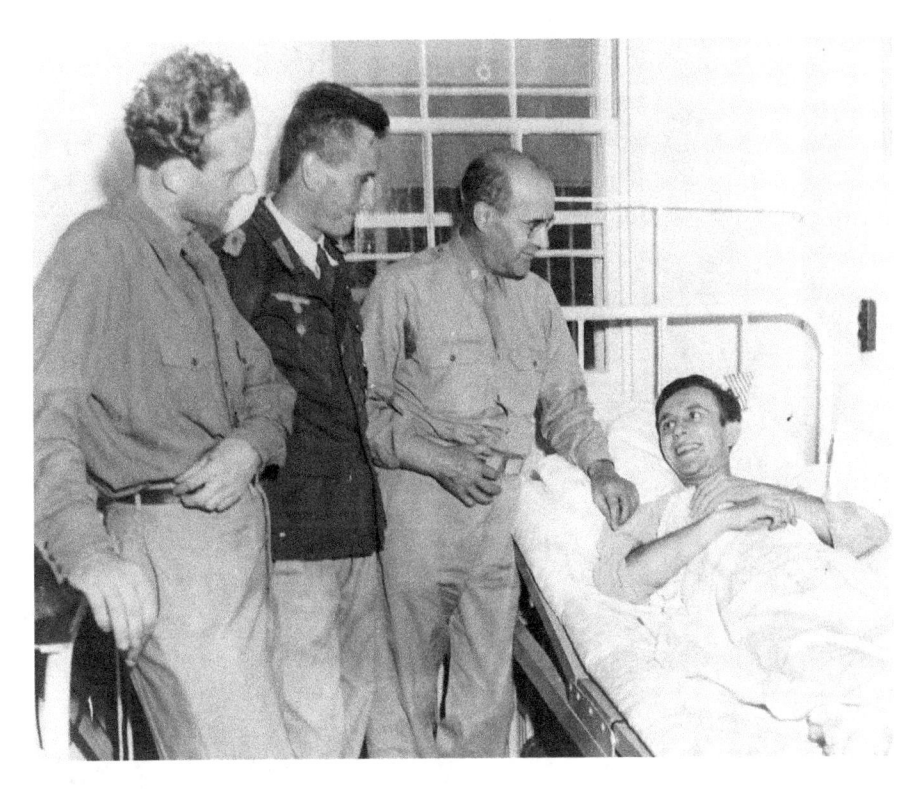

Above: U.S. Army doctors and nurses compose the staffs of prison camp hospitals. A U.S. Army doctor (*at bedside*) is shown with a war prisoner patient in the camp hospital. *Courtesy NARA collection.*

Opposite, top: War prisoners whose health was not perfect are shown here in the rest and convalescence room of a prison camp hospital. The room was designed primarily for prisoners whose illness did not require complete hospitalization. *Courtesy NARA collection.*

Opposite, bottom: A U.S. Army doctor is pictured as he supervises the dressing of a German soldier's leg in the camp hospital. *Courtesy NARA collection.*

Georgia POW Camps in World War II

Administration

Georgia POW Camps in World War II

Above: POWs read news bulletins printed in German and issued at regular intervals. This scene is the publication office. *Courtesy NARA collection.*

Opposite, top: A U.S. Army officer (*standing*) is shown conferring with captured German officers. *Courtesy NARA collection.*

Opposite, bottom: POWs working in their camp administration building. *Courtesy NARA collection.*

Georgia POW Camps in World War II

Top: POWs sorting mail, April 1944. *Courtesy NARA collection.*

Bottom: German prisoners of war working in the camp post office, sorting mail from Germany for delivery to fellow prisoners. This camp had about 2,500 prisoners and received an average of 2,000 letters and 160 packages daily from Germany, April 1944. *Courtesy NARA collection.*

Georgia POW Camps in World War II

Inspection

POWs interface with their U.S. Army guards through their own liaison officers. Three German liaison officers talk with an American army officer. *Courtesy NARA collection.*

Georgia POW Camps in World War II

Georgia POW Camps in World War II

Above: POWs being transported to work. *Courtesy NARA collection.*

Opposite, top: German POW officers inspect camp grounds with American officers and civilians. *Courtesy NARA collection.*

Opposite, bottom: A group of POWs, well fed and warmly clothed, marches out of camp to work on a nearby farm. *Courtesy NARA collection.*

Georgia POW Camps in World War II

Top: Utilization of animal transport in lieu of motor vehicles, November 23, 1944. *Courtesy NARA collection.*

Bottom: POWs working on farm, November 11, 1943. *Courtesy NARA collection.*

Opposite: POWs working on a farm. *Courtesy NARA collection.*

GEORGIA POW CAMPS IN WORLD WAR II

Georgia POW Camps in World War II

Above: POWs working in a cabbage patch, November 21, 1944. *Courtesy NARA collection.*

Opposite, top: POWs working on a nursery farm near their camp, where they gathered shrubs for replanting throughout the United States. *Courtesy NARA collection.*

Opposite, bottom: German POWs working on the camp farm. Enough vegetables for the 2,500 prisoners were raised on the farm, April 1944. *Courtesy NARA collection.*

Georgia POW Camps in World War II

Georgia POW Camps in World War II

Top: POWs working on farm with American guard. *Courtesy NARA collection.*

Bottom: POWs doing farm work. *Courtesy NARA collection.*

Georgia POW Camps in World War II

POWs picking cotton. *Courtesy NARA collection.*

POWs in a camp carpentry shop. Among prisoners were skilled carpenters who taught others who wished to learn the trade. *Courtesy NARA collection.*

Above: German POWs working in carpentry shop. *Courtesy NARA collection.*

Opposite, top: German POW at work packaging boxes. *Courtesy NARA collection.*

Opposite, bottom: POWs kept their own equipment in repair. Here two of them are repairing a broken stretcher. *Courtesy NARA collection.*

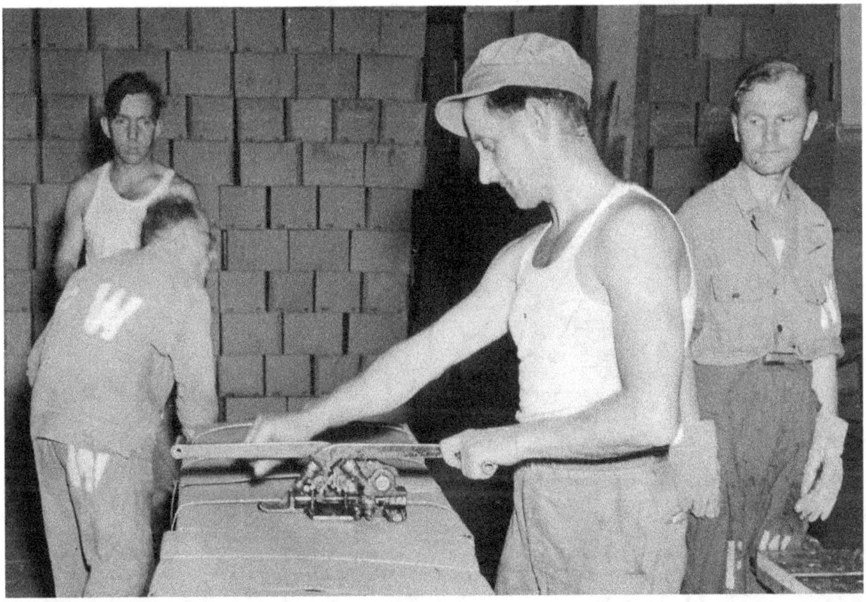

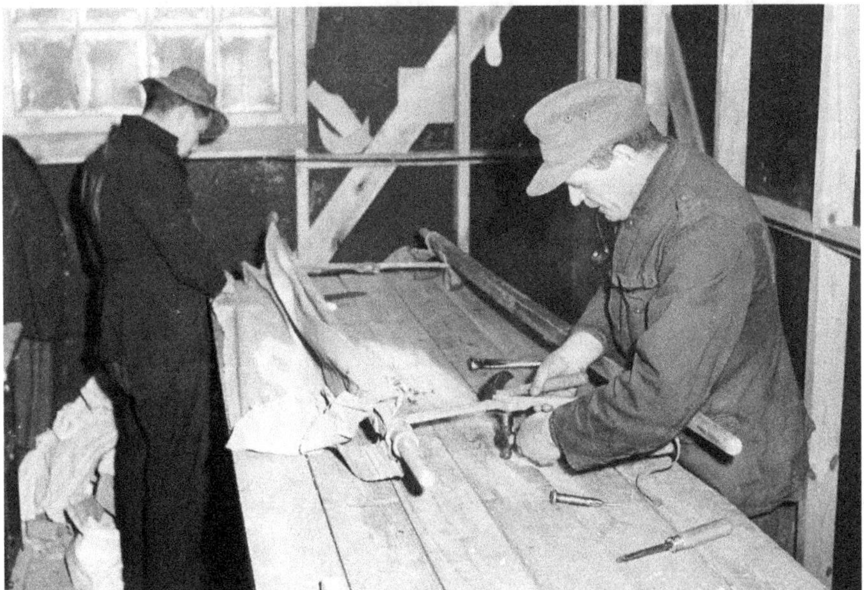

Georgia POW Camps in World War II

Above: German POWs repairing eating utensils. *Courtesy NARA collection.*

Opposite: POW at work in Camp Blanding, Florida, 1945. *Courtesy NARA collection.*

GEORGIA POW CAMPS IN WORLD WAR II

Georgia POW Camps in World War II

Georgia POW Camps in World War II

Above: German POWs load lumber. *Courtesy NARA collection.*

Opposite, top: POWs working on timber farm. *Courtesy NARA collection.*

Opposite, bottom: Three POWs cutting trees. *Courtesy NARA collection.*

Georgia POW Camps in World War II

Education

German POWs see films of German concentration camps, July 12, 1945. *Courtesy NARA collection.*

POWs in class. *Courtesy NARA collection.*

Georgia POW Camps in World War II

German POWs read a bulletin board with the latest developments on the world's war fronts. Accustomed to years reading in Germany only what their government wanted them to know, the prisoners show apparent interest in America's objective news presentation, November 6, 1944. *Courtesy NARA collection.*

GEORGIA POW CAMPS IN WORLD WAR II

RELIGION

Georgia POW Camps in World War II

Above: POW funeral, the details of which were entirely in the hands of the prisoners. *Courtesy NARA collection.*

Opposite, top: POWs singing at Lutheran church service. *Courtesy NARA collection.*

Opposite, bottom: POW funeral. *Courtesy NARA collection.*

Canteen

A German POW who runs the post exchange is adding cigarettes to his already well-stocked shelves. Prisoners earn scrip for what they wish to buy. *Courtesy NARA collection.*

A POW German officer is buying American-made cigarettes at an officers' post exchange. A second officer (*right*) has already bought a different brand. POW post exchanges were managed by the prisoners. *Courtesy NARA collection.*

POWs at their camp post exchange. *Courtesy NARA collection.*

Georgia POW Camps in World War II

POWs enjoy a soft drink at their POW post exchange. The post exchanges sell candy, cigarettes, beverages and small toilet luxuries to supplement regular equipment issued to prisoners. *Courtesy NARA collection.*

GEORGIA POW CAMPS IN WORLD WAR II

POWs in camp canteen. *Courtesy NARA collection.*

Georgia POW Camps in World War II

Recreation

Georgia POW Camps in World War II

Above: POWs in their barracks. *Courtesy NARA collection.*

Opposite, top: Clad in hot-weather attire, a German POW devotes his spare time to making models of old-time German sailing ships. *Courtesy NARA collection.*

Opposite, bottom: In camp, POWs kept their own equipment in repair. This is the inside of a POW clubhouse, built by POWs. *Courtesy NARA collection.*

Georgia POW Camps in World War II

Above: POWs in their barracks. *Courtesy NARA collection.*

Opposite, top: POWs lounge in their cots in hot-weather attire while they look at magazines. Pictures of American actresses adorn the walls of the barracks. The Germans liked American pin-up girls, and their walls were covered with their favorites. Camp Blanding, Florida, June 17, 1943. *Courtesy NARA collection.*

Opposite, bottom: A barracks scene during leisure hours. *Courtesy NARA collection.*

Georgia POW Camps in World War II

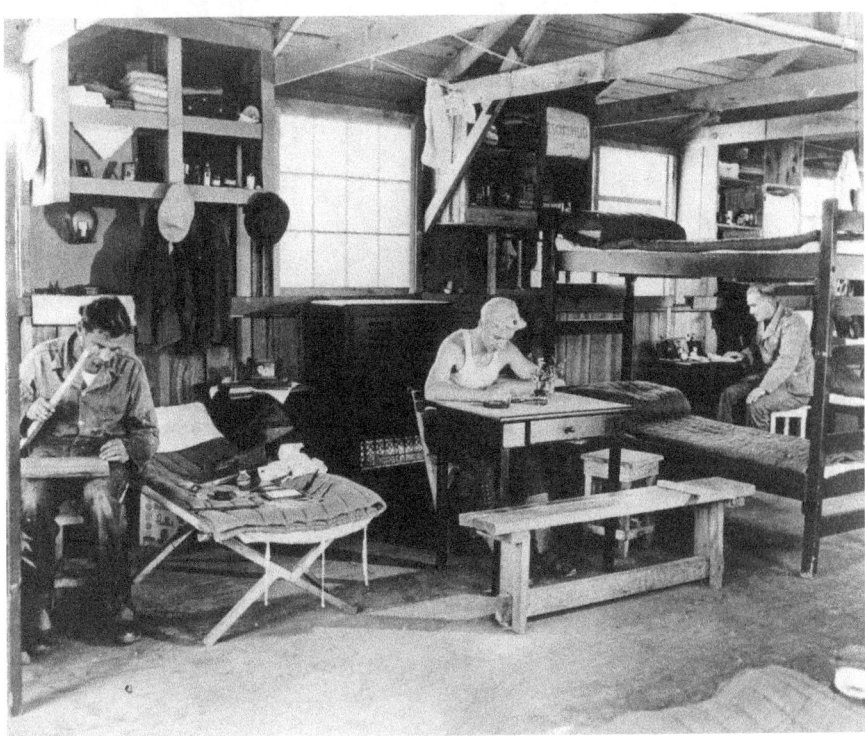

Georgia POW Camps in World War II

GEORGIA POW CAMPS IN WORLD WAR II

Above: POW in barracks. *Courtesy NARA collection.*

Opposite, top: POWs lounging in front of their clubrooms and recreation halls. They were encouraged to build them themselves with some used and new building materials. *Courtesy NARA collection.*

Opposite, bottom: German POWs working in their leisure time to improve their quarters. They spent much of their free time in beautifying the camp grounds and improving their barracks to make them more comfortable, April 1944. *Courtesy NARA collection.*

225

Georgia POW Camps in World War II

Entertainment

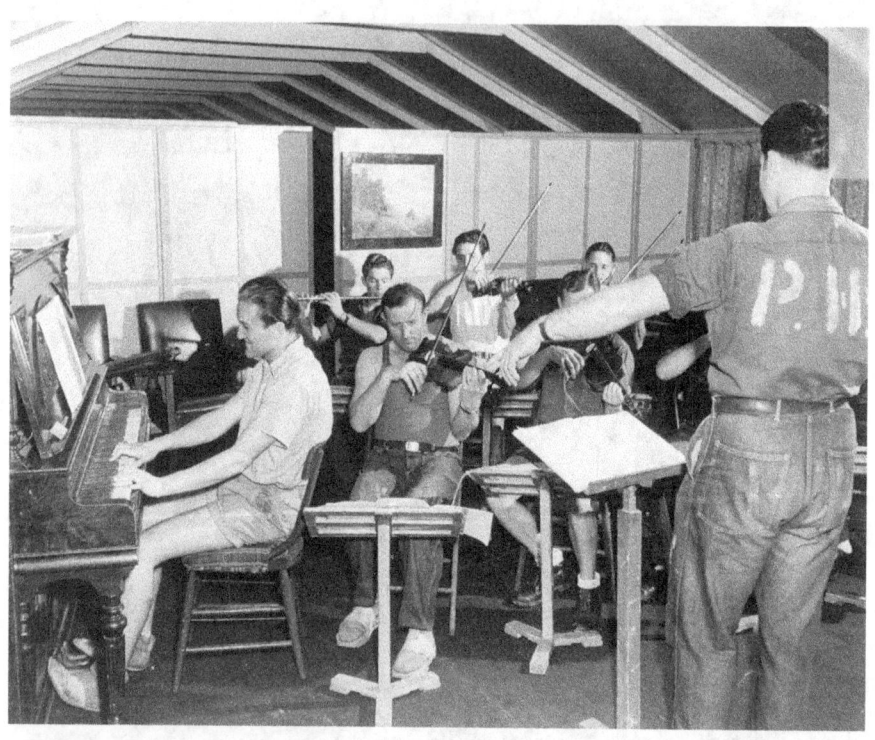

Georgia POW Camps in World War II

Above: German soldiers join in singing at a POW camp. The stage on which they stand also served for camp theatricals produced by POWs. *Courtesy NARA collection.*

Opposite, top: German POWs hold a rehearsal for a camp play. The orchestra leader conducting his group was formerly a well-known tenor in Germany, April 1944. *Courtesy NARA collection.*

Opposite, bottom: A German POW, who studied music in Berlin, conducts a symphony orchestra composed of German officers. The thirty-two-man orchestra played classics, while a smaller group played popular music. *Courtesy NARA collection.*

Georgia POW Camps in World War II

Georgia POW Camps in World War II

Above: An audience of POWs applauds a scene from one of the plays written and produced by their camp comrades. *Courtesy NARA collection.*

Opposite, top: POWs building a stage. Like the theater, most of the buildings in camp were built by prisoners with tools and materials furnished by the U.S. Army. Their small barrack houses, laid out like cottages in a small community, were fitted with fireplaces, tables, radios, pictures, couches and other items. *Courtesy NARA collection.*

Opposite, bottom: A theater building built by POWs in their woodworking shop, with seats for 250 persons and a modern projection booth for showing movies. They built and painted professional-quality sets and backdrops for shows. *Courtesy NARA collection.*

SPORTS

Above: Here one prisoner does a handstand on prisoner-made parallel bars as two others stand by. Sports clothing was supplied by the camp. *Courtesy NARA collection.*

Opposite, top: German prisoners engage in a lively game of soccer. *Courtesy NARA collection.*

Opposite, bottom: German POWs relax in the sun and watch a soccer game. Soccer was the most popular sport at many camps. There are eight soccer fields within the camp grounds. The camp was not identified due to wartime security, April 1944. *Courtesy NARA collection.*

GEORGIA POW CAMPS IN WORLD WAR II

Georgia POW Camps in World War II

Georgia POW Camps in World War II

Above: A German soldier pulls himself up on a chinning bar as fellow prisoners look on. *Courtesy NARA collection.*

Opposite, top: German prisoners watch a soccer match between teams of two rival companies organized by the prisoners. The competitive spirit between teams was strong. *Courtesy NARA collection.*

Opposite, bottom: Prisoner spectators show keen interest in a soccer match between teams of rival companies. Prisoners organized their own companies and chose their own leaders for work, study and recreation. *Courtesy NARA collection.*

Georgia POW Camps in World War II

Leaving for Home

Above: Italian POWs at Camp Wheeler, Georgia, joyfully celebrate the surrender of Italy to the Allies, September 1943. *Courtesy NARA collection.*

Opposite, top: A boatload of German POWs arrives in New York. POWs are clustered behind a wire fence at the pier. They were en route to the United States when Germany surrendered, May 13, 1945. *Courtesy NARA collection.*

Opposite, bottom: These Germans, part of 1,483 POWs being sent home to Germany, are on a harbor boat preparing to board the hospital ship *Francis Y. Slanger*, formerly the Italian liner *Saturnia*. Piermont, New York, July 26, 1946. *Courtesy NARA collection.*

Georgia POW Camps in World War II

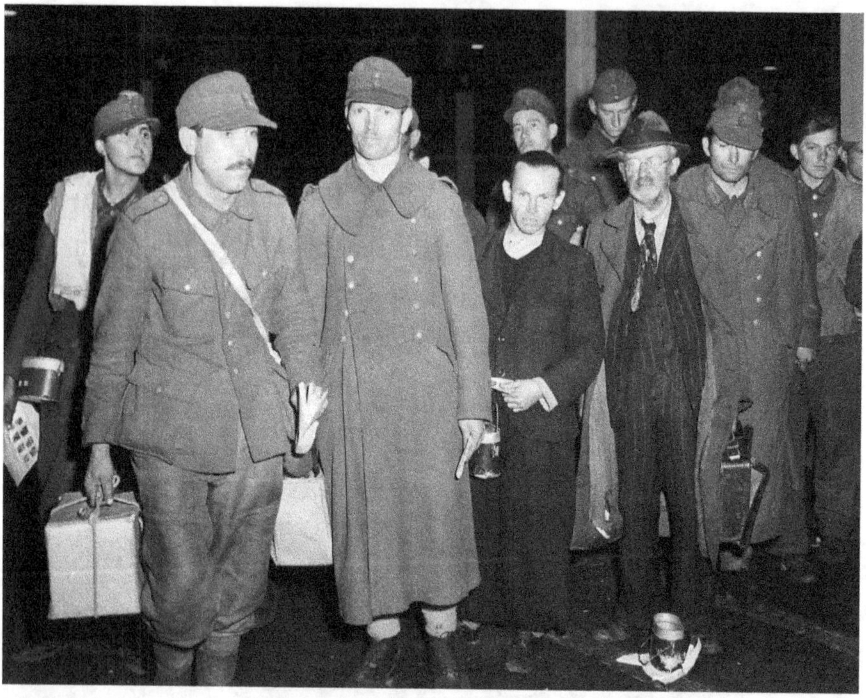

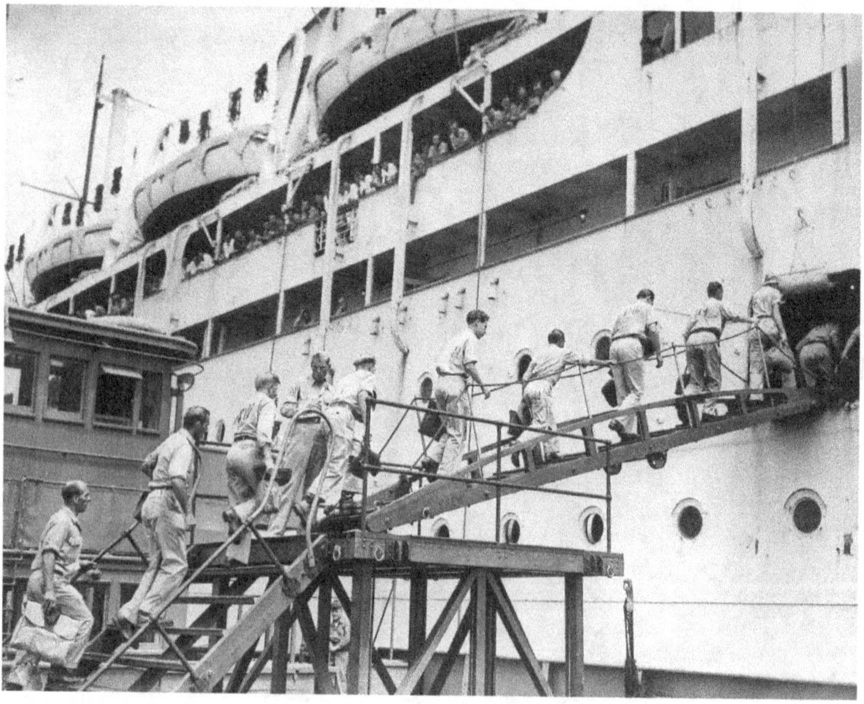

Georgia POW Camps in World War II

Top: German POWs sing as they march to work. *Courtesy NARA collection.*

Bottom: Four German soldiers who had just surrendered. *Courtesy NARA collection.*

Opposite, top: This motley assortment of German prisoners is made of regular soldiers as well as home guards in civilian clothes. They were going to the United States when Germany surrendered, May 13, 1945.

Opposite, bottom: German POWs going home, boarding hospital ship *Francis Y. Slanger.* Sixty American guards would make the trip with the POWs. *Courtesy NARA collection.*

Georgia POW Camps in World War II

POW German officer on a ship going to American captivity. *Courtesy NARA collection.*

CONCLUSION

Many Georgians—unfamiliar with the more than twelve thousand German and Italian prisoners of war detained in five base camps, dozens of smaller branch camps and a number of hospitals across the state—hopefully now have a better understanding of this significant homefront event of World War II. The POWs were not "coddled," as some contemporary Americans alleged. The Geneva Convention guaranteed certain rights for captured enemy combatants. The convention afforded POWs' fair treatment, educational and recreational opportunities and religious freedom, among other rights. In return, our government hoped that American POWs would receive similar treatment.

The Geneva Convention required enlisted POWs to work and to receive a fair wage. Without that stipulation, Georgia's economy would have been crippled. POW labor kept the agricultural industry afloat throughout the dire manpower shortage. Without POW laborers, Georgians would have found it almost impossible to harvest their peanuts and corn; pick cotton, tobacco and peaches; cut, stack and transport timber; operate sawmills; maintain the infrastructure of military installations; feed soldiers; and perform other essential tasks. These jobs were vital to Georgia's wartime economy.

Meanwhile, many Georgians gained a new understanding of their enemies. All Germans were no longer rabid Nazis. And many Italians served in Italian Service Units, helping to defend America. POWs in the backyards of Georgians helped paint a different "face" or perspective on the enemy— he was no longer impersonal. Some Georgians recalled the influence the

Conclusion

POWs had on them and the "positive cultural interchange that occurred, even under difficult war-time conditions." Ted Lesniak, who guarded POWs at Camp Wheeler, came to realize that he and the prisoners "shared more than a barbed wire enclosure."[412] He learned that "once you got to know them, they became people, just like you and me."[413]

As firsthand memories of this era fade, there are still some physical reminders. Georgia has at least four historical markers evidencing the location of POW camps at Bainbridge Army Air Field, Camp Wheeler, Finney General Hospital and Statesboro. The marker in Aiken, South Carolina, is proof of that branch camp's existence. The faint swastika and the displaced cell bars testify to POWs at the Dublin VA Hospital. There are POW monuments on Fort Benning.

Fort Benning and Fort Gordon each have a POW cemetery. Every year, the posts commemorate *volkstrauertag* ("people's day of mourning"). The German Consulate places a wreath honoring POWs from World Wars I and II buried at Fort Oglethorpe—the only place in America with graves of prisoners from both wars. A monument at the Chattanooga National Cemetery is dedicated to the German POWs who died in America.[414] Are these enough to preserve the history of World War II POWs in the Peach State? Barracks at Camp Wheeler recently were demolished. CCC camps used for POW camps are gone. The scant historical photographs are scattered and challenging to access. The authors hope that this small book will start a dialogue on safeguarding this era in the state's history.

It has been said that, at its best, preservation engages the past in a conversation with the present over a mutual concern for the future.
—William Murtagh,
first keeper of the National Register of Historic Places

Appendix A

DEATH RATES OF WORLD WAR II PRISONERS OF WAR

German POWs held by Americans	0.15%
American POWs held by Japanese	33.0%
German POWs held by Soviets	35.8%

Source: Niall Ferguson, "Prisoner Taking and Prisoner Killing in the Age of Total War: Towards a Political Economy of Military Defeat," War in History *11, no. 2 (2004): 186.*

American POWs held by Germans had a death rate of 1.2 percent. "In the European theater, 93,941 Americans were held as prisoners of war (POWs)....As prisoners of the Germans during World War II, life was difficult, often boring, and above all, uncertain—92,820 men lived to tell…their…stories." This means 1,121 died in captivity, or 1.2 percent.[415]

Appendix B

KEY TO MAP OF WORLD WAR II PRISONER OF WAR CAMPS IN GEORGIA

County	POW Camp	Map ID Number
Atkinson	Axson	39
Ben Hill	Fitzgerald	13
Bibb	**Camp Wheeler***	**2**
Bryan	**Camp Stewart***	**27**
Bulloch	Statesboro	26
Burke	Waynesboro	35
Catoosa	Fort Oglethorpe	4
Chatham	Chatham Field	8
Chatham	Savannah ASFD****	24
Clinch	Fargo	11
Colquitt	Moody Field	21
Colquitt	Spence Field	25
Decatur	Bainbridge AAF**	40
Dougherty	Albany	5
Dougherty	Turner Field	30
Early	Blakely	7
Emanuel	Swainsboro	43
Floyd	Battey General Hospital	6

Appendix B

County	POW Camp	Map ID Number
Fulton	Lawson General Hospital	36
Glynn	Glynco NAS***	41
Houston	Perry	22
Jasper	Monticello	19
Jefferson	Wadley	33
Laurens	Dublin	10
Liberty	**Camp Stewart***	**1**
Liberty	Hunter Field	16
Lowndes	Moody Field	20
Lowndes	Valdosta	32
Muscogee	**Fort Benning***	**3**
Pulaski	Hawkinsville	17
Richmond	**Camp Gordon***	**14**
Richmond	Daniel Field	9
Screven	Sylvania	44
Spalding	Griffin	15
Stephens	Toccoa	29
Sumter	Americus	37
Tattnall	Reidsville	23
Thomas	Finney General Hospital	12
Thomas	Thomasville	28
Tift	Tifton	31
Turner	Ashburn	38
Ware	Waycross	34
Washington	Sandersville	42
Wayne	Jessup	18

* Base Camp
** AAF (Army Air Field)
*** NAS (Naval Air Station)
**** ASFD (Army Supply Field Depot)

NOTES

Introduction

1. Auction Finds, "Simple Form Leads to History."
2. Ibid.
3. Ibid.; Gansberg, *Stalag: USA*, 1.
4. Auction Finds, "Simple Form Leads to History."
5. Ibid.
6. Interview, Father Radbert Kohlhaas, with Dr. Kathy Roe Coker, April 25, 1989, Radbert Kohlhaas Papers, U.S. Army Signal Corps and Fort Gordon (USASC&FG) Archives.
7. Hawaii Memory Project, Nisei Story: Americans of Japanese Ancestry, "Shiroku 'Whitey' Yamamoto."

Chapter 1

8. Gansberg, *Stalag: USA*, 2–3; Murphy, "Prisoners of War," CRS-11.
9. Lewis and Mewha, *History of POW Utilization*, 75–76; Krammer, *Nazi POWs in America*, 39–40; International Committee of the Red Cross, "Geneva Convention of 27 July 1929."
10. Gansberg, *Stalag: USA*, 3–4.
11. Ibid., 3; Wikipedia, "Army Service Forces."
12. Coker, *World War II Prisoners of War in Georgia*, 1.
13. Reiss, "Solidarity Among 'Fellow Sufferers,'" 534–36.

14. Gansberg, *Stalag: USA*, 4–5.
15. Krammer, *Nazi POWs in America*, 27; Krammer, "German POWs in the United States," 68–69; Brown, "German POWs in the United States," 205–6; HistoryNet, "World War II: North Africa Campaign."
16. Kohlhaas interview with Coker, April 25, 1989. On a trip to the United States in April 1989, Father Radbert Kohlhaas visited Fort Gordon and the former POW camp site. He consented to an interview on April 25 with Dr. Kathy Roe Coker. Prior to his visit, Dr. Coker had corresponded with Father Kohlhaas several times.
17. Lewis and Mewha, *History of POW Utilization*, 90–91; Krammer, *Nazi POWs in America*, 2–17; *Camp Gordon Cadence*, "Prisoners Prefer Prison," May 28, 1943, 7.
18. Hudnall, "Brief Overview of Camp Policy and Life"; Auction Finds, "Simple Form Leads to History."
19. Reiss, "Solidarity Among 'Fellow Sufferers,'" 537.
20. Hudnall, "Brief Overview of Camp Policy and Life."
21. Ibid.
22. Krammer, *Nazi POWs in America*, 16.
23. Ibid., 2–17; Lewis and Mewha, *History of POW Utilization*, 90–91; Byrd, "Captured by the Americans," 27
24. Letter, Father Radbert Kohlhaas to Dr. Kathy Roe Coker, November 17, 1989; Kohlhaas interview with Coker, April 25, 1989.
25. Krammer, *Nazi POWs in America*, 26; Krammer, "German POWs in the United States," 68–69; Lewis and Mewha, *History of POW Utilization*, 83–85.
26. Wikipedia, "Army Service Forces."
27. Study the Past, "Democracy and Diversity in Walker County, Texas."
28. Krammer, *Nazi POWs in America*, 26–27; Krammer, "German POWs in the United States," 68–69; Lewis and Mewha, *History of POW Utilization*, 83–85.
29. Hudnall, "Brief Overview of Camp Policy and Life."
30. Lewis and Mewha, *History of POW Utilization*, 83–84, 91, 112; Hudnall, "Brief Overview of Camp Policy and Life."
31. Brown, "German POWs in the United States," 206–7. There are discrepancies in the sources concerning the standard layout of the camps. See Krammer, *Nazi POWs in America*, 26–28, 30; Wyatt, "United States Policy Toward German POWs," 23.
32. Krammer, *Nazi POWs in America*, 26–28, 30; Coker, *World War II Prisoners of War in Georgia*, 8.

33. Vaughn, "German Hun in the Georgia Sun," 60; Hudnall, "Brief Overview of Camp Policy and Life."
34. Lewis and Mewha, *History of POW Utilization*, 84–85, 111, 112; Krammer, *Nazi POWs in America*, 27; Wyatt, "United States Policy Toward German POWs," 21–24; Moore, "Nazi Troopers in South Carolina," 306, 308.
35. Inspection Reports, Camp Gordon, Georgia, May 25, 1944, POW Division, Provost Marshal General Office (PMGO), Record Group (RG) 389, National Archives and Records Administration (NARA); Inspection Reports, Reidsville, Georgia, December 28, 1944, POW Division, PMGO, RG 389, NARA; Inspection Reports, Camp Gordon, Georgia, Waynesboro, Georgia, and Reidsville, Georgia, 31 December 1944, POW Division, PMGO, RG 389 NARA; Lieutenant Colonel R. Hipeuser, Assistant Adjutant General, to Commanding Officer, POW Camp, Camp Gordon, Subject: POW Branch Camps, July 22, 1944, Construction Correspondence, Camp Gordon, Georgia, PMGO, RG 389, NARA.
36. Moore, "Nazi Troopers in South Carolina," 306, 308.
37. Kohlhaas interview with Coker, April 25, 1989.
38. Ibid.
39. Krammer, *Nazi POWs in America*, 17–18; Lewis and Mewha, *History of POW Utilization*, 90, 91; Reiss, "Soliditarity Among 'Fellow Sufferers,'" 538.
40. Budanovic, "Georg Gartner."
41. Reiss, "Soliditarity Among 'Fellow Sufferers,'" 538.
42. Hamer, "Barbeque, Farming and Friendship," 62.
43. Saunders, "I Guard Nazi Prisoners," 16.
44. Letter, Kohlhaas to Coker, November 17, 1989; letter, Father Radbert Kohlhaas to Mr. and Mrs. Page, June 22, 1981; Kohlhaas interview with Coker, April 25, 1989.
45. Kohlhaas interview with Coker, April 25, 1989.
46. Krammer, *Nazi POWs in America*, 44.
47. Ibid.
48. Quoted in Krammer, *Nazi POWs in America*, 45.
49. Hamer, "Barbeque, Farming and Friendship," 65–66.
50. Ibid.
51. Krammer, *Nazi POWs in America*, 174.
52. Ibid.
53. Hudnall, "Brief Overview of Camp Policy and Life."
54. Vaughn, "German Hun in the Georgia Sun," 60, 61.
55. Krammer, *Nazi POWs in America*, 79–82; Hudnall, "Brief Overview of Camp Policy and Life."

56. Hudnall, "Brief Overview of Camp Policy and Life."
57. Krammer, *Nazi POWs in America*, 83–84; Wikipedia, "German Prisoners of War in the United States."
58. Vaughn, "German Hun in the Georgia Sun," 73.
59. Lewis and Mewha, *History of POW Utilization*, 102, 106; Krammer, *Nazi POWs in America*, 85–94.
60. John Ray Skates, "German Prisoners of War in Mississippi, 1943–1946"; Krammer, *Nazi POWs in America*, 88–90.
61. Hamer, "Barbeque, Farming and Friendship," 67.
62. Lewis and Mewha, *History of POW Utilization*, 108, 235, 335; Krammer, *Nazi POWs in America*, 82–83.
63. Ibid.
64. Ibid., 67–68.
65. Krammer, *Nazi POWs in America*, 61–64; Waters, *Lone Star Stalag*, 41, 62.
66. Thompson, "Winning the War Behind the Lines," 439; Coker, "World War II Prisoners of War in Georgia," 847; Waters, *Lone Star Stalag*, 40.
67. Moore, "Nazi Troopers in South Carolina," 309; Donald Law, "Wartime Aiken Roused by German POW Escape; Nazi Hoped to Steal Airplane," *Aiken Standard*, June 14, 1967, 10; *Smithsonian Magazine*, "German POWs on the American Homefront." For more details on POW escapes, see Krammer, *Nazi POWs in America*, 114–46.
68. Murphy, "Prisoners of War," CRS-11; Krammer, *Nazi POWs in America*, 237.
69. Krammer, *Nazi POWs in America*, 237.
70. Ibid., 235–38; Lewis and Mewha, *History of POW Utilization*, 77–79, 86–90, 102–13.
71. Krammer, *Nazi POWs in America*, 241–42.
72. Wikipedia, "German Prisoners of War in the United States."
73. *Smithsonian Magazine*, "German POWs on the American Homefront."

Chapter 2

74. Billinger, *Hitler's Soldiers in the Sunshine State*, 60.
75. Ibid., 28–29.
76. Ibid., 32; Koop, *Stark Decency*, 30; Krammer, *Nazi POWs in America*, 153.
77. Croley, "American Reeducation of German POWs," 32; Krammer, *Nazi Prisoners of War in America*, 154.

78. Waters, *Lone Star Stalag*, 111; Krammer, *Nazi POWs in America*, 167–68; Croley, "American Reeducation of German POWs," 30–33.
79. Croley, "American Reeducation of German POWs," 30.
80. Thompson, "Winning the War Behind the Lines," 21–34.
81. Ibid., 31.
82. Ibid., 34.
83. Ibid., 32–33.
84. Ibid., 34; James H. Powers, "What to Do With German Prisoners." *Atlantic Monthly* (November 1944): 50.
85. Croley, "American Reeducation of German POWs," 35; Krammer, *Nazi POWs in America*, 190.
86. Waters, *Lone Star Stalag*, 81.
87. Croley, "American Reeducation of German POWs," 35.
88. Ibid., 37; Billinger, *Hitler's Soldiers in the Sunshine State*, 140–41; Smith, *War for the German Mind*, 19; Gansberg, *Stalag: USA*, 62.
89. Croley, "American Reeducation of German POWs," 35; Krammer, *Nazi POWs in America*, 177.
90. Smith, *War for the German Mind*, 19; Croley, "American Reeducation of German POWs," 38.
91. History Experience, "German POWs in the Southern United States."
92. Croley, "Reeducation in America of German POWs," 39–40; Gansberg, *Stalag: USA*, 59–60; Krammer, *Nazi POWs in America*, 198–99, 194.
93. Croley, "Reeducation in America of German POWs," 39–40.
94. Ibid., 54–56, 67; Gansberg, *Stalag: USA*, 68, 70–71.
95. Gansberg, *Stalag: USA*, 76.
96. Ibid., 63; Croley, "Reeducation in America of German POWs," 68; Krammer, *Nazi POWs in America*, 197.
97. Croley, "Reeducation in America of German POWs," 51.
98. Ibid.
99. Croley, "Reeducation in America of German POWs," 54–56.
100. Ibid., 64; Gansberg, *Stalag: USA*, 74, 76.
101. Croley, "Reeducation in America of German POWs," 66.
102. Ibid.
103. Ibid.
104. Ibid., 65–66.
105. Ibid., 66.
106. Ibid., 69–71.
107. Thompson, "Winning the War Behind the Lines," 417–18, 453–54.
108. Ibid., 453–54.

109. Ibid., 454.
110. Croley, "Reeducation in America of German POWs," 77–78; Gansberg, *Stalag: USA*, 86.
111. Croley, "Reeducation in America of German POWs," 80–88.
112. Ibid., 78–79; Krammer, *Nazi POWs in America*, 198–99.
113. Croley, "Reeducation in America of German POWs," 74–75.
114. Ibid., 72–74; Gansberg, *Stalag: USA*, 13.
115. Croley, "Reeducation in America of German POWs," 79–83.
116. Ibid., 66; Robin, *Barbed-Wire College*, 127.
117. Croley, "Reeducation in America of German POWs," 95; Gansberg, *Stalag: USA*, 124.
118. Gansberg, *Stalag: USA*, 124–25; Croley, "Reeducation in America of German POWs," 95.
119. Croley, "Reeducation in America of German POWs," 96.
120. Ibid., 96–97. See also Robin, *Barbed-Wire College*, 47.

Chapter 3

121. Inspection Reports, Camp Gordon, Georgia, December 31, 1943–January 2, 1944, POW Division, PMGO, RG 389, NARA; Colonel Walter L. Anderson, Commanding Officer, Camp Gordon Internment Camp, to Commanding General, Fourth Service Command, Subject: Deficiencies and Proposed Changes in Camp Gordon Internment Camp, February 27, 1943; Lieutenant Colonel Earl Edwards, POW Division, PMGO, to Chief of Engineers, Subject: Guard Towers, February 18, 1944, Construction Correspondence, Camp Gordon, Georgia, PMGO, RG 389, NARA.
122. Memorandum for the Chief of Engineers from Headquarters, Services of Supply, War Department, October 4, 1942; Major E. Seelans, Corps of Engineers, South Atlantic Division Engineer, November 11, 1942; Colonel Walter L. Anderson, Commanding Officer, Camp Gordon Internment Camp, to Commanding General, Fourth Service Command, February 27, 1943; Captain Harold W. Smith, Aliens Division, PMGO, to Major Earl Edwards, PMGO, April 12, 1943; Construction Correspondence, Camp Gordon, Georgia, PMGO, RG 389, NARA; Camp Gordon Historical Data Reference Card, Military Reservations, no date, Military History Institute.
123. Memorandum for the Chief of Engineers from Headquarters, Services of Supply, War Department, October 4, 1942, POW Division, PMGO, RG 389, NARA; Inspection Reports, Camp Gordon, Georgia, November

28, 1943; December 31, 1943–January 2, 1944; May 25, 1944; July 21, 1944; and March 7, 1945, POW Division, PMGO, RG 389, NARA; letter, Father Kohlhaas to Dr. Kathy Roe Coker, July 19, 1989, Father Radbert Kohlhaas Papers, USASC&FG Archives.
124. Inspection Reports, Camp Gordon, Georgia, December 31, 1943–January 2, 1944, POW Division, PMGO, RG 389, NARA; Colonel Walter L. Anderson, Commanding Officer, Camp Gordon Interment Camp, to Commanding General, Fourth Service Command, Subject: Deficiencies and Proposed Changes in Camp Gordon Internment Camp, February 27, 1943, NARA; Lieutenant Colonel Earl Edwards, POW Division, PMGO, to Chief of Engineers, Subject: Guard Towers, February 18, 1944, Construction Correspondence, Camp Gordon, Georgia, PMGO, RG 389, NARA.
125. Kohlhaas interview with Coker, April 25, 1989.
126. Ibid.
127. Todd Conger, "Freedom Behind Barbed Wire: Former German POW Recalls Old Memories," *The Signal*, May 3, 1989, 11, USASC&FG Newspaper Collection, Public Affairs Office, USASC&FG Archives; letter, Kohlhaas to Coker, November 17, 1989; Kohlhaas interview with Coker, April 25, 1989.
128. Kohlhaas interview with Coker, April 25, 1989.
129. Letter, Kohlhaas to Mr. and Mrs. Page, September 30, 1986, Kohlhaas Papers, USASC&FG Archives; letter, Kohlhaas to Coker, July 19, 1988, Kohlhaas Papers, USASC&FG Archives; Conger, "Freedom Behind Barbed Wire," 11.
130. Kohlhaas interview with Coker, April 25, 1989.
131. Ibid.; Inspection Reports, Camp Gordon, Georgia, December 31, 1943–January 2, 1944, and March 7, 1945, POW Division, PMGO, RG 389, Box 2668, NARA. Also see Fickle and Ellis, "POWs in the Piney Woods," 723. The Library of Congress retains many of the POW newspapers on microfilm. The fifteen-reel series is titled "German POW Camp Newspapers, 1943–1946." The Camp Gordon POW newsletter is missing.
132. Inspection Reports, Camp Gordon, Georgia, November 28, 1943; July 21, 1944; March 7, 1945, POW Division, PMGO, RG 389, NARA.
133. Inspection Reports, Edouard J. Patte, Camp Gordon, Georgia, December 1944, PMGO, POW Division, RG 389, NARA.
134. Inspection Reports, Camp Gordon, Georgia, November 23, 1943, and March 7, 1945, POW Division, PMGO, RG 386, Box 2668, NARA; Inspection Report, Oliver General Hospital, Maurice Perrett, June 20,

1944, POW Division, PMGO, RG 386, Box 2668, NARA; letter with copies of Basic Personnel Records and Death Certificates, POWs, Camp Gordon, Georgia, from German Federal Archives, to Command Historian Office, USASC&FG, December 22, 1989.
135. Inspection Report, Edouard J. Patte, Camp Gordon, Georgia, December 1944, PMGO, POW Division, RG 389, NARA.
136. Ibid.
137. Ibid.
138. Inspection Reports, Camp Gordon, Georgia, June 21, 1944; July 5–6, 1944; July 8, 1944, POW Division, PMGO, RG 389, NARA; letter, Kohlhaas to Coker, July 19, 1988; Kohlhaas interview with Coker, April 25, 1989.
139. Kohlhaas interview with Coker, April 25, 1989.
140. Ibid.
141. *Augusta Chronicle*, "Prisoners Begin Farm Work Today," August 30, 1943, 1; Lester Moody to General Blackshear M. Bryan, Assistant Provost Marshal, War Department, September 11, 1943, POW Operations Division, RG 389, NARA; Colonel John E. Hatch, Director, Internal Security Division, Army Service Forces, Fourth Service Command, to Provost Marshal, War Department, January 20, 1945, POW Operations, RG 389, NARA.
142. Maurice Getchell, "German Prisoners Harvest Peanut Crop in Aiken Area: War Captives Go About Tasks in Fields with Will; None Shows Displeasure at Work," *Augusta Chronicle*, September 12, 1943.
143. John F. Battle Jr. and Maurice Getchell, "American Soldiers Do Honor to German Killed at Gordon," *Augusta Chronicle*, October 31, 1943, 1, 16.
144. *Augusta Chronicle*, "German Listed as 'Escapee' Concealed Himself in Attic," May 11, 1944, 1.
145. *Augusta Chronicle*, "Nazis Recaptured in Bibb County," February 17, 1945, 5.
146. *Augusta Chronicle*, "German War Prisoner Chased from Yard by Irate Woman," December 19, 1944, 3.
147. *Augusta Chronicle*, "Arsenal Employees Are Warned Against Fraternization with PWs," April 3, 1945, 5.
148. Ibid.
149. Letters, Kohlhaas to Coker, November 17, 1988, and July 19, 1988, Kohlhaas Papers, USASC&FG Archives; letter, Kohlhaas to Mr. and Mrs. Page, September 30, 1986, Kohlhaas Papers, USASC&FG Archives; interview, Mr. Joe Buck, with Dr. Kathy Roe Coker, November 7, 1988,

Oral History Collection, USASC&FG Archives; interview, Mr. Albert D. Cromer, with Dr. Kathy Roe Coker, November 8, 1988, Oral History Collection, USASC&FG Archives.
150. Letter, Kohlhaas to Coker, July 19, 1988; Inspection Reports, Camp Gordon, Georgia, November 28, 1943; December 31, 1943; January 2, 1944, RG 389, NARA; POW Camp Labor Reports, Camp Gordon, Georgia, 1944, RG 389, NARA.
151. *Augusta Chronicle*, "War Prisoners Used for Labor: Captives Work on Farms and in Industry Here," December 10, 1933, 6.
152. Letter, Kohlhaas to Coker, July 19, 1988; Inspection Reports, Camp Gordon, Georgia, December 31, 1943–January 2, 1944, POW Division, PMGO, RG 389, NARA.
153. *Augusta Chronicle*, "War Prisoners Used for Labor," 6; letter, Kohlhaas to Coker, July 19, 1988; interview, Mrs. Edna Tatter, with Dr. Kathy Roe Coker, November 4, 1988, Oral History Collection, USASC&FG Archives; Cromer interview with Coker, November 8, 1988; Cashin, *Story of Augusta*, 269.
154. *Augusta Chronicle*, "War Prisoners Used for Labor," 6.
155. Kohlhaas interview with Coker, April 25, 1989; Cromer interview with Coker, November 8, 1988.
156. Strege, *When War Played through Golf*, 43, 115–16, 243; Steadman, "When Cattle Made Rounds at Old Augusta"; Busbee, "When Cows Ruled Augusta."
157. Strege, *When War Played through Golf*, 243.
158. Ibid.
159. Ibid.; Busbee, "When Cows Ruled Augusta."
160. Strege, *When War Played through Golf*, 243.
161. Ibid.; Cutmore, "Yes, This Really IS Augusta."
162. Busbee, "When Cows Ruled Augusta."
163. Steadman, "When Cattle Made Rounds at Old Augusta."
164. Inspection Reports, Camp Gordon, Georgia, June 21, 1944; July 5–6, 1944; July 8, 1944, POW Division, PMGO, RG 389, NARA.
165. Inspection Reports, Camp Gordon, Georgia, June 21, 1944; Billinger, *Hitler's Soldiers in the Sunshine State*, 21.
166. Hunnicutt, "German POWs in Dade City."
167. Ibid.
168. Ibid. Manion, "Historian Sheds Light on German POWs."
169. Inspection Reports, Camp Gordon, Georgia, December 31, 1943–January 2, 1944, POW Division, PMGO, RG 389, NARA.

170. Ibid.; Krammer, *Nazi POWs in America*, 6; Other Inspection Reports, Camp Gordon, Georgia, May 10, 1944, POW Division, PMGO, RG 389, NARA.

171. Inspection Reports, Camp Gordon, Georgia, March 1944, POW Division, PMGO, RG 389, NARA; Krammer, *Nazi POWs in America*, 172–74.

172. Inspection Reports, Camp Gordon, Georgia, March 1944, POW Division, PMGO, RG 389, NARA.

173. Inspection Report, Camp Gordon, Georgia, December 31, 1944, POW Division, PMGO, RG 389, NARA.

174. Inspection Reports, Camp Gordon, Georgia, March 7, 1945, POW Division, PMGO, RG 389, NARA.

175. Kohlhaas interview with Coker, April 25, 1989.

176. Buck interview with Coker, November 7, 1988.

177. Colonel Callie H. Palmer, Director, Security and Intelligence Division, Army Service Forces, Office of the Commanding General, Headquarters Fourth Service Command, POW Instructions and Information Letter No. 23, August 21, 1945, RG 160, NARA.

178. Letter, Kohlhaas to Coker, November 17, 1989, Kohlhaas Papers, USASC&FG Archives. For related information, see, for example, *Newsweek*, "Anger at Nazi Atrocities Is Rising but U.S. Treats Prisoners Fairly," issue no. 25 (May 7, 1945), 58; *Augusta Chronicle*, "POW Fare Is Changed," April 29, 1945, 4.

179. Kohlhaas interview with Coker, April 25, 1989.

180. Ibid.

181. Moore, "Nazi Troopers in South Carolina," 314.

182. Conger, "Freedom Behind Barbed Wire," 11.

183. Letter, Kohlhaas to Coker, July 19, 1988; Kohlhaas interview with Coker, April 25, 1989.

184. Colonel Catesby Jones, Director of Security and Intelligence Division, Army Service Forces, Headquarters Fourth Service Command, Atlanta, Georgia, to Commanding General, Army Service Forces, Washington, D.C., May 7, 1946, Army Service Forces, Fourth Service Command, RG 160, NARA; Moore, "Nazi Troopers in South Carolina," 311.

185. Letter, Kohlhaas to Coker, November 17, 1989.

186. Ibid.

187. Ibid.; letter, Kohlhaas to Mr. and Mrs. Page, September 30, 1986; Conger, "Freedom Behind Barbed Wire," 11.

188. Conger, "Freedom Behind Barbed Wire," 11.

189. Most of the one Italian and twenty-one German POWs buried at the Fort Gordon cemetery died of accidental or natural causes while prisoners either in South Carolina or Georgia POW camps. POWs Interred in the United States, Camp Gordon, Georgia, POW Division, PMGO, RG 389, NARA; letter, with copies of Basic Personnel Records and Death Certificates, POWs, Camp Gordon, Georgia, from German Federal Archives, to Dr. Kathy Roe Coker, Command Historian Office, USASC&FG, December 22, 1985.
190. Jeffery, "Remembering German POW Camp in Aiken."
191. Hamer, "Barbeque, Farming and Friendship," 61.
192. Ibid., 65–66.
193. Ibid., 68–69.
194. Ibid., 69.
195. Carl Langley, "Repp Returns to Aiken and Site of POW Camp," *Aiken Standard*. Peter changed his last name to that of his stepfather, Repp.
196. Ibid.
197. Hamer, "Barbeque, Farming and Friendship," 64.
198. Ibid.; Jeffery, "Remembering German POW Camp in Aiken."
199. Jeffery, "Remembering German POW Camp in Aiken."
200. Ibid.
201. Ibid.
202. Ibid.
203. Ibid.
204. Inspection Report, Camp Gordon, Georgia, May 25, 1944, POW Division, PMGO, RG 389, NARA.
205. Inspection Reports, Camp Gordon, Georgia, December 31, 1943–January 2, 1944, POW Division, PMGO, RG 389, NARA; Inspection Reports, Camp Gordon, Georgia, March 7, 1945, POW Division, PMGO, RG 386, NARA.
206. Letter, Kohlhaas to Coker, July 19, 1988.
207. Krammer, *Nazi POWs in America*, 172–73; Hamer, "Barbeque, Farming and Friendship," 71; Hamer, "Nazi Troopers in South Carolina," 309.
208. Krammer, *Nazi POWs in America*, 173.
209. Ibid.; Thompson, *Men in German Uniform*, 40–41; Mike Stroud, "Murder at Aiken Branch Camp," *Aiken Standard*, September 28, 2010.
210. Thompson, *Men in German Uniform*, 40–41; Militarian, "Murder at Aiken POW Camp."
211. Mike Stroud, "The Escape," *Aiken Standard*, September 28, 2010.
212. Hamer, "Nazi Troopers in South Carolina," 308–9.

213. Ibid., 308.
214. Ibid.
215. Ibid., 309.
216. Ibid.
217. Ibid.
218. Ibid., 309–10; Listman, Baker and Goodfellow, "Historic Context," C-41.
219. Jeffery, "Remembering German POW Camp in Aiken"; Latitude 34 North, "Historical Markers Across South Carolina."
220. Prisoner of War Camp Labor Report, Waynesboro, Georgia, June 13–14, 1944, RG 389, Box 2495, NARA; Inspection Reports, Camp Waynesboro, Georgia, December 1944, PMGO, POW Division, RG 389, NARA; Copeland, "Foreign Prisoners of War."
221. Inspection Reports, Camp Reidsville, Georgia, December 28, 1944, PMGO, POW Divisions, RG 389, NARA.

Chapter 4

222. Listman, Baker and Goodfellow, "Historic Context," July 10, 2007, Appendix C: Documentation Reports, C-65; Wikipedia, "Fort Stewart."
223. Lewis and Mewha, *History of POW Utilization*, 93–95, 97, 100; Listman, Baker and Goodfellow, "Historic Context," Appendix C-69; Billinger, "Enemies and Friends"; Kelly, "Army Patch of the Italian Service Unit."
224. Inspection Report, Parker Buhrman, Prisoner of War Camp, Camp Stewart, Georgia, July 3, 1944, Box 2673, RG 389, NARA; Listman, Baker and Goodfellow, "Historic Context," C-69, C-76; Cook, *Guests Behind Barbed Wire*, 337.
225. Waymarking, "Fort Stewart POW Camps—Hinesville, GA."
226. Inspection Report, Parker Buhrman, Prisoner of War Camp, Camp Stewart, Georgia, July 3, 1944, Box 2673, RG 389, NARA.
227. Ibid.; Memorandum for Director, Prisoner of War Operations Division, Subject: Report of Visit to P/W Camp, Camp Stewart, Georgia; PW Branch Camp, Chatham Field, Georgia; PW Branch Camp, Hunter Field, Georgia, December 22–26, 1944; December 26, 1944, Box 1427, RG 389, NARA; Listman, Baker and Goodfellow, "Historic Context," C-71.
228. Inspection Report, Parker Buhrman, Prisoner of War Camp, Camp Stewart, Georgia, July 3, 1944, Box 2673, RG 389, NARA.
229. Listman, Baker and Goodfellow, "Historic Context," C-71.

230. Memorandum with enclosures for Director, Prisoner of War Operations Division, from Major Edward C. Shannahan, Subject: Report of Visit to P/W Camp, Camp Stewart, Georgia; PW Branch Camp, Chatham Field, Georgia; PW Branch Camp, Hunter Field, Georgia, December 22–26, 1944; December 26, 1944, Box 1427, RG 389, NARA; Waymarking, "Fort Stewart POW Camps—Hinesville, GA."
231. Inspection Report, Parker Buhrman, Prisoner of War Camp, Camp Stewart, Georgia, July 3, 1944, Box 2673, RG 389, NARA.
232. Inspection Report, Maurice Perret, Prisoner of War Camp, Camp Stewart, Georgia, July 4, 1944, Box 2673, RG 389, NARA.
233. Inspection Report, Charles Eberhardt, Prisoner of War Camp, Camp Stewart, Georgia, December 15, 1944, Box 2673, RG 389, NARA.
234. Ibid.
235. Memorandum for Director, Prisoner of War Operations Division, Subject: Report of Visit to P/W Camp, Camp Stewart, Georgia; PW Branch Camp, Chatham Field, Georgia; PW Branch Camp, Hunter Field, Georgia, December 22–26, 1944; December 26, 1944, Box 1427, RG 389, NARA.
236. Memorandum for Director, Prisoner of War Special Projects Division, Subject: Field Service Report on Visit to Prisoner of War Camp, Camp Stewart, Georgia, February 8–9, 1945, by Captain Robert L. Kunzig, March 21, 1945, Box 2673, RG 389, NARA.
237. Listman, Baker and Goodfellow, "Historic Context," C-69.
238. Memorandum with enclosures for Director, Prisoner of War Operations Division, from Major Edward C. Shannahan, Subject: Report of Visit to P/W Camp, Camp Stewart, Georgia; PW Branch Camp, Chatham Field, Georgia; PW Branch Camp, Hunter Field, Georgia, December 22–26, 1944; December 26, 1944, Box 1427, RG 389, NARA.
239. Waymarking, "Fort Stewart POW Camps—Hinesville, GA."
240. Memorandum with enclosures for Director, Prisoner of War Operations Division, from Major Edward C. Shannahan, Subject: Report of Visit to P/W Camp, Camp Stewart, Georgia; PW Branch Camp, Chatham Field, Georgia; PW Branch Camp, Hunter Field, Georgia, December 22–26; December 1944, December 26, 1944, Box 1427, RG 389, NARA.
241. 475th Military Police Guard Escort Company, "Keep Your Confederate Money Folks."
242. Listman, Baker and Goodfellow, "Historic Context," C-73, C-74.
243. Waymarking, "Fort Stewart POW Camps—Hinesville, GA"; Listman, Baker and Goodfellow, "Historic Context," C-69, C-70.

Chapter 5

244. Memorandum with Attachments, Captain Hardison, to the Provost Marshal General, Subject: Closing of Prisoner of War Camps, May 16, 1946, RG 389, NARA; Thompson, "Winning the War Behind the Lines," 417; Krammer, *Nazi POWs in America*, 3–6.
245. Thompson, "Winning the War Behind the Lines," 417.
246. Ibid., 421–24.
247. *Macon Telegraph*, "War Prisoners May Be Used in Some Areas," July 15, 1943, 2.
248. Ibid.
249. Thompson, "Winning the War Behind the Lines," 426.
250. Ibid.
251. Ibid.
252. *Macon Telegraph*, "Prisoners to Harvest Peanut Crop—Hundreds Moving to Goober Fields," August 28, 1943, 1.
253. George Bonetti and R.W. Roth, Inspection Report, Prisoner of War Camp, Fort Benning, Georgia, October 15–17, 1943, RG 389, 1609, NARA; Thompson, "Winning the War Behind the Lines," 426.
254. Thompson, "Winning the War Behind the Lines," 426.
255. Ibid., 426–27.
256. Ibid.
257. Ibid., 427–28.
258. Ibid., 428.
259. Ibid., 428–29.
260. Bonetti and Roth, Inspection Report, October 15–17, 1943, RG 389, Box 1609, NARA.
261. Ibid.
262. Ibid.
263. Thompson, "Winning the War Behind the Lines," 451. Consensus about the humane treatment of POWs in America appears in most all the primary and secondary literature and interviews with prisoners, guards or civilian employers. For general references, see Krammer, *Nazi POWs in America*, and Keefer, *Italian Prisoners of War in America*.
264. Bonetti and Roth, Inspection Report, October 15–17, 1943, RG 389, Box 1609, NARA.
265. Ibid.
266. Ibid.
267. Reiss, "Solidarity Among 'Fellow Sufferers,'" 539.

268. Haas, "History of the Army Medical Service," 48; Listman, Baker and Goodfellow, "Historic Context," July 10, 2007, 6-3 to 6-31, 6-33.
269. Listman, Baker and Goodfellow, "Historic Context," 6-3 to 6-31.
270. Thompson, "Winning the War Behind the Lines," 429.
271. Ibid., 430.
272. Bonetti and Roth, Inspection Report, October 15–17, 1943, RG 389, Box 1609, NARA.
273. Thompson, "Winning the War Behind the Lines," 429–31.
274. Ibid., 431–32.
275. Ibid., 432.
276. Ibid.
277. *Columbus Enquirer*, "Army Chaplains Re-Enact Pioneer Preachers' Role," December 22, 1944, 17.
278. Thompson, "Winning the War Behind the Lines," 432–33.
279. Ibid., 433.
280. Ibid., 434.
281. Ibid.
282. Ibid., 435.
283. Ibid., 436.
284. Thompson, "Winning the War Behind the Lines," 432–33.
285. Ibid., 437; Maurice Ed. Perret, Fort Benning, Georgia, Inspection Report, September 21, 1945, RG 389, Box 1609, NARA.
286. Thompson, "Winning the War Behind the Lines," 437.
287. Ibid., 439. According to an article dated May 7, 1944, in the *Sunday Ledger-Enquirer*, 90 percent of the 3,000 Italian POWs at Fort Benning volunteered to join ISUs. At that time, there were 50,136 Italian prisoners in America. See *Sunday Ledger-Enquirer*, "Italian Prisoners Offered Chance to Volunteer for Non-Combat Duty: Most at Fort Benning Accept," May 7, 1944, 1.
288. *Columbus Enquirer*, "Nazis Treat US Prisoners Well, Post Officer States," September 6, 1944, 10; Perret Inspection Report, Fort Benning, Georgia, September 21, 1945; Thompson, "Winning the War Behind the Lines," 439. Camp Opelika's construction began in September 1942; it closed in September 1945. The first prisoners, captured by the British, were part of General Erwin Rommel's Afrika Corps. At any given time, the camp held about three thousand German POWs. See Wikipedia, "Camp Opelika."
289. *Columbus Enquirer*, "Nazis Treat US Prisoners Well," 10.
290. Thompson, "Winning the War Behind the Lines," 439.
291. Ibid.

292. Perret Inspection Report, Fort Benning, Georgia, September 21, 1945; Moore, review of Klaw's *Faustball Tunnel*.
293. *Columbus Enquirer*, "Nazis Treat US Prisoners Well," 10.
294. Perret Inspection Report, Fort Benning, Georgia, September 21, 1945.
295. Thompson, "Winning the War Behind the Lines," 444.
296. Ibid.
297. Ibid., 445.
298. *Columbus Enquirer*, "Four Prisoner Camps Come Under Benning," July 26, 1944, 2.
299. *Macon Telegraph*, "German Prisoners Are Not Available," July 28, 1944, 2.
300. Thompson, "Winning the War Behind the Lines," 445–46.
301. Ibid., 446.
302. Ibid., 447–48.
303. Ibid., 451.
304. Ibid.
305. Ibid., 417–18.
306. Ibid., 454–55.
307. Ibid., 455–57.
308. Memorandum with Attachments, Captain Hardison, to the Provost Marshal General, Subject: Closing of Prisoner of War Camps, May 16, 1946, RG 389, NARA.
309. Dr. Rudolph Fischer, Inspection Report, Prisoner of War Camp: Bainbridge Army Air Field, Bainbridge, Georgia, July 6, 1944, RG 186, Box 1609, NARA.
310. Ibid.
311. Ibid.
312. Ibid.
313. Ibid.
314. Ibid.
315. Ibid.
316. Ibid.
317. Ibid.
318. Ibid.
319. Interview, Faye Beazley, with Dr. Kathryn Roe Coker, December 14, 2018; interview, Dr. Ed Heard, with Dr. Kathryn Roe Coker, December 14, 2017.
320. Ray City History Blog, "Nazi Prisoners at Moody Field." See also *Valdosta Times*, "Nazi Prisoners Now at Moody," November 22, 1943.

321. Ray City History Blog, "Nazi Prisoners at Moody Field." See also the *Atlanta Constitution*, November 28, 1943, 14A.
322. Ray City History Blog, "Nazi Prisoners at Moody Field."
323. Ibid.
324. Ibid.
325. Ibid.
326. Minor, "Many German POWs Were in Southern Camps."
327. Ibid.
328. Memorandum with Attachments, Captain Hardison, to the Provost Marshal General, Subject: Closing of Prisoner of War Camps, May 16, 1946, RG 389, NARA.

Chapter 6

329. Bob Fackleman, "Enemy Alien Camp Started Near Macon," *Macon Telegraph*, November 17, 1942, 1; *Macon Telegraph*, "Labor Needed at Alien Camp," November 21, 1942, 1.
330. Memorandum with Attachments, Captain Hardison, to the Provost Marshal General, Subject: Closing of Prisoner of War Camps, May 16, 1946, RG 389, NARA; Waymarking, "Camp Wheeler-Macon, Georgia."
331. Inspection Report, Captain Edward C. Shannahan, POW Division, OPMG, POW Camp, Camp Wheeler, Georgia, December 22–24, 1943, RG 389, Box 2675, NARA; *Macon Telegraph*, May 19, 1943.
332. Ben E. Adams, "Italian War Prisoners Here Seem Cheerful but Stick to Roman Salute for Officers," *Macon Telegraph*, June 14, 1943, 1.
333. Ibid.
334. Ibid.
335. Ibid.
336. *Macon Telegraph*, "Peanut Farmers Face Serious Labor Shortage," July 15, 1943, 2.
337. Memorandum, Major Earl Edwards, POW Division, OPMG, for Director, POW Division, PMGO, Subject: Inspection Report on Prisoner of War Camp, Camp Wheeler, Georgia, September 10, 1943, RG 389, Box 2675, NARA.
338. Ibid.
339. Ibid.
340. Ibid.

341. *Macon Telegraph*, "War Prisoners Grin at Italy's Capitulation," September 9, 1943, 10.
342. *Macon Telegraph*, "Captive Italians May Farm Here," September 1944.
343. Inspection Report, Captain Edward C. Shannahan, POW Camp, Camp Wheeler, Georgia, December 22–24, 1943, RG 389, Box 2675.
344. Ibid.
345. Ibid.
346. Lieutenant Colonel R. Hipeuser, Assistant Adjutant General, to Commanding Officer, POW Camp, Camp Gordon, Subject: POW Branch Camps, July 22, 1944, PMGO, RG 389, NARA.
347. Ibid.
348. Ibid.
349. Ibid.
350. Inspection Report, Major Edward C. Shannahan, POW Camp, Camp Wheeler, Georgia, December 12–16, 1944, 1943, RG 389, Box 2675.
351. Ibid.
352. Memorandum, Major Paul A. Neuland, Chief, Field Service Branch, OPMG, POW Special Projects Division, to Director, POW Special Projects Division, Subject: Field Service Report on Visit to POW Camp, Camp Wheeler, Georgia, February 10, 1945, by Captain Robert L. Kunzig, March 7, 1945, RG 399, Box 2675, NARA.
353. Ibid.
354. Ibid.
355. Linton Burkett, "German Prisoner's Break Frustrated by Two Women," *Macon Telegraph*, January 6, 1945, 1A.
356. *Macon Telegraph*, "Nearly 3,000 Germans Leave Wheeler; Work in Area Valued at $3,500,000," December 25, 1945, 14.
357. Albrecht, "Parma Heights World War II Veteran."
358. Ibid.
359. Ibid.
360. Ibid.
361. Ibid.
362. Ibid.
363. Ibid.
364. Ibid.
365. *Macon Telegraph*, "Prisoners to Harvest Peanut Crop," 1. Members of the Farm Labor Advisory Committee were Walter B. Daniel, Bob Hodges, Wade Dominy, TC Waldrep, D.I. Parker, J.L. Allen, M.F. Beall,

Dennis Rawls, C.L. Thigpen, R.T. Gilder, H.W. Dozier, Frank Clark, D.W. Allgood and Oswell Hadden.
366. Ibid.
367. Memorandum with Attachments, Captain Hardison, to the Provost Marshal General, Subject: Closing of Prisoner of War Camps, May 16, 1946, RG 389, NARA; Inspection Report, Major Shannahan, Camp Wheeler, December 12–16, 1944, 1943, RG 389, Box 2675.
368. Inspection Report, Major Shannahan, Camp Wheeler, December 12–16, 1944, 1943, RG 389, Box 2675; J.S. Wilson, "German POW Camp in Monticello," *Monticello News*, July 2, 2009, http://themonticellonews.com/german-pow-camp-in-monticello-p6011-116.htm.
369. Inspection Report, Shannahan, Camp Wheeler, December 12–16, 1944, 1943, RG 389, Box 2675.
370. Ibid.; Wilson, "German POW Camp in Monticello."
371. Inspection Report, Major Shannahan, Camp Wheeler, December 12–16, 1944, 1943, RG 389, Box 2675.
372. Ibid.
373. Memorandum with Attachments, Captain Hardison, to the Provost Marshal General, Subject: Closing of Prisoner of War Camps, May 16, 1946, RG 389, NARA; Wilson, "German POW Camp in Monticello."
374. Pieces of Our Past, "German Italian Prisoner of War Camp"; Thompson, "Images of Our Past."
375. Pieces of Our Past, "German Italian Prisoner of War Camp"; Thompson, "Images of Our Past."
376. Pieces of Our Past, "German Italian Prisoner of War Camp."
377. Inspection Report, Major Shannahan, Camp Wheeler, December 12–16, 1944, 1943, RG 389, Box 2675.
378. Ibid.
379. Pieces of Our Past, "German Italian Prisoner of War Camp"; Memorandum with Attachments, Captain Hardison, to the Provost Marshal General, Subject: Closing of Prisoner of War Camps, May 16, 1946, RG 389, NARA.
380. Crenshaw, "Dublin Hospital Played a Little-Known Role."
381. Ibid.
382. Ibid.
383. Ibid.

Chapter 7

384. News Release 383.6, First Lieutenant Charles Hundt, Subject: Prisoners of War, March 20, 1944, Fourth Service Command, Fort Oglethorpe, Georgia, RG 389, Box 2668, NARA; Memorandum with Attachments, Captain W.M. Hardison, to the Provost Marshal General, Subject: Closing of Prisoner of War Camps, May 16, 1946, RG 389, NARA.
385. News Release 383.6, First Lieutenant Charles Hundt, Subject: Prisoners of War, March 20, 1944, Fourth Service Command, Fort Oglethorpe, Georgia, RG 389, Box 2668, NARA.
386. Depken and Powell, *Images of America: Fort Oglethorpe*, 8.
387. Report, Charles C. Eberhardt, Subject: Visit to Prisoner of War Camp Oglethorpe, Georgia, December 9, RG 389, Box 2668, NARA.
388. Report, Charles C. Eberhardt, Subject: Visit to Prisoner of War Camp Oglethorpe, Georgia, November 8, 1944, RG 389, Box 2668, NARA.
389. Ibid.
390. Ibid.; Depken and Powell, *Images of America: Fort Oglethorpe*, 8.
391. Report, Eberhardt, Subject: Visit to Prisoner of War Camp Oglethorpe, Georgia, November 8, 1944, RG 389, Box 2668, NARA.
392. Report, Edouard Patte, Subject: Visit to Prisoner of War Camp Oglethorpe, Georgia, November 8, 1944, RG 389, Box 2668, NARA.
393. Ibid.
394. Ibid.
395. Ibid.; Report, Edouard Patte, Subject: Visit to Prisoner of War Camp Oglethorpe, Georgia, December 7, 1944, RG 389, Box 2668, NARA.
396. Patte Report, December 7, 1944.
397. Memorandum for the Director, Prisoner of War Special Projects Division, Major Paul Neuland, Chief, Field Service Branch, POW Special Projects Division, OPMG, Subject: Field Service Report on Visit to the Prisoner of War Camp, Fort Oglethorpe, Georgia, January 8–9, 1945, by Captain William F. Raugust, RG 389, Box 2668, NARA.
398. Ibid.
399. Ibid.
400. Ibid.
401. Ibid.
402. Report, Edouard Patte, Subject: Visit to Prisoner of War Camp Oglethorpe, Georgia, February 26, 1945, RG 389, Box 2668, NARA.
403. Report, Edouard Patte, Subject: Visit to Prisoner of War Camp Oglethorpe, Georgia, May 8, 1945, RG 389, Box 2668, NARA.

404. Report, Edouard Patte, Subject: Visit to Prisoner of War Camp Oglethorpe, Georgia, September 15, 1945, RG 389, Box 2668, NARA.
405. Ibid.
406. Report, Captain Alexander Lakes, Prisoner of War Special Projects Division, to Commanding Officer, Prisoner of War Camp, Fort Oglethorpe, Georgia, Subject: Report on Field Service Visit, October 19, 1945, RG 389, Box 2668, NARA.
407. Report, Captain Lyle T. Dawson, Liaison Officer, Office of Provost Marshal General, of Prisoner of War Camp, Fort Oglethorpe, Georgia, to Commanding Officer, Fort Oglethorpe, Georgia, Subject: Report of Inspection, August 6, 1945, RG 389, Box 2668, NARA.
408. Ibid.; Memorandum with Attachments, Captain Hardison, to the Provost Marshal General, Subject: Closing of Prisoner of War Camps, May 16, 1946, RG 389, NARA.
409. Report, Captain Dawson, to Commanding Officer, Fort Oglethorpe, Subject: Inspection, August 6, 1945, RG 389, Box 2668, NARA; Memorandum with Attachments, Captain Hardison, to the Provost Marshal General, Subject: Closing of Prisoner of War Camps, May 16, 1946, RG 389, NARA.
410. Report, Captain Dawson, to Commanding Officer, Fort Oglethorpe, Subject: Inspection, August 6, 1945, RG 389, Box 2668, NARA.
411. Ibid.; Memorandum with Attachments, Captain Hardison, to the Provost Marshal General, Subject: Closing of Prisoner of War Camps, May 16, 1946, RG 389, NARA.

Conclusion

412. Albrecht, "Parma Heights World War II Veteran."
413. Coker, *World War II Prisoners of War in Georgia*, 861; Albrecht, "Parma Heights World War II Veteran."
414. *Augusta Chronicle*, "Fort Gordon Commemorates German POWs," November 18, 1999; *NBC News*, "Day of Mourning"; Vaughn, "German Hun in the Georgia Sun," 125; Depken and Powell, *Images of America: Fort Oglethorpe*, 44.

NOTE TO PAGE 241

Appendix A

415. National World War II Museum, "Guests of the Third Reich: American POWs in Europe," http://www.guestsofthethirdreich.org/home.

BIBLIOGRAPHY

PRIMARY SOURCES

NATIONAL ARCHIVES AND RECORDS ADMINISTRATION (NARA)
Headquarters Fourth Service Command, Army Service Forces, (ASF), Record Group (RG) 160
Office of the Chief of Ordnance, RG 156
    Atlanta Ordnance Depot (Atlanta, NARA Branch)
    Augusta Arsenal (Atlanta, NARA Branch)
Provost Marshal General Office, RG 389
    Construction Correspondence
    Inspection Reports, POW Division
    Labor Reports
    Letters, Aliens Division
    Letters, Fourth Service Command
    Memorandums, Internal Security Division, Army Service Forces, Fourth Service Command
    Memorandums, Services of Supply, Corps of Engineers, South Atlantic Division Engineer
    Memorandums, POW Operations Division
    Memorandums, POW Special Projects Division
    News Releases, Fourth Service Command
    Standard Operating Procedures, POW Division

Bibliography

U.S. Army Heritage & Education Center
  Camp Gordon Historical Data Reference Card, Military Reservations
  World War II POW Camp Newspapers

U.S. Army Signal Corps & Fort Gordon Archives (USASC&FG)
  Letters, Father Radbert Kohlhaas Papers
  Letter with copies of POW Basic Personnel Records and Death Certificates from German Federal Archives
  Photographs, Father Radbert Kohlhaas Papers

Interviews, Oral History Collection, USASC&FG Archives
  Joe Buck with Dr. Kathy Roe Coker, November 7, 1988
  Albert D. Cromer with Dr. Kathy Roe Coker, November 8, 1988
  Father Radbert Kohlhaas with Dr. Kathy Roe Coker, April 25, 1989
  Edna Tatter with Dr. Kathy Roe Coker, November 4, 1988

Interviews, Author's Private Collection
  Faye Beazly with Dr. Kathryn Roe Coker, December 14, 2017
  Dr. Ed Heard with Dr. Kathryn Roe Coker, December 14, 2017

Newspapers

Aiken Standard
Atlanta Journal Constitution
Augusta Chronicle
Camp Gordon Cadence
Columbus Enquirer
Macon Telegraph
Monticello News
Newsweek
The Signal
Sunday Ledger-Enquirer
Tar Heel Junior Historian
Valdosta Times

BIBLIOGRAPHY

SECONDARY SOURCES

Theses

Croley, Pamela. "American Reeducation of German POWs, 1943–1946." *Electronic Theses and Dissertations.* Paper 2233, 2006. http://dc.etsu.edu/etd/2233.
Salgado, Rebecca C. "Rebuilding the Network: Interpretation of World War II Prisoner of War Camps in the United States." MA Thesis, Columbia University, May 2012.
Vaughn, Leisa. "The German Hun in the Georgia Sun: German Prisoners of War in Georgia." Master's thesis, Georgia Southern University, 2016.
Wyatt, Judy. "United States Policy Toward German POWs and Its Application in South Carolina." MA thesis, University of South Carolina, 1985.

Books

Billinger, Robert. *Hitler's Soldiers in the Sunshine State: German POWs in Florida.* Gainesville: University of Florida, 2000.
Cashin, Edward J. *The Story of Augusta.* Augusta, GA: Richmond County Board of Education Historical Society, 1980.
Coker, Kathy Roe. *World War II Prisoners of War in Georgia: Camp Gordon's POWs.* Fort Gordon, GA: Command Historian Office, 1994.
Cook, Ruth Beaumont. *Guests Behind Barbed Wire: German POWs in America—A True Story of Hope and Friendship.* Birmingham, AL: Crane Hill Publishers, 2007.
Cowley, Betty. *Stalag Wisconsin: Inside WWII Prisoner-of-War Camps.* Oregon, WI: Badger Books Inc., 2002.
Depken, Gerry, and Julie Powell. *Images of America: Fort Oglethorpe.* Charleston, SC: Arcadia Publishing, 2009.
Fiedler, David. *The Enemy Among US: POWs in Missouri During World War II.* Columbia: University of Missouri Press, 2010.
Gansberg, Judith M. *Stalag: USA: The Remarkable Story of German POWs in America.* New York: Thomas Y. Crowell, 1977.
Keefer, Louis. *Italian Prisoners of War in America, 1942–1946: Captives or Allies?* New York: Praeger, 1992.
Kirkpatrick, Kathy. *Prisoner of War Camps Across America.* Salt Lake City, UT: GenTracer, 2012.

Bibliography

Koop, Allen V. *Stark Decency: German Prisoners of War in a New England Village.* Lebanon, NH: University Press of New England, 1998.

Krammer, Arnold. *Nazi POWs in America.* Lanham, MD: Scarborough House, 1992.

Lewis, Lieutenant Colonel George G., and Captain John Mewha. *History of POW Utilization by the United States Army, 1776–1945.* Department of the Army Pamphlet No. 20-213. Washington, D.C.: Department of the Army, June 1955.

Robin, Ron. *The Barbed-Wire College: Reeducating German POWs in the United States During World War II.* Princeton, NJ: Princeton University Press, 1995.

Smith, Arthur L. *The War for the German Mind: Reeducating Hitler's Soldiers.* Providence, RI, 1996.

Stokesbury, James L. *A Short History of World War II.* New York: HarperCollins, 1980.

Strege, John. *When War Played through Golf During World War II.* New York: Penguin Group, 2005.

Thomas, Kenneth H., Jr. *Images of America: Fort Benning.* Charleston, SC: Arcadia Publishing, 2003.

Thompson, Antonio. *Men in German Uniform: POWs in America During World War II.* Knoxville: University of Tennessee Press, 2010.

Waters, Michael R. *Lone Star Stalag: German Prisoners of War at Camp Hearne.* College Station: Texas A&M University Press, 2004.

Periodicals

Brown, John Mason. "German Prisoners of War in the United States." *American Journal of International Law* 39, no. 2 (1945), 198–215.

Byrd, Martha H. "Captured by the Americans." *American History Illustrated* 11 (February 1977), 26–27.

Coker, Kathy Roe. "World War II Prisoners of War in Georgia: German Memories of Camp Gordon, 1943–1945." *Georgia Historical Quarterly* 76, no. 4 (Winter 1992): 837–61.

Fickle, James E., and Donald W. Ellis. "POWs in the Piney Woods: German POWs in the Southern Lumber Industry, 1942–1945." *Journal of Southern History* 56, no. 4 (November 1990): 695–24.

Hamer, Fritz. "Barbeque, "Farming and Friendship." *Proceedings of the South Carolina Historical Association* (1994): 61–74.

———. "Nazi Troopers in South Carolina." *South Carolina Historical Magazine* 81, no. 4 (October 1980): 306–15.

Heisler, Barbara Schmitter. "Returning German Prisoners of War and the American Experience." *German Studies Review* 31, no. 3 (October 2008): 537–56.

Krammer, Arnold P. "German POWs in the United States." *Military Affairs* 40, no. 2 (April 1976): 68–73.

Moore, John Hammond. "Nazi Troopers in South Carolina." *South Carolina Historical Magazine* 81, no. 4 (October 1980): 306–15.

Murphy, Charles. "Prisoners of War: Repatriation or Internment in Wartime American and Allied Experience, 1775 to Present." Congressional Research Report, Library of Congress, July 20, 1971.

Reiss, Matthias. "Icons of Insult: German and Italian Prisoners of War in African American Letters during World War II." *American Studies* 49, no. 4 (2004): 539–62.

———. "The Importance of Being Men: The Afrika-Korps in American Captivity." *Journal of Social History* 46, no. 1 (Fall 2012): 23–47.

———. "Solidarity Among 'Fellow Sufferers': African Americans and German Prisoners of War in the United States During World War II." *Journal of African American History* 98, no. 4 (n.d.): 531–61.

Thompson, Antonio. "Winning the War Behind the Lines: Colonel George M. Chescheir and the Axis POWs at Fort Benning, Georgia." *Register of the Kentucky Historical Society* 105, no. 3 (Summer 2007): 417–60.

Ward, Jason Morgan. "Nazis Hoe Cotton: Planters, POWs, and the Future of Farm Labor in the Deep South." *Agricultural History* 81, no. 4 (Fall 2007): 471–92.

Internet Sources

Albrecht, Brian. "Parma Heights World War II Veteran Recalls Guarding German POWs." Metro News. http://blog.cleveland.com/metro/2011/10/vet_recalls_duty_as_german_pow.html.

Auction Finds. "Simple Form Leads to History of POW Camps in U.S." April 18, 2016. http://myauctionfinds.com/2016/04/18/simple-form-leads-to-history-of-pow-camps-in-u-s.

Billinger, Robert, Jr. "Enemies and Friends." Reprinted with permission from the *Tar Heel Junior Historian* (Spring 2008). Tar Heel Junior Historian

Bibliography

Association, North Carolina Museum of History, www.ncpedia.org/history/20th-Century/wwii-pows.

Boyette, John. "Masters Took Break during World War II." The Masters. http://www.augusta.com/masters/story/history/masterstook-break-during-world-war-ii.

Budanovic, Nikola. "Georg Gartner: A German Soldier Who Lived in the US for 40 Years Under a False Identity After He Escaped from a POW Camp." War History Online, April 13, 2018. https://www.warhistoryonline.com/instant-articles/georg-gartner-german-soldier-pow.html.

Busbee, Jay. "When Cows Ruled Augusta: The World's Most Famous Golf Course Was a Cow Pasture in WWII." Yahoo! Sports, April 12, 2013. https://sports.yahoo.com/blogs/golf-devil-ball-golf/cows-ruled-augusta-national-world-most-famous-golf-175954183—golf.html.

Copeland, Susan. "Foreign Prisoners of War." Georgia Encyclopedia, August 12, 2002. https://www.georgiaencyclopedia.org/articles/government-politics/foreign-prisoners-war.

Crenshaw, Wayne. "Dublin Hospital Played a Little-Known Role in World War II." *Macon Telegraph*, January 3, 2016. http://www.macon.com/news/local/article52874345.html.

Cutmore, Chris. "Yes, This Really IS Augusta, but Not as You Know It… but Why Was It Once Home to 200 Cattle and 1,400 Turkeys (but No Tigers)?" *Daily Mail*, April 10, 2013. http://www.dailymail.co.uk/sport/golf/article-2306832/MASTERS-2013-Why-Augusta-home-200-cattle-1-400-turkeys-Tigers.html.

475th Military Police Escort Guard Company. "Keep Your Confederate Money Folks the South Will Rise Again." 475thmpeg.memorieshop.com/CHAPTERS/FIVE/chapter5.html.

Haas, Major Robert F. "A History of the Army Medical Service Fort Benning, Georgia." U.S. Army Fort Benning and the Maneuver Center of Excellence. http://www.benning.army.mil/Library/content/Virtual/Fort%20Benning%20History/Martin%20Army%20Hospital%20-%20May%201964.pdf.

Hawaii Memory Project. The Nisei Story: Americans of Japanese Ancestry During WWII. "Shiroku 'Whitey' Yamamoto, 442nd Antitank Company." http://nisei.hawaii.edu/page/whitey.

The History Experience. "German POWs in the Southern United States: Reeducation and Reactions during World War II." May 3, 2014. https://leverettmb.wordpress.com/2014/05/03/german-pows-in-the-southern-united-states-reeducation-and-reactions-during-world-war-ii.

BIBLIOGRAPHY

HistoryNet. "World War II: North Africa Campaign." http://www.historynet.com/world-war-ii-north-africa-campaign.htm.

Hudnall, Amy. "A Brief Overview of Camp Policy and Life." Appalachian State University. http://www.appstate.edu/~hudnallac/pow.htm.

Hunnicutt, J.W. "German POWs in Dade City." History of Pasco County, Florida. http://www.fivay.org/pow.html.

International Committee of the Red Cross. "Geneva Convention of 27 July 1929 Relative to the Treatment of Prisoners of War." June 4, 1998. https://www.icrc.org/eng/resources/documents/misc/57jnws.htm.

Jeffery, Ashley. "Remembering German POW Camp in Aiken." WRDW News, September 21, 2008. http://www.wrdw.com/home/headlines/29201149.html.

Kelly, Clement. "Army Patch of the Italian Service Unit." Military Trader. http://www.militarytrader.com/military-trader-news/italian_service_unit_insignia.

Latitude 34 North. "Historical Markers Across South Carolina: World War II POW Camp." http://www.lat34north.com/HistoricMarkersSC/MarkerDetail.cfm?KeyID=02-41&MarkerTitle=World%20War%20II%20%20POW%20Camp.

Listman, John, Christopher Baker and Susan Goodfellow. "Historic Context: World War II Prisoner-of-War Camps on Department of Defense Installations." Department of Defense, Legacy Resource Management Program, July 10, 2000, Project No. 05-256. Available at Scribd, https://www.scribd.com/document/105343368/Military-POW-Camp-Buildings.

Manion, B.C. "Historian Sheds Light on German POWs." *Laker/Lutz News*, July 22, 2015. http://lakerlutznews.com/lln/?p=28099.

Militarian. "Murder at Aiken POW Camp." http://www.militarian.com/threads/murder-at-aiken-pow-camp.608.

Minor, Elliott. "Many German POWs Were in Southern Camps." Stormfront, https://www.stormfront.org/forum/t20689.

Moore, John Hammond. Review of Barbara Klaw's *The Faustball Tunnel: German POWs in America and Their Great Escape*. American Heritage. http://www.americanheritage.com/content/faustball-tunnel-german-pows-america-and-their-great-escape.

NBC News. "Day of Mourning Will Honor German POWs Held in U.S." http://www.nbcnews.com/id/6491844/ns/us_news/t/day-mourning-will-honor-german-pows-held-us.

Bibliography

Pieces of Our Past. "The German Italian Prisoner of War Camp, Dublin." March 2009. http://dublinlaurenscountygeorgia.blogspot.com/2009/03/german-italian-prisoner-of-war-camp.html.

Ray City History Blog. "Prisoners at Moody Field Worked Ray City Farms." https://raycityhistory.wordpress.com/tag/edward-t-lillis.

Saunders, Private First Class Norm. "I Guard Nazi Prisoners." *National Picture Monthly*, November 1943, 16. Reprinted article from oldmagazinearticles.com.

Smithsonian Magazine. "German POWs on the American Homefront." https://www.smithsonianmag.com/history/german-pows-on-the-american-homefront-141009996.

Steadman, John. "When Cattle Made Rounds at Old Augusta." *Baltimore Sun*, April 6, 1994. http://articles.baltimoresun.com/1994-04-06/sports/1994096188_1_augusta-national-golf-golf-club-masters.

Study the Past. "Democracy and Diversity in Walker County, Texas: The Four Freedoms: Teaching Democracy at Huntsville's Prisoner of War Camp." http://studythepast.com/democracy/pow_camp_home.

Thompson, Scott. "Images of Our Past—German and Italian POWs in Dublin, Georgia, 1943." Pieces of Our Past, April 2017. http://dublinlaurenscountygeorgia.blogspot.com/2017/04/images-of-our-past-german-and-italian.html.

Waymarking. "Camp Wheeler—Macon, Georgia—WWII Prisoner of War Camps." http://www.waymarking.com/waymarks/WM7F0W_Camp_Wheeler_Macon_Georgia.

———. "Fort Stewart POW Camps—Hinesville, GA." http://www.waymarking.com/waymarks/WM3ERR_Fort_Stewart_POW_camps_Hinesville_GA.

Wikipedia. "Army Service Forces." https://en.wikipedia.org/wiki/Army_Service_Forces.

———. "Camp Opelika." https://en.wikipedia.org/wiki/Camp_Opelika.

———. "German Prisoners of War in the United States." https://en.wikipedia.org/wiki/German_prisoners_of_war_in_the_United_States.

INDEX

A

accidents 39, 53, 97
Adams, Ben 115, 116, 121, 261
African Americans 13, 14, 75, 96, 121, 132
Afrika Korps 23, 37, 38, 50, 70, 73, 104, 129, 130
Aiken, South Carolina 70, 73, 74, 75, 76, 124, 240
Aiken Standard 74
Alabama 80, 89, 97, 107, 146
Albany, Georgia 91, 105, 131
Allen, Marilyn May 133
Allgood, D.W. 133
Allies 8, 41, 79, 100, 101, 258
American soldiers. *See* U.S. soldiers
Americus, Georgia 100, 105
Anderson, Colonel Walter 49, 56, 65, 66, 73
Anderson, Pierce 61
Anthony, Howard 98

anti-Nazis 26, 38, 39, 43, 46, 82, 83, 145
Army Service Forces 34, 79, 89, 91
Ashburn, Georgia 131, 165
Atlanta Constitution 110, 261
Atlanta, Georgia 50, 74, 80, 104, 105
Atlanta Ordnance Depot 80
Augusta Arsenal, Georgia 60, 62
Augusta Chronicle 58, 60, 61
Augusta, Georgia 53, 57, 58, 59, 60, 61, 62, 63, 64, 66, 75
Augusta National. *See* Augusta National Golf Club
Augusta National Golf Club 62, 63
Austin, Jack 80, 85
Axson, Georgia 105

B

Badoglio, Marshal Pietro 100, 125
Bainbridge Army Air Field 107, 108, 109

Index

Bainbridge, Georgia 9, 100, 105, 107, 108, 109, 240
barracks 28, 49, 50, 51, 52, 53, 67, 70, 74, 76, 81, 84, 85, 90, 115, 116, 117, 118, 119, 122, 126, 136, 137, 140, 141, 142, 143, 240
base camps 43, 47, 56, 62, 76, 85, 103, 104, 105, 107, 113, 123, 124, 239
Battey General Hospital 144, 146
Baughman, Chaplain Captain Alden C. 51
Bauknight, Lewis 111
Bauknight, Loudell 111
Beazly, Faye 9, 109
Bennett, Oliver 134
Bibb County 58, 115
Blumenberg, Horst 106
Boscolo, Armando 101
Boudreaux, Captain Henry J. 131
branch camps 32, 34, 47, 64, 66, 70, 73, 76, 83, 84, 85, 89, 96, 100, 105, 106, 110, 124, 127, 128, 131, 132, 139, 144, 146, 239
Brewer, Colonel Carlos 126
Bryan, Lieutenant General Blackshear 34
Buck, Joe 66
Buckley, First Lieutenant John J. 65
Buhrman, Parker 80, 81, 82, 94, 140
Burch, Captain Curtis T. 141, 142
Burns, Ken 128

C

Callahan, Captain Howard E. 83
Callan, Warner 135
Cammaert, Monseigneur Ferdinand 69
camp administration 66, 82, 95
Camp Alva, Oklahoma 143
camp arrival 23, 50, 64, 69, 70, 71, 90, 97, 98, 100, 103, 110, 129, 133, 141
Camp Blakely, Georgia 32
Camp Blanding, Florida 64, 66
camp construction 47, 49, 62, 85, 94, 96, 122
Camp Croft, South Carolina 76
Camp Forrest, Tennesse 69, 139
Camp Gordon, Georgia 23, 33, 49, 50, 52, 53, 57, 58, 62, 63, 64, 65, 66, 67, 68, 69, 73, 75, 76, 125
Camp Hearne, Texas 42
camp newspapers 42, 46
Camp Opelika, Alabama 103, 259
Camp Shanks, New York 69, 87
camp specifications 26
Camp Stewart, Georgia 79, 80, 82, 83, 85, 86, 87
Camp Wabaunsee, Kansas 32
Camp Wheeler, Georgia 8, 43, 57, 66, 69, 91, 115, 121
canteen 29, 71, 81, 82, 84, 95, 108, 116, 122, 123, 127, 129, 140, 144
Carl Vinson Veterans' Administration Medical Center, Georgia 136
Castleberry Food Company 61
Catoosa County, Georgia 139
cemetery 70, 74, 240, 255
Central Labor Union 98
Chambers, J.W. 57

276

INDEX

Charleston, South Carolina 64, 68, 123, 124
Chatham Army Air Field, Georgia 85
Chatham Field, Georgia 43
Chattanooga, Tennessee 145
Chavous, Bill 62. *See* guards
Chescheir, Colonel George M. 43, 89, 90, 91, 92, 94, 97, 98, 100, 101, 102, 104, 105, 106, 107
Civilian Conservation Corps 84, 87, 119, 240
Clark, Captain Myrvin C. 43, 107, 263
Clark, Frank 133
Columbia, South Carolina 75
Columbus Enquirer 103
Columbus, Georgia 89, 90, 95, 98, 105, 259, 260
Columbus Ledger 90, 95
concentration camps 35, 46, 62, 67, 68
Concord, North Carolina 70
Cromer, Albert J. 62
Cullens, Robert 135
Cummer Sons Cypress Company 64

D

Dade City, Florida 64
daily operations 12, 27, 28, 31, 47, 51, 52, 62, 65, 70, 73, 112, 121, 122, 140, 145
Damer, Josef 135
Daniel Field, Georgia 59, 62, 66, 69, 131

Daniel, Walter B. 133, 262
Davison, Major Edward 41
Dawson, Captain Lyle 145, 146
deaths 53
Department of State 12
Der Ruf 42, 43
De Stefano, Sergeant Carlo 102
discipline 39, 60, 65, 83, 94, 126, 129, 135
Dominy, Wade 133
Dozier, H.W. 133
Dryden, Lieutenant Colonel Charles 96
Dublin, Georgia 131, 133, 135, 136, 137, 240

E

Eastern Europe 67
East Germany 72
Eberhardt, Charles C. 66, 73, 82, 83, 94, 126, 140, 143
economy 8, 34, 36, 128, 239
Edge, Harry 133
education 32, 33, 39, 41, 42, 44, 45, 46, 47, 56, 68, 72, 95, 103, 106, 107, 126, 127, 140, 142, 143, 144, 145, 146
 curriculum 41, 142
Edwards, Major Earl L. 118, 119, 120, 121, 122, 125
Eisenhower, Major General Dwight David 13
Emory University 127
England 13
Erichsen, Heino 39
escapes 29, 33, 34, 58, 59, 66, 72, 74, 75, 110, 129, 132, 134

Index

F

facilities 42, 49, 50, 51, 55, 69, 70, 72, 82, 84, 85, 86, 89, 107, 108, 118, 119, 122, 127, 131, 136, 143
"Factory, the" 41, 42
Fargo, Georgia 100, 105, 110, 113
farmers 25, 58, 61, 86, 90, 97, 105, 110, 111, 117, 118, 121, 129
Fascism 96, 101, 125
Federal Bureau of Investigation (FBI) 74, 75
Finney General Hospital 240
Fischer, Dr. Rudolph 80, 82, 107, 108, 109, 126, 140, 260
Fitzgerald, Georgia 131
Florida 64, 76, 89
Florida Times-Union 64
food 11, 28, 35, 51, 52, 60, 67, 68, 72, 73, 79, 82, 85, 98, 108, 111, 113, 115, 116, 118, 122, 125, 134, 136
Fort Benning, Georgia 42, 43, 69, 91, 106, 107, 240
  Martin Army Hospital 96
Fort Custer, Michigan 65, 73
Fort Eustis, Virginia 86
Fort Getty, Rhode Island 43
Fort Jackson, South Carolina 76
Fort Kearny, Rhode Island 41, 42
Fort Leavenworth, Kansas 74
  Southeastern Branch of the United States Disciplinary Barracks 67
Fort McPherson, Georgia 74
Fort Moultrie, South Carolina 124
Fort Oglethorpe, Georgia 139
442nd Antitank Company 9

475th Military Police Escort Guard Company 86
Fourth Service Command 49, 57, 89, 98, 100, 105, 106, 132, 135, 139
France 34, 70, 71, 104, 132, 133, 141
Fredericks, Lieutenant Colonel Horace 142
Freer, Dr. Edward A. 73
Fries, Jeorge 135
Frits Ritz 71

G

Gaertner, Heinz 32
Ganoe, Colonel William 10
Gansberg, Judith 39, 41, 47
Gartner, Georg 247
Gauss, Sergeant Erick 73, 74
Geneva Convention 11, 26, 27, 28, 29, 31, 32, 34, 41, 51, 62, 65, 91, 92, 97, 98, 104, 139, 140, 239
Georgia-Carolina Tile and Brick Company 61
Germany 34, 38, 39, 40, 41, 42, 43, 46, 50, 51, 56, 57, 59, 67, 72, 74, 75, 79, 82, 87, 102, 105, 106, 113, 121, 128, 130, 144, 145, 146
Gilder, R.T. 133, 263
Glynco, Reidsville 43
Griffin, Georgia 131
Grovania, Georgia 128
Grovetown, Georgia 61
guards 9, 12, 13, 14, 23, 25, 35, 39, 49, 59, 60, 62, 65, 66,

INDEX

70, 72, 74, 76, 80, 82, 84, 85, 92, 94, 104, 105, 106, 107, 108, 109, 111, 112, 118, 122, 124, 125, 126, 127, 129, 130, 131, 132, 133, 134, 135, 139, 140, 143
  baseball 135
  basketball 135
  football 135
guard towers 49, 70, 107, 118, 122
Gullion, Major General Allen W. 12
Gunther, Horst 73
Guztat, Gurd 74

H

Hadden, A.O. 133
Hamer, Fritz 25, 74, 75
Hammack, Simk 63
Hawkinsville, Georgia 131
health 40, 76, 108, 122, 136
Heard, Ed 6, 9
Heard, Edgar 109, 110
Hemingway, S.M. 112
Hendrickson, Major Anselm 127
Hitler, Adolf 37, 38, 39, 42, 111, 112
Hobson, Brigadier General William H. 98
Hodges, Bob 133
Holmes, Zilla 71
Holstein, Dick 72
homefront 8, 9, 25
Homerville, Georgia 113
Hunter Field, Georgia 85

I

inspections 56, 65, 66, 91, 94, 97, 115
Intellectual Diversion Program. *See* Reeducation Program
International Red Cross 11, 12, 51, 56, 65, 67, 100
International Red Cross Committee 11, 51, 65, 100
International YMCA 12, 52, 106
Irwin, Colonel S.L. 133
Italian Service Units 79, 80, 87, 96, 100, 101, 239
Italy 70, 71, 79, 84, 104, 121

J

Jackson, Georgia 133
Japan 7, 8, 10, 11
Jasper County 131
Jasper Middle School 131
Jessup, Georgia 124
Joe Buck 252, 254
Johnson County 134
Johnson, Major Clarence T. 105
Jordon, Frank 136

K

Keefer, Louis 258
Keen, Lehman P. 134
Knight, Elias M. 111
Knight, Judge W.D. 111
Kohlhaas, Radbert 8, 23, 36, 50, 51, 56, 57, 60, 62, 66, 67, 68, 69, 73

INDEX

Krammer, Arnold 25, 41, 74, 245, 246, 247, 248, 249, 250, 254, 255, 258
Krestchmer, Alfred 103
Kunzig, Captain Robert L. 42, 83, 84, 127

L

laborers. *See* prisoner of war labor
Lacoochee, Florida 64
lagersprecher 27
Lakes, Captain Alexander 145, 265
Langdale, Harley 110
Lanier, Rufus 62
Laurens County 133
Leibelt, Gunther 72
Lesniak, Ted 128, 129, 130, 240
libraries 29, 32, 39, 45, 51, 53, 56, 81, 82, 84, 92, 103, 123, 127, 140, 143, 145
  Life 95
  magazines 46, 51, 108, 109, 143
  newspapers 42, 43, 46, 51, 55, 58, 59, 65, 74, 75, 108, 109, 121, 143, 145
  New York Times 95
  Time 95
Lillis, Lieutenant Edward T. 110
Louisville, Kentucky 89, 106
Lovett, Herschel 133
Lowndes County 110, 111

M

MacEachen, Chaplain (Captain) Roderick 98, 100

Macon, Georgia 8, 58, 66, 90, 91, 115, 117, 121, 128
Macon Telegraph 90, 91, 115, 121
MacWilliams, Second Lieutenant Thomas A 142
Maria Laach 69
Marshall, Brigadier General S.L.A. 41
McKnight, Major Maxwell 40, 41, 45
medical treatment 53, 76, 82, 94, 96, 97, 103, 108, 118, 132, 140
Merry Brick 66
mess hall 30, 42, 50, 60, 68, 70, 81, 108, 116, 130, 132, 135, 141
Mexia, Texas 25
military personnel 13, 14, 46, 49, 50, 58, 64, 65, 70, 71, 94, 96, 104, 117, 118, 129, 140, 145, 239
  enlisted soldiers 26, 30, 45, 50, 65, 79, 85, 116, 120, 122, 125, 140
  guards 122, 126, 127
  Military Police 65, 73, 75, 86, 105, 109, 110, 111, 122, 132, 139
  Military Police Escort Guard Company 13, 14, 122
Milledgeville, Georgia 133
Milner, Renate 113
Mitchell, Walter 65
Monticello, Georgia 96, 131
Moody Army Air Field, Georgia 110
morale 62, 66, 68, 82, 84, 94, 108, 109, 143
Moran, Captain Richard J. 127
Moultrie, Georgia 105, 124

Index

Mueller, Hermann 75
Muldrow, Colonel J.A. 131
murder 53, 255
murders 38, 53, 73, 74

N

National Catholic Welfare
    Association 122
National Guard 23
Nazis 8, 25, 26, 27, 34, 37, 38, 39,
    40, 41, 42, 45, 46, 56, 58,
    59, 62, 67, 68, 73, 82, 83, 91,
    102, 103, 112, 143, 239
Nazism 25, 40, 42, 46, 106
Nehfischer, Karl 128
Neuland, Major Paul A. 125, 127,
    142, 143
newspapers 147. *See* camp
    newspapers
New York Times 40, 95
Noel, Margaret Holmes 71
Norfolk, Virginia 16, 86
North Africa 13, 14, 37, 63, 71, 91
North Carolina 76

O

Ochs, Colonel William V. 83
Oglethorpe, Georgia 141, 146
O'Hara, Father Gerald P. 50
Okefenokee Swamp 110
Oliver General Hospital, Augusta
    53, 62, 66, 67, 251
Opelika, Alabama 108
Osborn, Jim 72
Owens, Jesse 133

P

Pace, Stephen 90, 98, 117
Panucci, Francesco 101
Pape, Willi 135
Pasco Packing Association 64
Patte, Edouard J. 52, 53, 55, 56, 76,
    77, 141, 143, 144, 146
Patterson, Lieutenant Colonel
    Ralph E. 120, 122, 125, 126,
    128, 131, 132, 133
Pearl Harbor 12
Perret, Maurice 82, 103, 104
Pete, Dr. Marc 100, 101
Peters, Audrey 112
Peter, Wolfgang 71, 72
Pige, Lieutenant Robert R. 107
Powder House Polo Field 70
Pretscher, S. 134
prisoner of war camps
    construction 259
prisoner of war employment review
    board 29
prisoner of war labor 7, 9, 11, 12,
    26, 28, 29, 30, 31, 34, 36, 51,
    52, 56, 57, 58, 60, 61, 62, 63,
    64, 66, 67, 70, 71, 72, 73, 74,
    79, 82, 85, 92, 97, 98, 103,
    104, 105, 106, 108, 109, 111,
    112, 113, 115, 116, 117, 121,
    122, 124, 125, 126, 127, 128,
    129, 130, 131, 132, 133, 134,
    135, 136, 137, 139, 140, 141,
    143, 145, 146, 239
    agriculture 66
    bakery 60, 82, 122
    brickyard 66
    carpentry 118, 123
    citrus industry 64

Index

Class I 30
Class II 30
Class III 31
cooks 60
corn 110
cotton 57, 61, 71
dairying 64
factories 61
farmers 261
farms 30, 61, 105, 110, 111, 112, 131, 253
fertilizer plant 64, 70
forestry 62
kitchen detail 68
laundry 30, 57, 60, 65, 81, 82, 83
logging 62, 106
lumber 53, 70, 71, 105, 106, 108, 118, 131, 132, 133, 136, 145
machine shop 82
mosquito abatement 64
motor pool 57, 60, 82, 110
motor shop 68
motor vehicle shop 60
orderlies 60
peaches 70
peanuts 29, 58
planting trees 70
post maintenance 82
pulpwood 26, 53, 62, 70, 110, 132, 135, 136
salvage 82
sawmills 30, 64, 131, 239
shoe repair 118
stables 82
sugar cane 111
tailoring 118
tent repair 140
timber 62
tobacco 29, 76, 111, 113, 239
tree pruning 132
turpentine 136
wood cutting 53, 67
woodcutting 64
work details 62
prisoner of war policy 12, 13
prisoners of war
  agriculture 30
  contracts 30
  death rates 241
  Germans 7, 8, 9, 10, 13, 25, 26, 28, 32, 34, 36, 37, 38, 39, 40, 41, 42, 43, 44, 45, 47, 50, 51, 52, 53, 55, 56, 57, 58, 59, 60, 61, 62, 63, 64, 65, 66, 68, 69, 70, 71, 74, 75, 76, 80, 81, 82, 83, 85, 86, 89, 96, 100, 103, 104, 105, 106, 107, 108, 109, 110, 112, 113, 126, 127, 128, 129, 130, 131, 132, 134, 135, 136, 137, 140, 141, 143, 144, 145, 146, 239, 240
  Italians 53, 57, 79, 84, 87, 89, 90, 91, 92, 94, 97, 98, 100, 101, 102, 103, 104, 105, 115, 116, 117, 118, 121, 124, 125, 126, 133
  manual 12
  policy 91, 98, 108, 109, 133, 136, 139
processing 23, 29, 69, 92
Progresso Italo-Americana 95
Provost Marshal General Office 12, 13, 14, 26, 30, 34, 38, 39, 41, 46, 49, 71, 74, 85, 89, 91, 96, 100, 118, 119, 121, 122, 123, 124, 125, 127, 131
  administrative executive officer 43, 44, 45

INDEX

Special Projects Division 41, 43, 44, 45, 46, 47, 145
public perceptions 37
PX. *See* canteen
Pydd, Sergeant Alex 96

R

Raber, Captain 146
Raugust, Captain William F. 142
recreation 11, 29, 36, 49, 51, 53, 55, 73, 77, 80, 81, 82, 83, 84, 92, 95, 104, 106, 108, 109, 122, 123, 126, 127, 129, 132, 135, 136, 143, 144, 146, 239
  choir 55, 82, 119
  concerts 32, 53, 72, 92, 104, 144
  crossword puzzles 42
  films 32, 39, 42, 44, 46, 126, 127
  guitar 92, 146
  mouth-organs 146
  music 42
  orchestra 53, 82, 84, 104, 119, 123, 127, 143
  theater 53, 72, 95, 123
Red Cross 27, 45, 51, 103, 141, 143
Reeducation Program 37, 40, 41, 42, 43, 45, 46, 47, 68, 83, 106, 107, 128
Reidsville, Georgia 76, 247
religion 11, 55, 98, 104, 108, 109, 134, 136, 140, 146, 239
  Catholic 50, 51, 56, 57, 66, 98, 100, 103, 140
  chaplain 50, 51, 55, 56, 69, 141
  Lutheran 100, 108, 140
repatriation 11, 34, 35, 53, 56, 69

Richards, Lieutenant Mason F. 83, 84
Richmond County 57
Rivers, L. Mendel 34
Roberts, Jack 70
Rockenbach, Brigadier General Samuel 12
Rodgers, Colonel Ralph W. 100
Roehrs, Heinz 113
Rome, Georgia 144
Rommeswinkel, Walter 113
Roosevelt, Eleanor 40, 41
Roosevelt, Franklin D. 12, 41, 112
Rossville, Georgia 145
Rudesheim, Germany 69
Russia 11, 113

S

Sandersville, Georgia 131
Saunders, Private First Class Norm 247
Savage, Colonel Mills S. 107
Savannah, Georgia 50, 79, 85
Schroer, Herman 111
Schroer, Walter 111
Scott, Georgia 135
Second Italian Engineer Regiment 102
security 67, 68, 122, 124, 132
Shannahan, Major Edward C. 66, 83, 85, 121, 122, 123, 125, 126, 131, 132, 135, 136
Shepherd, J. Quintis 145
Sicily 91
side camps 66, 86, 107, 123, 124, 125
Silcox, Harold 139

Index

Sims, Fred 57
Smith, Arthur 42
Snellgrove Plantation 135
South Carolina 25, 34, 58, 64, 68, 71, 124
   Monetta 72
sports 32, 42, 53, 82, 104, 119, 140
   badminton 146
   boxing 82
   cards 26, 95
   chess 32, 95, 146
   cricket 32
   faustball 32, 82, 104
   handball 32, 53, 104
   ping-pong 32, 104, 146
   shuttlecocks 146
   soccer 32, 82, 92, 144
   track and field 32
   wrestling 104
State Department 12, 73, 80, 94
Staten Island, New York 23, 69
Statesboro, Georgia 86, 240
Stimson, Henry 40
St. Mary on the Hill, Augusta, Georgia 66
Straub, Rudolph 73
suicides 38, 39, 40, 53
Summers, Colonel I.B. 133
Swainsboro, Georgia 86
Swiss Legation 11, 12, 27, 73, 80, 82, 94, 96, 97, 107

T

Tatter, Staff Sergeant Percy 61
Tennessee 69, 139, 145
tent camps 97, 107, 131

10th Italian Ordnance Materiel Acquisiton Management Company 84
tents 76, 77, 107, 108, 131, 136
Thigpen, C.L. 133
Thomasville, Georgia 105, 113
Thompson, Antonio 89, 90, 94, 97
Thompson, Colonel J. 60
Thompson, Dorothy 40
Thompson, Scott 137
315th Military Police Escort Guard Company 110
357th Military Police Escort Guard Company 122
356th Military Police Escort Guard Company 122
Todte, Gerhard 112
transportation 29, 31, 63, 69, 72, 84, 86, 104, 109, 110, 118
treatment 8, 11, 53, 67, 86, 89, 92, 94, 96, 98, 100, 102, 107, 118, 125, 126, 239
Truman, Harry S 34
Tunisia 73
Turner Field, Georgia 131, 156, 164
Twaddle, Brigadier General Harry L. 13
25th Italian Dump Truck Company 84
typhus 136

U

Uhl, Major General Frederick E. 98
"University of Democracy". *See* Reeducation Program

Index

U.S. Army 12, 13, 14, 26, 27, 30, 34, 44, 49, 51, 58, 66, 67, 69, 74, 75, 79, 91, 100, 107, 115, 116, 124, 129, 131, 133, 135
U.S. Navy 12, 135, 136

V

Valdosta, Georgia 105, 110, 112, 113, 260
Valdosta Times 110, 260
Vinson, Carl 133
Vulliet, Andre 91, 92, 101, 104, 105

W

Wadley, Georgia 61
wages 29, 31, 61, 97, 108, 121, 128, 132, 140, 165
War Department 12, 26, 29, 30, 34, 42, 43, 46, 49, 57, 76, 80, 89, 95, 97, 104, 107, 115, 126, 128, 143
  War Manpower Commission 30, 61
Ward, Lieutenant William Arthur 25
War Prisoners' Aid 122
War Production Board 132
Washington, D.C. 39, 59
Waynesboro, Georgia 76, 131
Wehrmacht 26, 105
West Germany 73
Wille und Weg (*Will and Way*) 42, 43, 47
Williams, Janice W. 134

Wilmington Island, Georgia 64
Wilmington, North Carolina 124
women 60, 79, 113, 125, 163
work detachments 103, 104, 131
work details 108
World War I 8, 11, 40, 115
Wrightsville, Georgia 134
Wyman, Mayor E.H. 70

Y

Yamamoto, Shiroku "Whitey" 9, 245
Young Men's Christian Association (YMCA) 11, 12, 27, 52, 91, 106, 146

ABOUT THE AUTHORS

Dr. Kathryn Roe Coker received a doctorate in history from the University of South Carolina. She served for thirty years as a historian for the Department of the Army (DA). Her interest in World War II POWs began at Fort Gordon while serving as the deputy command historian. She has published various articles in professional journals like the *Georgia Historical Quarterly*. While a DA historian, she published numerous books and pamphlets, including *A History of Fort Gordon*, *World War II Prisoners of War in Georgia: Camp Gordon's POWs* and *The Indispensable Force: The U.S. Army Reserve (1990–2010)*. She now resides in Richmond, Virginia, with her Miniature Schnauzer and Puggle.

Jason Wetzel has an MA in education and history from Georgia State University. The bulk of his working life was in telecommunications, with side forays as a high school teacher and a Department of the Army historian. His interest is World War II history. He was born in Australia during World War II. His mother was an Australian war bride, and he is an Australian war baby. Dahlonega, Georgia, is home.

Visit us at
www.historypress.com

Printed in the USA
CPSIA information can be obtained
at www.ICGtesting.com
LVHW021441230624
783804LV00003B/132